S0-CXU-648

# THE UNITED STATES:
## PEOPLE AND LEADERS

# THE UNITED STATES:
## PEOPLE AND LEADERS

LOUIS H. ABRAMOWITZ AND JACK ABRAMOWITZ

Conceived and created by TRI-ED CORPORATION

Modern Curriculum Press, Inc.
Cleveland • Toronto

**Louis H. Abramowitz, M.A.**
Mr. Abramowitz has extensive experience as an educator in the New York City public schools. He is a noted teacher-trainer, and has taught special courses for administrators. Mr. Abramowitz has developed curriculum in reading and social studies and most recently served as an elementary school principal.

**Jack Abramowitz, Ph.D.**
Dr. Abramowitz has had a distinguished career as a teacher of social studies. His work includes over twenty years of classroom experience at a variety of levels, and curriculum development and consulting for school districts in Oregon, Ohio, New York, Texas, California, Indiana, Georgia, and New Hampshire. Dr. Abramowitz is the author of numerous texts and journal articles in the social sciences, and speaks frequently to teacher and other professional groups. He was Visiting Professor at the University of London's Goldsmith's College.

Project Editor:

**Elizabeth A. Grossman**

Editorial Consultants:

**Richard Gallin**
**Dorothy Kirk**

Editorial Assistance:

**Elaine Wellin and Philip St. Clair**
**Western Reserve Publishing Services; Kent, Ohio**

Book Design and Illustrations by:

**Edward J. Sinnott**
**John D. Firestone & Associates, Inc./Bob Russo/**
**Kevin Nichols**

**Copyright © 1981 MODERN CURRICULUM PRESS, INC.**
13900 Prospect Road, Cleveland, OH 44136

Original Copyright © 1975 TRI-ED CORPORATION

All rights reserved. Printed in the United States of America. This book or parts thereof may not be reproduced in any form or mechanically stored in any retrieval system without written permission from the publisher.

Published simultaneously in Canada by Globe/Modern Curriculum Press, Toronto.

ISBN 0-87895-704-9     3  4  5  6  7  8  9  10     84

# CONTENTS ☆☆☆☆☆☆☆☆☆☆☆☆☆☆☆☆☆☆

☆☆☆☆☆☆☆☆☆☆☆☆☆☆☆☆☆☆☆☆☆☆☆☆☆☆

# INTRODUCTION
# The United States: People and Leaders

The United States of America is the fourth largest country in the world. It is about 3,000 miles from east to west coast. Nearly 2,000 miles separate the northern border from the southern border. All of this land, together with Alaska and Hawaii, makes up the fifty states of the United States.

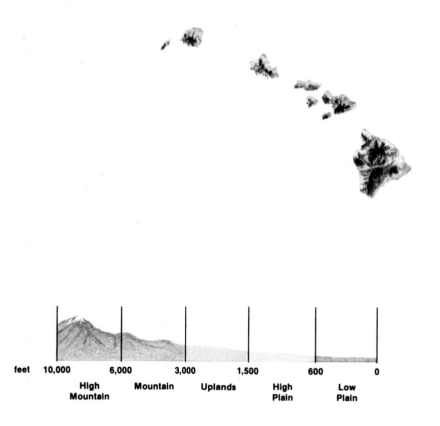

| feet | 10,000 | 6,000 | 3,000 | 1,500 | 600 | 0 |
|---|---|---|---|---|---|---|
| | High Mountain | Mountain | Uplands | High Plain | Low Plain | |

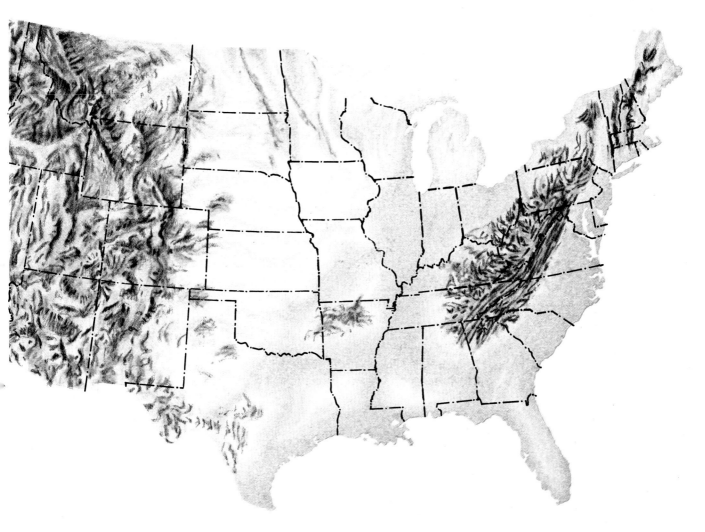

The United States is rich in resources. It has some of the most fertile soil on earth and the water supply is plentiful. Our country is also rich in minerals, such as coal, copper, iron, natural gas, and oil. The nation's factories produce a variety of goods and the farms are very productive. All these things help to make the United States the richest nation in the world.

The United States is a land of many kinds of people. These people are alike in many ways, but they are different in other ways. Citizens of the United States have given the world such things as the Salk vaccine, nuclear energy, the telephone, and even the hot dog. These people have helped to make the United States one of the great nations of the world.

This book tells the story of the United States, its people, and the women and men who have helped make the nation great.

# THE PEOPLE OF THE UNITED STATES

# CONTENTS ☆ ☆ ☆ ☆ ☆ ☆ ☆ ☆ ☆ ☆ ☆ ☆ ☆ ☆ ☆

☆ ☆ ☆ ☆ ☆ ☆ ☆ ☆ ☆ ☆ ☆ ☆ ☆ ☆ ☆ ☆ ☆ ☆ ☆ ☆ ☆ ☆ ☆ ☆

☆ ☆ ☆ ☆ ☆ ☆ ☆ ☆ ☆ ☆ ☆ ☆ ☆ ☆ ☆ ☆ ☆ ☆

☆ ☆ ☆ ☆ ☆ ☆ ☆ ☆ ☆ ☆ ☆ ☆ ☆ ☆ ☆ ☆ ☆ ☆ ☆ ☆

# Who are the people of the United States?

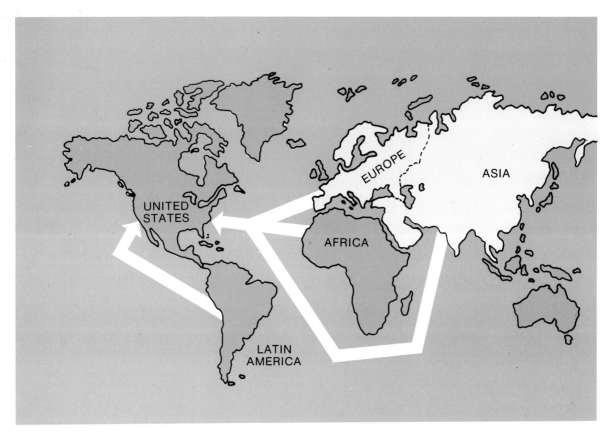

More than 225 million people live in the United States. These people are alike in many ways. They live and work in the same country. They have many of the same customs and celebrate many of the same holidays. As Americans they are protected by the United States government. As good citizens, they obey the laws of the country.

Americans are alike in some ways, but different in other ways. Most Americans are light-skinned, or white in color. Other Americans have skin color that is black, brown, or yellow. Many Native Americans, or Indians, are copper-skinned.

Americans, or their ancestors, come from many different lands. The United States is a land of immigrants. These immigrants came from Europe, Asia, Africa, and Latin America. They brought different religions, languages, and customs to the United States.

Today the American people are different in many ways. Their skins are of many different colors. They have many different religions and customs. But all Americans are alike in their love for their country.

# Who were the people of Europe who came to the United States?

Europe is a continent to the east of the United States, across the Atlantic Ocean. There are many different people and countries in Europe. They speak many languages and have many different customs.

The first Europeans came to America as settlers nearly 500 years ago. At that time only the Native Americans, the people we call Indians, lived in America. They lived in all parts of North and South America.

European nations sent settlers to establish colonies in America. Spain, France, Portugal, Holland, and England started colonies in America. English colonies were mainly located along the Atlantic coastline. These colonies later joined together to become the United States.

Later, millions of Europeans came to live in the United States. They came from Great Britain, Ireland, Germany, Italy, Russia, and other European countries. They started a new life in America.

The millions of immigrants who came to the United States from Europe spoke many languages. They dressed in different ways and had different customs.

*What were some of the languages the immigrants spoke?*

*How did the people of Europe who came to America differ in dress and customs?*

*What were some reasons people from Europe came to America?*

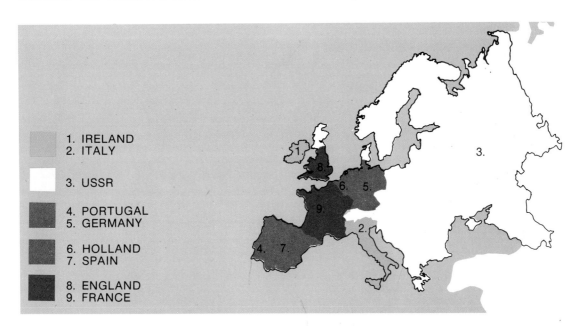

1. IRELAND
2. ITALY

3. USSR

4. PORTUGAL
5. GERMANY

6. HOLLAND
7. SPAIN

8. ENGLAND
9. FRANCE

# Why did the people of Europe come to the United States?

Europeans came to the United States to find a better life. Many Europeans wanted their own land or they wanted better jobs. Land was hard to get in Europe. The United States had plenty of cheap farmland. There were also jobs in the mines, factories, and offices of the United States.

Some Europeans came to the United States because they wanted to worship God in their own way. This could not be done in many European countries.

Europeans also came because they wanted freedom of speech and the press. They wanted the right to vote for leaders and not to be ruled by kings or dictators. They wanted the right to be free.

Millions of Europeans moved to the United States to start a new life. They felt they could find new opportunities in the United States. Many immigrants hoped that their children would be able to gain an education and a better life.

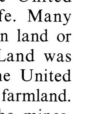

## Who were the people of Asia who came to the United States?

Asia is the largest continent in the world. More than one-half of the people of the world live in Asia. China, Japan, India, Vietnam, and many countries of the Middle East are located in Asia.

Most of the Asian people who came to the United States were Chinese. Another large group was the Japanese. Both groups settled mainly on the west coast of our country. However, there are many Chinese-Americans living in most of the big cities of the United States. There are also many Japanese-Americans living in Hawaii.

## Why did the people of Asia come to the United States?

Most Asian people who moved to the United States wanted a better life. Many people in China, Japan, and the other Asian lands were very poor. They came to the United States to find jobs.

Many thousands of Chinese came to the United States about one hundred years ago. They worked as laborers building America's first cross-country railroad. Chinese workers helped to lay tracks over the deserts and mountains of the West.

Today there are many Chinese people in the United States. They live in such cities as San Francisco and New York. Some live in small towns and rural areas. Though they are proud to be Americans, they still keep many of their Chinese customs.

# Who were the people of Africa who came to the United States?

Once there were great kingdoms in Africa. The most famous were the great kingdoms of Ghana, Mali, and Songhay. These kingdoms were located in the western bulge of Africa. They were in the area below the Sahara Desert. The Arabs of North Africa called these lands **bilad-al-sudan,** or "the land of the black people." These parts of Africa are still known as the Sudan.

The great kingdoms of Africa lost their power many years ago. Later, the European nations ruled most of Africa. Today most of Africa is independent and is ruled by Africans.

The first black Africans came to America more than three hundred years ago. They were brought to America as slaves. Slavery was ended in the United States in 1863. Today there are more than twenty-five million Americans of African descent. Many black Americans are studying the history of Africa. They are becoming familiar with many of the languages and customs of Africa.

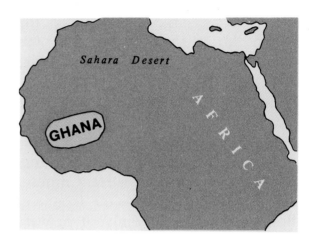

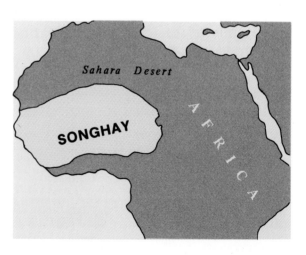

# Why did the people of Africa come to the United States?

Most of the people from other lands have come to the United States willingly. This is not true of black Africans. For about 200 years black Africans were brought to the United States as slaves.

Many slave ships from Europe and America raided African villages. Many African people were put on these ships and sold into slavery. They were used as field hands and workers in distant lands. These Africans lost everything—their families, their languages, their customs, religions, and their freedom.

Slavery was ended in the United States more than one hundred years ago. The descendants of the black Africans are now American citizens.

They have served the nation in war and peace. Black citizens are farmers, workers, teachers, and doctors. Black people vote and are elected to office.

Black Americans are working to win equal rights and a better life. Many black Americans also want to know more about Africa. They are proud to be Americans, but they are also proud of their African heritage.

## Who were the people of Latin America who came to the United States?

The lands of Latin America lie to the south of the United States. They include such places as Mexico, Panama, Puerto Rico, Brazil, and Chile. The region is called Latin America because the people speak Spanish or Portuguese. These languages grew out of the Latin language. Latin was spoken by the ancient Romans.

1. MEXICO
2. PANAMA
3. CHILE
4. PUERTO RICO
5. BRAZIL

Many Latin American immigrants in the mainland United States are from Mexico and Puerto Rico. More than five million Mexican-Americans live in the United States. There are also about one and one-half million Puerto Ricans living in the mainland United States.

## Why did the people of Latin America come to the United States?

Many Latin American countries were poor. Their people often moved to other lands to find a better life for their families.

Most Mexican people who came to the United States lived in the Southwest. This part of the United States once belonged to Mexico. It was lost to the United States in war. After the war Mexicans in these lands became citizens of the United States. Since then other Mexican people have immigrated to the United States. They live mainly in California, New Mexico, Arizona, Texas, and Colorado. They work as farm laborers, office workers, teachers, doctors, lawyers, and business people.

Puerto Rico is a beautiful island in the Caribbean Sea. It has its own government, but it is part of the United States. The people of Puerto Rico are citizens of the United States.

Puerto Rico is very poor. Many of its people come to the mainland United States in search of jobs. They want good homes and better schools for their children. About one million Puerto Ricans live in New York City. They bring the language, songs, and customs of Latin America to New York.

## LEARNING EXERCISES

### I. Remembering What We Have Read

Pick the best answer.

1. Black people of Africa came to America
   a. to find jobs.
   b. for religious freedom.
   c. as slaves.
2. The first American colonies were started by
   a. Africans.
   b. Europeans.
   c. Latin Americans.
3. The greatest number of Puerto Ricans in the United States live in
   a. the Southwest.
   b. New York City.
   c. San Francisco.
4. The first people to live in the Americas were the
   a. Europeans.
   b. Latin Americans.
   c. Native Americans, or Indians.

### II. True or False

1. Parts of the southwestern United States were once English colonies.
2. Latin Americans speak Spanish or Portuguese.
3. The great kingdoms of Africa were located in the Sudan area.
4. Most Chinese and Japanese immigrants settled in the eastern United States.

### III. Thinking About Things

Can you guess the answers to these questions? They are based on what you have been reading, but the answers are not in the book.

1. What might have been some problems facing the immigrants who moved to the United States?
2. From which parts of the world did your family come to the United States?
3. What might be some reasons immigrants want to keep some of their old customs?

11

BORN IN
GERMANY

# ALBERT EINSTEIN

Albert Einstein will always be remembered by Americans. He was a great scientist whose ideas were used to produce atomic energy.

Einstein was born and educated in Germany. He was not a good student in mathematics in his early school years. As he grew older, he improved as a mathematician. Einstein went on to a university where his teachers recognized his abilities. Many of his teachers felt that he would become one of the great people of science. They were right, but fame did not come easily to Einstein.

Because he was a Jew, he found it hard to get a job in Germany. For a time he worked in nearby Switzerland as a clerk in a government office. He continued to study on his own and he developed new ideas in science. Einstein's success in mathematics soon made him famous. He returned to Germany as a teacher in a university.

Einstein was only twenty-six years old when he made his great scientific discovery. Seventeen years later he was awarded the Nobel Prize. This prize is given only to the outstanding scientists in the world. It is a very great honor.

In 1933 Albert Einstein was forced to flee from Germany. The country was then ruled by Adolf Hitler and his followers. They hated Jews and took away their jobs and homes. Without reason they put them in jail. Even a world-famous person like Albert Einstein was in danger of losing his life.

Einstein left Germany and came to the United States where he was welcomed warmly. He became an American citizen and continued his studies at Princeton University. This was to be his home for the rest of his life. Albert Einstein became an American in every sense of the word.

BOSTON

# THE KENNEDY FAMILY

The people of Ireland faced ruin in 1850. The Irish potato crop was spoiled that year. Because potatoes were so important to Ireland, there was actual starvation in many parts of the country.

Thousands of Irish people decided to move to the United States. They hoped to find a better life in the New World. One of those who moved to the United States was a young farmer named Patrick Kennedy. He settled in Boston, got a job, and married. He never dreamed that his great-grandson would be president of the United States.

Kennedy and other Irish immigrants had to take low-paying jobs at first. But they worked hard, saved their money, and encouraged their children to go to school. They believed this was the way to succeed.

Patrick Kennedy's grandson was named Joseph Kennedy. He graduated from Harvard University and became a wealthy businessman. He married the daughter of a mayor of Boston and they had nine children. One son, John F. Kennedy, became president. Two other sons became United States Senators.

President John F. Kennedy was elected to office in 1960. He was the first Catholic to be chosen president of the United States. President Kennedy was only forty-three years old when elected president. This made him the youngest elected president in history.

The story of the Kennedy family is the story of part of the greatness of our country. It opened its doors to those who sought a better life. In return, immigrants like the Kennedy family helped make America great.

13

# FIORELLO LA GUARDIA

He was very short, about 5 feet 2 inches in height, and was almost as wide. He always wore a black hat with a wide brim that almost covered his face. He could speak seven different languages in a high-pitched voice. His name was Fiorello La Guardia and he was the Mayor of New York City for three terms. To the more than one million Italian-Americans of the city he was "The Little Flower."

Mayor La Guardia got his nickname because Fiorello means "little flower" in Italian. He was the son of Italian immigrants. His father died in 1898 in the Spanish-American War. Sixteen-year-old Fiorello had to go to work in order to finish school. He was a good student and became a lawyer. Before long, he entered politics and was elected to Congress. Congressman La Guardia was still "The Little Flower" to Italian-Americans.

La Guardia served in Congress from 1923 to 1933. In 1933 he was elected Mayor of New York City. As Mayor he set out to give the city clean government. Gamblers and crooks were warned to reform or get out of town. Efforts were made to tear down many of the slum houses in poor neighborhoods. Low-rent housing projects were built for poor people.

Mayor La Guardia led other steps to improve the city. Airplanes were a fairly new means of transportation in the 1930s, but La Guardia knew their importance. After all, he had been a flier during World War I. He led the fight for an airport in New York. When the airport was built, it was given his name. Today, hundreds of jet planes land daily at La Guardia Airport.

Fiorello La Guardia was one of the great Mayors of New York City. He was the son of Italian immigrants and his life showed that America can be a land of opportunity for all people.

# CHIEN-SHIUNG WU

As a child growing up in a rural area of China, Chien-Shiung Wu had no higher ambition than to become a school teacher and lead the same simple cultural lifestyle that her parents and their parents before them had lived. But while studying to become a teacher, she received an invitation to attend the National Central University, one of the best universities in China. This was a great honor for the young girl, and her parents were very proud of her.

She decided that she would like to study physics at the University, but she was afraid that her teaching studies had not prepared her to become a scientist. Her father, who had always had a strong belief in democracy and the equality of women, brought her books on algebra, chemistry, and physics. She studied hard all summer, and when she got to the University that fall, she found herself on her way to becoming a physicist, just as she had dreamed. In 1936, she came to the United States to continue her education at the University of California—a courageous adventure for this girl from the Chinese countryside.

Soon after she graduated from the University of California in 1940, she became a professor at Smith College, sharing her knowledge and her love for science with students only slightly younger than herself.

Even though she had not been born in this country, she had quickly come to love it. When the United States entered World War II, she wanted to help in any way she could. So she volunteered to join other brilliant scientists in finding ways for science to help America win the war.

When the war was over, Chien-Shiung Wu went to Columbia University in New York City, where she performed many experiments, hoping to learn more about the world and the way it works. In 1956 she conducted her most famous experiment, which proved that a basic idea about the way the pieces of the world are put together was wrong. This experiment helped to win a Nobel Prize for the other scientists who had asked Chien-Shiung Wu to help them. It also proved, just as Chien-Shiung Wu's father had said, that a young girl could grow up to become a great scientist, and maybe even change the way we view the world.

15

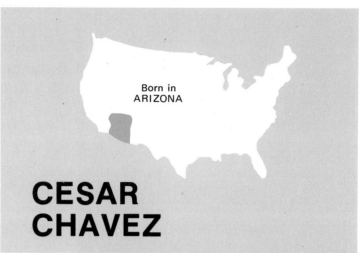

Born in
ARIZONA

# CESAR CHAVEZ

Five million Chicanos, or Mexican-Americans, know him as the leader of la causa—"the cause." His name is Cesar Chavez and he is the leader of Chicano migrant farm workers. Most of these workers live in the southwestern United States.

Cesar Chavez was born in Arizona in 1927. His parents were Mexican-American farm workers and he also worked in the fields. He attended more than thirty different elementary schools. This was because his family kept moving to follow the harvests in different states. Cesar Chavez left school in the seventh grade, but continued to study on his own. The boy who once could barely read and write grew up to be a self-educated man.

Cesar Chavez was a farm worker and also served in the United States Navy. After he left the Navy he tried to help his fellow migrant farm workers. Chavez wanted them to organize into unions to gain better wages and work conditions.

It was no easy job to organize migrant farm workers. Some farm owners refused to deal with the farm union. Strikes, called huelgas, by the Spanish-speaking Chicanos had to be used. They stopped work until their demands were met. At such times Cesar Chavez stood for nonviolence. He did not believe in fighting with fists. Instead, he spoke to people and tried to win them to his side. Sometimes he went without food to win support for his cause. Once he did not eat for twenty-five days.

Cesar Chavez has been recognized as the leader of la causa for Chicano farm workers for many years.

Born in CALIFORNIA

MEXICO

# NANCY LOPEZ

In 1978 the name of a young woman golfer began appearing in newspapers. Her name was soon familiar to millions of people watching sports events on television. The name of the young woman was Nancy Lopez. She gained thousands of fans as she won eight tournaments in 1978. By the end of the year, Lopez was one of the stars of the Ladies Professional Golf Association. What made her more remarkable was that she was only twenty-one years old.

Nancy Lopez was born in California in 1957. Her parents were Mexican-Americans who encouraged her interest in golf. She started playing the game at the age of seven. Nancy was still using junior-size clubs when she became a better golfer than her father. In high school she was the number-one player on the golf team. She was the only woman member of the team.

Nancy went on to the University of Tulsa in Oklahoma and played golf there. In 1977 she became a professional golfer and soon had won a string of major tournaments. Today Nancy Lopez is one of the leaders in women's golf in the world. Her cheerful smile and steady play on the golf course mark her as a real champion.

# ANNA JULIA HAYWOOD COOPER

Anna Julia Haywood Cooper was born in North Carolina in 1859. Her mother was a slave. When she was only eleven years old, she was already working as a student teacher at her school.

Anna was a bright child who always did well in school, and who enjoyed studying. After high school, she attended Oberlin College in Ohio, which was one of the few colleges in those days that would accept black students.

Her first job was as a teacher at Wilberforce University, where she worked for two years. In 1892, she wrote a book called *A Voice From the South By a Black Woman of the South,* which described the thoughts and feelings of black people, and told about what it was like to be a slave.

In 1901, Anna moved to Washington, D.C., and became the principal of the M Street High School, which was later renamed Dunbar High School. This made Anna only the second female school principal that Washington had ever had. In those days, black children and white children were not allowed to go to school together. The M Street School was the best school for black children in our nation's capital. Many prominent Americans graduated from the M Street School, including Benjamin O. Davis, the first black general in the U.S. Army; Judge William H. Hastie, the first black governor of the U.S. Virgin Islands; and U.S. Senator Edward Brooke.

While Anna was principal of the M Street School, some people wanted to lower the standards at the school. They felt that they could save money by doing this, and that black children did not need a good education anyway. Anna Cooper fought hard to stop this from happening. She knew that black children, like all children everywhere, wanted and needed the finest education they could get.

When she was sixty-six years old, Anna received the highest degree possible, a Ph.D., from the Sorbonne in Paris, France. At the same time, she cared for five homeless children. She was leading a busy life at an age when most people are thinking about retiring.

At the age of seventy, Anna started a new school in her own home, which was called Frelinghuysen University. The purpose of this school was to teach black men and women what they needed to know to find better jobs.

Anna Julia Haywood Cooper died when she was 105 years old. She spent her long life helping black children get the education they needed.

# ROBERTO CLEMENTE

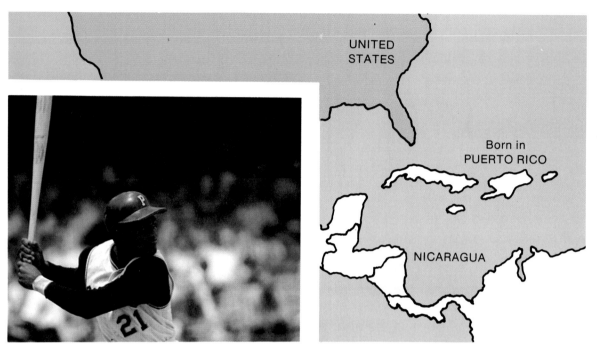

Baseball is the most popular sport in Puerto Rico. Many Puerto Ricans have become major league baseball players. One of the greatest of these baseball players was Roberto Clemente. He is honored in Puerto Rico because of his athletic skill and his love for others.

Roberto Clemente was born in Puerto Rico in 1934. When he was twenty years old he became a right fielder for the Brooklyn Dodgers. In 1955 he was traded to the Pittsburgh Pirates. Clemente remained with the Pirates for the next seventeen years. As a big league baseball player he hit 240 home runs.

Clemente was the leading hitter of the National League four times. He played on two All-Star teams and was voted Most Valuable Player in 1966.

By 1972 Roberto Clemente was one of the great stars of baseball. But he was also concerned about people who needed help. In 1972 the country of Nicaragua suffered a terrible earthquake. Clemente organized help for the people who were suffering. On December 31, 1972, Clemente was on an airplane bringing food and medical supplies to the people of Nicaragua. He was killed when the airplane crashed after taking off. Roberto Clemente died trying to help the people who had loved and honored him as an athlete and a person. In 1973 he was made a member of baseball's Hall of Fame.

Born in U.S.A.

Born in POLAND

# JONAS SALK

# ALBERT SABIN

Albert Sabin was born in Poland in 1906. He was bright, but had little chance to go to a good school. His parents decided to leave Poland in 1921. They moved to the United States. In the United States it was possible for Albert to study medicine.

Albert Sabin became a special kind of doctor. He studied ways of preventing diseases. One disease was called polio and often led to death. It was sometimes called infantile paralysis. This was because it mainly affected young people and infants.

In the 1920s another boy was growing up in New York. His name was Jonas Salk. The Salk family had immigrated from Poland. Jonas was born in the United States in 1914. The family was poor and Jonas had to

work after school. After many years of study he became a doctor. Like Albert Sabin, Jonas also wanted to prevent polio.

Jonas Salk and Albert Sabin each looked for a way to stop polio. Each used his own ideas to find different methods of preventing the disease. Dr. Salk worked to find a way of vaccinating people against the disease. Dr. Sabin developed a different type of vaccine that can be taken with a lump of sugar.

Both methods proved successful. Polio has almost disappeared where they are used. Albert Sabin was an immigrant, Jonas Salk was the son of immigrants. Together they added another page to the story of our nation's greatness.

# ROSALYN YALOW

Rosalyn Sussman was born in New York City in 1921. She was a good student who wanted to study to be a scientist. Her parents were European immigrants who encouraged her. Rosalyn's father often told her that "girls can do as much as boys." She believed her father. But she also knew young women were not taken seriously as scientists. In spite of this, she went ahead with her studies.

In 1941 Rosalyn graduated from Hunter College in New York with the highest honors. Her plan was to go on for a doctor's degree in science. She was first offered a job as an office worker at a college. If she took the job she would also be allowed to use the library and laboratories. Another school, the University of Illinois, learned of her abilities. They offered her a teaching and learning position. She declined the office job and went to the University of Illinois. From then on she devoted her life to science.

At the University of Illinois, Rosalyn was the only woman teacher in the engineering college. For the next four years she studied and taught in her field of science. She also met and married Aaron Yalow in 1943. They both graduated in 1945 and returned to New York. She was soon doing research studies in the field of nuclear medicine. From 1950 to 1972 Rosalyn Yalow conducted research studies with Solomon Berson, a medical doctor. After he died in 1972 she went on alone in the work they had started.

In 1977 Dr. Yalow was awarded the Nobel Prize for medicine. The world was charmed when she reminded everyone of the importance of Dr. Berson. The Nobel Prize is awarded only to living scientists. For this reason it did not include Dr. Berson. But Dr. Yalow, as a true scientist, has always paid tribute to him.

FAMILY from JAPAN

JAPAN

born in HAWAII

# DANIEL INOUYE

## "Nisei Hero"

Nisei (nee-say) means "second generation" in Japanese. The Nisei are the descendants of Japanese who moved to the United States. The Inouye family of Hawaii are Nisei.

Daniel Inouye's grandfather left Japan and moved to Hawaii to seek a better life. The family was proud to be Japanese, but they also thought of themselves as Americans. The Inouye family felt that they owed much to their adopted homeland.

Daniel was born in Hawaii, and he was in high school when Japan attacked the United States in 1941. For a time, the American government did not trust any Japanese. Many Japanese living in the United States were forced to stay in special camps. This action was protested by Japanese-Americans and others. They declared that most Japanese living in the U.S. were loyal to the government.

In order to prove loyalty to the United States, a special unit of Nisei soldiers was formed. Daniel joined it. Lieutenant Daniel Inouye lost his right arm while leading a charge in Europe. Many other Nisei soldiers were killed or wounded in battle. Their bravery won the respect of all Americans.

Daniel Inouye did not let the loss of his arm keep him from doing what he wanted. He was elected as the first U.S. Representative from Hawaii when it became a state in 1959. Three years later, he was elected a U.S. Senator.

# ELLA T. GRASSO

Ella Grasso was the eighty-third governor of Connecticut. Her parents had come to America from Italy. Although times were not always easy for Ella and her family, she sometimes said, with typical good cheer, that "father was a baker, so we always had enough to eat." Ella's mother told her often how important it was to get a good education, and Ella made her mother and father proud by graduating with honors from Mount Holyoke College in 1940.

Her interest in politics soon led Ella to run for public office, and it was not long before she was elected to serve in the House of Representatives of the Connecticut General Assembly. After that, she worked for twelve years as the Connecticut Secretary of State, and became known by everyone as one of the best politicians in the state. While she was Secretary of State, she turned her office into what she called a "people's lobby." It was a place where ordinary people could go to seek advice or talk about what they thought the government should be doing.

Although Ella Grasso was a kind and gentle person, she could also be tough when she had to be. In 1968, she walked out of the Democratic National Convention in Chicago to protest the violent actions of the police toward people who were demonstrating against the Vietnam War. She did this even though she knew it might make her less popular with other politicians. Some people were angry with her, but most admired her honesty.

In 1970, Ella was elected to Congress. As a Congressional Representative from Connecticut's Sixth District, she sponsored the Fair Labor Standards Amendment of 1971, which increased the minimum wage to $2.00 per hour, and served on both the Education and Labor Committee and the Veteran Affairs Committee.

When she began running for Governor of Connecticut in 1974, her opponent said that she might not make a good governor because she was a woman. But Ella felt that the people would vote for her because of all the good things she had accomplished. And she was right!

On January 8, 1975, Ella T. Grasso became the first woman governor of Connecticut. She was the first woman ever to be elected governor without her husband having been governor first. One of the first things she did as governor was to turn down a raise in pay. She did this to demonstrate that she was willing to make personal sacrifices for the good of the people of Connecticut.

# A million dollars
# for black justice

The National Association for the Advancement of Colored People is more easily known as the N.A.A.C.P. It was founded in 1909 and has helped to lead the fight for full civil rights for black Americans.

The N.A.A.C.P. does much of its work in court. Its lawyers challenge laws that discriminate against black people. The N.A.A.C.P. has won hundreds of cases, but court cases can be very expensive. Raising money for this purpose has always been a big problem for the N.A.A.C.P.

During the 1930s the N.A.A.C.P.

had a special need for money. There were many cases of discrimination to be taken into court. But times were bad and it was hard to raise money. It seemed that the work of the N.A.A.C.P. might be halted.

Charles Garland was not a black man, but he believed in the work of the N.A.A.C.P. He was a young man who had just been left a million dollars. Most people would have kept that money for themselves. Charles Garland was a very different sort of person. He was happy with the life he was leading, and had no wish to keep the million dollars for himself. Instead, he intended to use the money to help others. He wanted to bring greater justice to black Americans.

Mr. Garland met with black leaders and told them of his plans. He sought no praise or notice as he arranged to give his million dollars to the cause of black freedom. His gift helped the N.A.A.C.P. continue its fight in court against discrimination and segregation.

# SHIRLEY CHISHOLM

Born in
NEW YORK

Parents from
BARBADOS

Shirley Chisholm was the first black woman to be elected to the Congress of the United States. It was not easy for her to win election. She had to face problems as a woman and as a black person. Hard as it was, she fought—and won.

Her parents had come to the United States from the island of Barbados. This is an island in the West Indies. Shirley Chisholm was born in New York. She grew up in the borough of Brooklyn.

She was an outstanding student in high school and college. After graduating from college, she worked as director of a children's school. Next, she decided to go into politics. Before long, Mrs. Chisholm was elected to the

New York State Assembly and served for four years. She became well-known as a fighter for the rights of all people, black or white. People began calling her Fighting Shirley Chisholm.

In 1968 Mrs. Chisholm became the first black woman elected to Congress. In her first term in office she showed herself still a fighter for the people. Representative Chisholm became a spokeswoman for the poor and for women's rights. She fought to be placed on important committees of Congress. Her words and actions convinced the leaders of Congress of the justice of her demands. Today, Shirley Chisholm is still fighting for the rights of all people though she is no longer a member of Congress.

# JIM THORPE

James F. Thorpe was known to millions of Americans as Jim Thorpe. As a Sac and Fox Indian, he also had the name of Wo-Tho-Huch or "Bright Path." He was truly a bright path in the world of athletics. Jim Thorpe was probably the greatest all-around athlete in the history of the United States.

As a young man, Jim Thorpe attended the Carlisle Indian Industrial School in Pennsylvania. Thorpe's skill soon made this small school famous. He was an all-American football player in 1911 and 1912. But football was only one of the sports for which he became known.

In 1912 Thorpe was on the United States Olympic team. He won the gold medals for the decathlon and pentathlon events. The decathlon consists of ten events. It includes running, shot-put, discus throw, javelin throw, and pole vault. The pentathlon involves five events. It includes running, swimming, horseback riding, fencing, and pistol shooting. Thorpe scored the most points to win his two gold medals. No wonder the king of Sweden called him "the greatest athlete in the world."

Jim Thorpe went on to play major league baseball for six years. At the same time he played professional football. Thorpe was one of the great football players in the early years of professional football from 1915 to 1925. He is honored by the Football Hall of Fame. A film of his life carries the perfect title. It is called *Jim Thorpe: All-American.*

# LEARNING EXERCISES

## I. Remembering What We Have Read

Pick the best answer.

1. Albert Einstein was a
   a. medical scientist.
   b. mathematician and scientist.
   c. politician.
2. Cesar Chavez is active in
   a. political office.
   b. medicine.
   c. organizing migrant workers.

3. A person known for work in nuclear medicine is
   a. Rosalyn Yalow.
   b. Nancy Lopez.
   c. Daniel Inouye.
4. The N.A.A.C.P. is active in the field of
   a. science.
   b. atomic energy.
   c. black people's rights.

## II. Thinking About Things

Can you guess the answers to these questions? They are based on what you have been reading, the answers are not in the book.

1. What do we mean when we say that immigrants have given much to America?
2. What are some of the foods that immigrants have made a part of American life?
3. What advice would you give to an immigrant who is coming to the United States today?

# LEARNING EXERCISES

## III. True or False

Is each of the following true or false?

1. Shirley Chisholm was elected to Congress.
2. Jim Thorpe's parents were immigrants.
3. Charles Garland was a black man who gave money to the N.A.A.C.P.
4. Jonas Salk and Albert Sabin were both immigrants.
5. Anna Julia Haywood Cooper was the principal of M Street High School.
6. Roberto Clemente is in the Baseball Hall of Fame.
7. Fiorello La Guardia was a congressman and a mayor.

## IV. Matching

Match Column B with Column A

COLUMN A
1. Ella T. Grasso
2. Cesar Chavez
3. Albert Sabin
4. Chien-Shiung Wu
5. Jim Thorpe
6. Shirley Chisholm
7. John F. Kennedy
8. Albert Einstein
9. Daniel Inouye

COLUMN B
a. Mexican-American
b. Chinese-American
c. Italian-American
d. Polish immigrant
e. German immigrant
f. Indian American
g. Japanese-American
h. black American
i. Irish-American

# DISCOVERING AND EXPLORING THE AMERICAS

UNIT

# 2

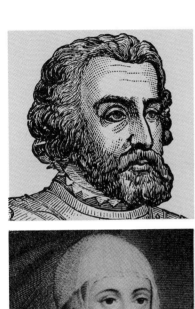

# CONTENTS ☆☆☆☆☆☆☆☆☆☆☆☆☆☆☆☆☆

☆☆☆☆☆☆☆☆☆☆☆☆☆☆☆☆☆☆☆☆☆☆☆

# UNIT 2

# Geographic Overview: What are maps and globes?

Globes and maps show us what the earth looks like. The globe is a round map. It is called a globe because it is shaped round like a sphere. A half of a globe is called a hemisphere. If we divide the earth evenly at an east-west line, we have a Northern Hemisphere and a Southern Hemisphere. If we divide the earth evenly on a north-south line, we have an Eastern Hemisphere and a Western Hemisphere.

Globes are shaped like small models of the earth. That is why the globe is the most accurate type of map. But globes are not always easy to use.

A flat map can show the whole world at one time. That is why flat maps are easier to read than globes. Flat maps are also easier to carry. However, flat maps are not as accurate as globes. This is because a flat map does not have the same shape as the earth.

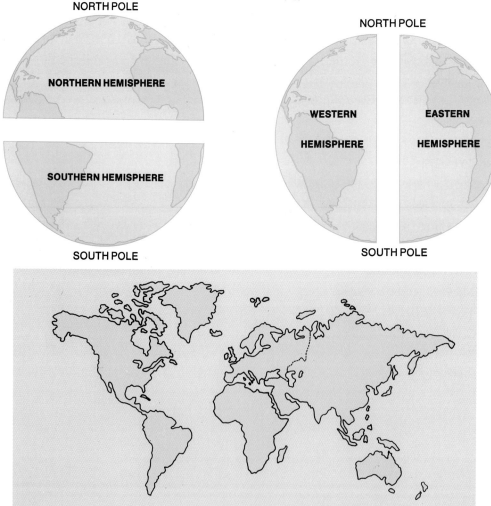

# How do we use keys and scales on a map?

A map is a special way of showing the earth. Maps use symbols to give us information about an area. In order to get the information, we must know how to read the symbols on the map. This is done by using the key to the map. The key explains what the symbols on the map stand for. A key is usually found at the bottom of the map. On the map below, the key is found in the lower left-hand corner.

A map is also used to learn the distance between two places on the map. To help us do this, maps show a scale of distance. The scale is often found at the bottom of the map. It shows how many miles on earth are equal to one inch on a map. An inch may stand for one mile, 500 miles, or 1,000 miles. Sometimes the scale is shown in metrics. A metric scale of distance shows how many kilometers on earth are equal to one centimeter on the map. A centimeter may stand for one kilometer (km), 1,000 kilometers, or 5,000 kilometers.

The map below shows a key and scale. It is a map of the United States. Use the key to locate two state capitals. Next use the scale of distance to find the distance in miles from New York to Chicago and from Atlanta to San Francisco.

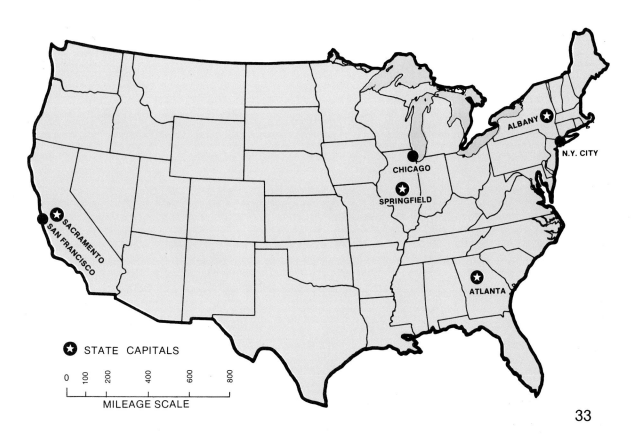

⭐ STATE CAPITALS

0  100  200  400  600  800
MILEAGE SCALE

# What are landforms?

The word landforms is used to describe the surface of the land. The surface of the earth's land masses is not the same in all places.

In some places the land is low and flat. These flat lands are called plains.

There is also land that is flat, but high. Such high, flat land is known as a plateau.

Some parts of the earth go up and down, forming hills. Hills are usually rounded at the top. They are not as high as mountains.

The highest places on the earth are mountains. Mountains are higher than hills. The tops of some high mountains are often snow-capped all year round.

The map below shows the four landforms that have been described.

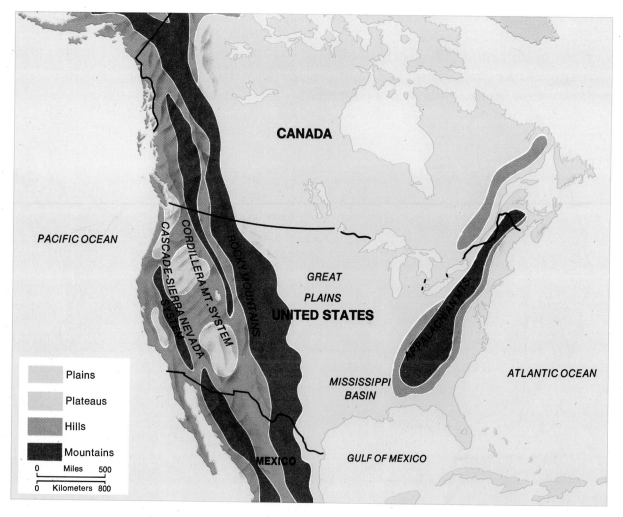

CANADA

PACIFIC OCEAN

CORDILLERA MT. SYSTEM

CASCADE-SIERRA NEVADA SYSTEM

ROCKY MOUNTAINS

GREAT PLAINS

UNITED STATES

APPALACHIAN MTS.

ATLANTIC OCEAN

MISSISSIPPI BASIN

Plains
Plateaus
Hills
Mountains

0    Miles    500
0    Kilometers    800

MEXICO

GULF OF MEXICO

# What are the different types of maps?

Many different kinds of maps are used to give many different kinds of information.

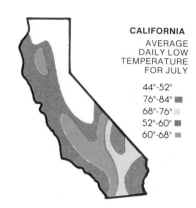

A climate map shows the different climates of an area. It can tell us whether the area has cold or mild winters. It also can tell whether the area has warm or cool summers.

A political map shows the nations of the world, or the states of a nation. A political map can also show the cities or counties within a state.

The most commonly used map is a road map. It helps automobile drivers get from one place to another without getting lost. Road maps show drivers the distances between places listed on the road map.

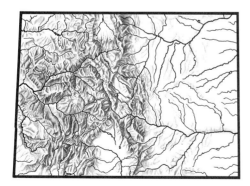

A relief map shows the plains, plateaus, hills, and mountains of an area.

There are many other kinds of maps. These include population distribution maps, land usage maps, and weather maps.

# How is the earth affected by rotation?

We know that the earth has no light of its own. It gets its light from the sun. We also know that the earth is shaped like a sphere. Because of this, the sun's light covers only one-half of the earth at a time. The half of the earth facing the sun has sunlight, or daytime. The other half of the earth is dark. It has nighttime.

If the earth did not spin, or rotate on its axis, the same half of the earth would always have sunlight. The other half of the earth would always have darkness. But we know that all parts of the earth get sunlight for part of the day and have darkness for part of the day. This takes place because the earth rotates, or spins, on its axis. The axis of the earth is an imaginary, or make-believe, line. It extends from the North Pole to the South Pole.

The earth makes one complete rotation in one day, or every twenty-four hours. This rotation on its axis causes day and night. It also creates time zones. We will learn more about time zones in a later lesson.

The three diagrams below show the changes that take place during one complete rotation of the earth.

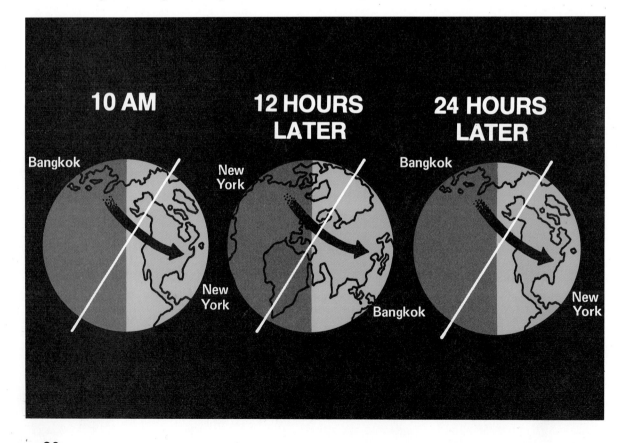

# How is the earth affected by revolution?

The rotation of the earth on its axis causes day and night. The picture shows that the axis does not run straight up and down, but is tilted to a side. If the north end of the axis were always tilted to the sun, we would always have summertime in the Northern Hemisphere. At the same time, we would always have winter in the Southern Hemisphere. But we know that we have different seasons in the Northern and Southern Hemispheres. We have different seasons at different times of the year. *Why is this so?*

Rotation is only one movement of the earth. There is another movement of the earth called revolution. This happens when the earth moves, or revolves, around the sun. One revolution of the earth around the sun takes one year, or about 365 days. The picture on this page shows the revolution of the earth around the sun. It shows the path, or orbit, of a complete revolution.

*Which pole is tilted toward the sun when we have summer? When we have winter? In March it is springtime in the Northern Hemisphere. What season is it in the Southern Hemisphere?*

The combination of the tilt of the earth's axis, and its revolution around the sun, causes us to have seasons.

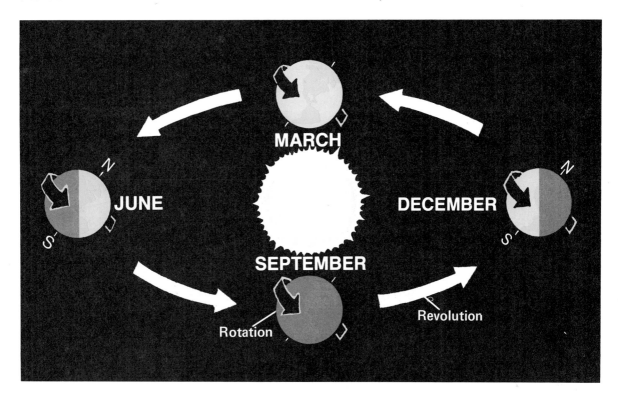

# What are the time zones?

Has this ever happened to you? It is five p.m. in New York or Boston in the month of November. The sun is down and it is quite dark outside. You turn on the television to watch a football game being played in California. It is sunny and bright in California. The television announcer says that it is now two p.m. and the game is about to begin. Have you ever wondered how it can be two p.m. in California when it is five p.m. in New York? To understand how this can happen, we need to know something about the sun and the earth. We need to know about the time zones on the earth.

The sun is always shining and the earth is always rotating. It rotates counterclockwise, or from west to east. A complete rotation takes one day, or twenty-four hours. As the earth rotates, half of the earth has daytime while the other half has nighttime.

As the earth rotates, the entire United States does not move into daylight at once. It moves into daylight in stages. First the eastern part of the United States begins to move into daylight. This is the Eastern Time Zone. One hour later the central part of the United States begins to move into daylight. This is the Central Time Zone. An hour later the western mountain area gets daylight. This is the Mountain Time Zone. One hour after that, the Pacific area gets daylight. This is the Pacific Time Zone. This process produces the time zones that are shown in the map on this page.

The United States is divided into four time zones. The Soviet Union has eleven time zones. *What does this tell us about the size of the Soviet Union?*

*When it is twelve o'clock in your city or town, what time is it in San Francisco? in Chicago? in New Orleans? and in Atlanta?*

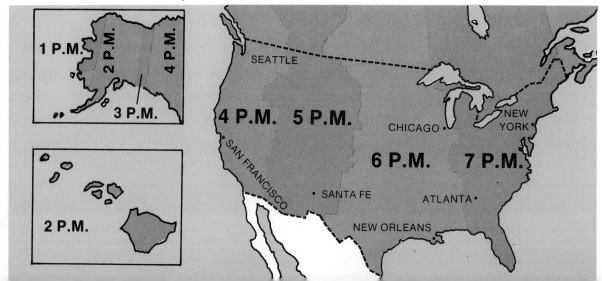

## LEARNING EXERCISES

### I. Remembering What We Have Read

Pick the best answer.

1. Flat maps are
   a. more accurate than globes.
   b. easier to read than globes.
   c. able to show only one-half of the world.
2. High, flat lands are called
   a. hills.
   b. plains.
   c. plateaus.
3. The earth makes one complete rotation in a
   a. year.
   b. day.
   c. month.
4. To get a Northern and Southern hemisphere, we divide the earth evenly
   a. in any direction.
   b. at an east-west line.
   c. at a north-south line.

### II. Learning About Seasons

Look at the drawing below. It shows the earth in orbit around the sun. The four stages of the orbit are labeled.

1. In which stage is it winter in the southern half of the world?
2. In which stage is it winter in the northern half of the world?

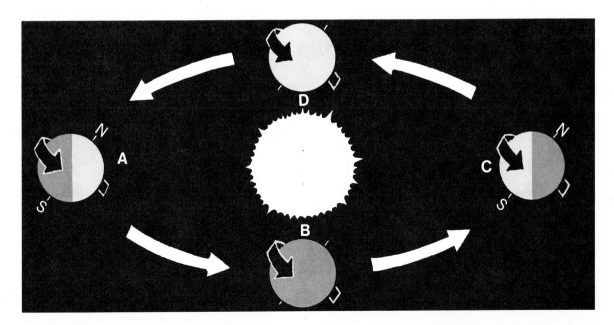

39

## III. Learning To Use Time Zones

1. If it is 3 p.m. in Chicago, what time is it in
   a. San Francisco?
   b. New Orleans?
   c. Atlanta?

2. If it is 6 a.m. in New York, what time is it in
   a. Santa Fe?
   b. Seattle?
   c. Chicago?

## IV. True or False

1. The metric scale uses kilometers to measure distance.
2. Hills are as high as mountains.
3. A relief map is like a political map.
4. The earth rotates from west to east.
5. The earth's axis is tilted to a side.

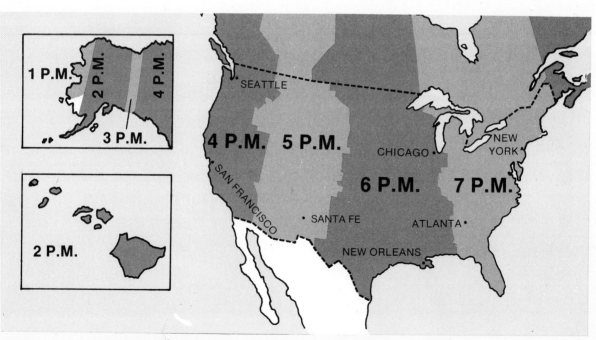

# What are the main directions?

We need to know directions in order to find places on a map. Many of the maps and globes that we use have north at the top of the globe. However this does not mean that north is at the top, or up. Nor does it mean that south is at the bottom, or down. Up and down are directions, but they have nothing to do with north and south. Up is a direction away from the center of the earth. Down is a direction toward the center of the earth. Up and down are not the main directions on a map.

There are four main directions that are used on maps. North, east, south, and west are the four main directions. North is the direction toward the North Pole. South is the direction opposite north and is toward the South Pole. East is the direction to our right when we are facing the north direction. West is the direction to our left when we are facing north.

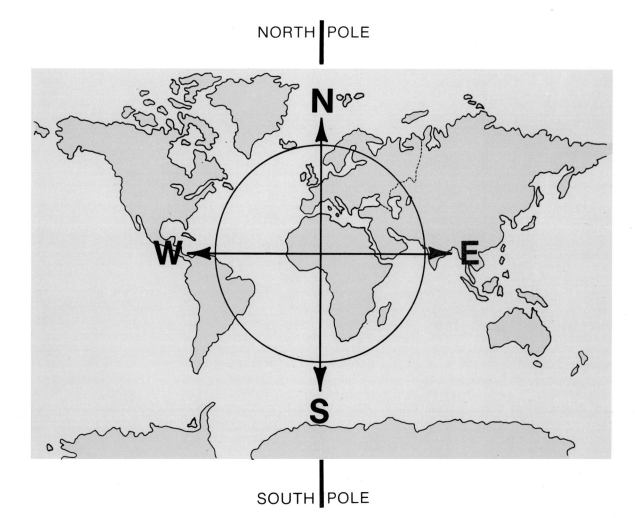

NORTH POLE

SOUTH POLE

# What are the intermediate directions?

North, east, south, and west are the main directions. These directions are useful in locating places on a map. But there are many parts of the earth that lie between these main directions. These are known as the intermediate directions. The compass shown on this page shows these intermediate directions. The four intermediate directions are northeast, southeast, southwest, and northwest.

Northwest lies halfway between north and west. Northeast lies halfway between north and east. Southwest lies halfway between south and west. Southeast lies halfway between south and east.

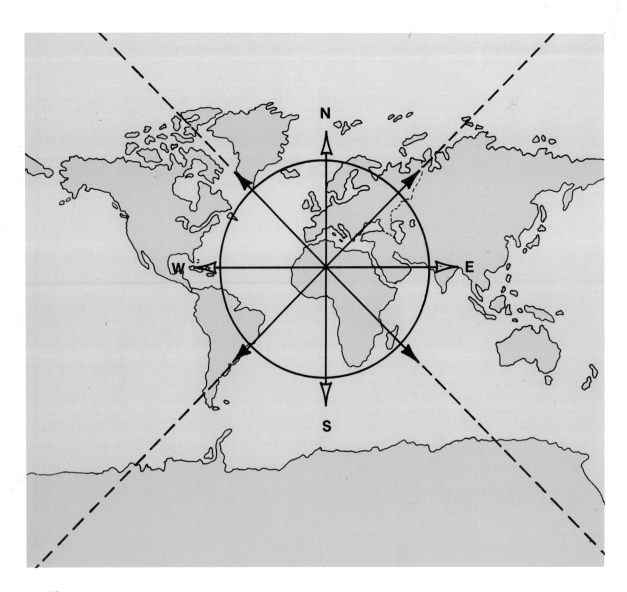

# What is meant by latitude and longitude?

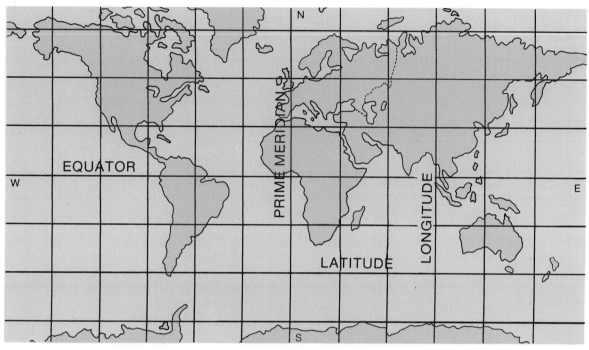

Maps are used to find, or locate, places on earth. This is done by using imaginary lines on the maps. Some of the lines circle the earth in an east-west direction. These east-west imaginary lines are known as lines of latitude. The equator is an imaginary east-west line. The equator divides the earth in half. One-half of the earth lies north of the equator, the other half lies south of the equator. All the lines of latitude are measured north and south of the equator.

The earth is also divided by north-south imaginary lines. The north-south lines are known as the lines of longitude. One of the north-south imaginary lines is drawn through western Africa and Europe. This line of longitude is called the Prime Meridian. Imaginary lines of longitude lie to the east or the west of the Prime Meridian.

Latitude and longitude are used to locate ships on the high seas. If you are in a car that needs help, you can phone a garage. You can give the garage your location as "15th Street and Anderson Place." But there are no streets on the oceans. Latitude and longitude take the place of streets. A ship that needs help has to give its location in latitude and longitude.

Suppose a ship needs help and gives its location as 30° south and 60° east.

*Can you locate this position on the map on page 44?*

# How do we measure latitude and longitude?

The map on this page shows the imaginary east-west lines and north-south lines. These are the lines of latitude and longitude. These lines on a globe or map are called a grid.

The lines on a grid map are numbered. The equator is numbered 0. It is the starting point for measuring lines of latitude. All east-west lines, or lines of latitude, are numbered from 0 to 90 north of the equator. They are also numbered 0 to 90 south of the equator.

The Prime Meridian is also numbered 0. It is the starting point for measuring longitude. All north-south lines, or lines of longitude are numbered 0 to 180 east of the Prime Meridian. They are also numbered 0 to 180 west of the Prime Meridian.

The small ° to the right of the number stands for degrees. The line of latitude marked 30°N stands for thirty degrees north latitude. The line of longitude marked 60°E stands for sixty degrees east longitude.

*What does 120° W stand for?*

*What country is crossed by the lines 30° N and 90° W?*

*What country is crossed by the lines 150° E and 30° S?*

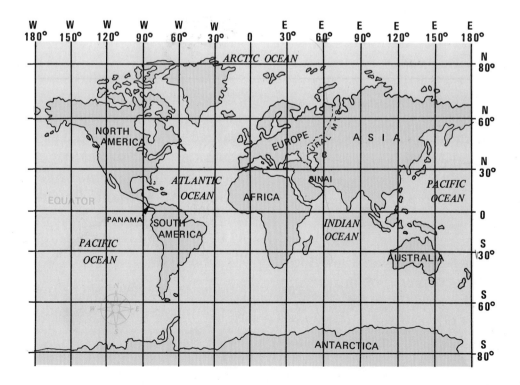

44

# LEARNING EXERCISES

## I. Remembering What We Have Read

Pick the best answer.

1. An example of an intermediate direction is
   a. north.
   b. southeast.
   c. east.
2. An example of a main direction is
   a. north.
   b. southwest.
   c. northeast.

3. The Prime Meridian is
   a. an east-west line.
   b. a north-south line.
   c. a main direction.
4. A grid shows
   a. directions.
   b. distance.
   c. lines of latitude and longitude.

## II. Directions and Locations on Maps

Look at the grid map below. Study the compass located in the lower left corner of the map. There are six letters on the map.

1. Which letter is located at 30°N and 30°E?
2. Which letter is located at 30°S and 60°W?

3. Which letter is located at 60°N and 120°E?
4. In which direction would you be traveling if you went from A to E?
5. In which direction would you be traveling if you went from C to E?
6. In which direction would you be traveling if you went from F to B?

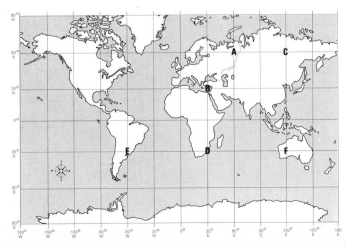

45

# What are the continents of the world?

A continent is a large land mass. The map on this page shows the world's seven large land masses or continents. They are North America, South America, Europe, Asia, Africa, Australia, and Antarctica.

North America and South America are joined together by a narrow strip of land. The southern boundary of Panama is the boundary between North and South America.

Asia is the largest continent and Australia is the smallest continent. Asia and Europe are separated by natural barriers in two places. The Ural Mountains separates them in the east. In the south, Europe is separated from Asia by the Caucasus Mountains. Because Europe and Asia are so closely joined together, they are sometimes called the Eurasian land mass.

*Why do you suppose they are given the name Eurasian?*

Africa is separated from Europe by the Mediterranean Sea. These two continents are only a few miles apart in some places. Africa and Asia are joined together at the Sinai Peninsula. The lands around the Sinai Peninsula are called the Middle East.

Australia is a large island that lies southeast of Asia.

Antarctica is a large land mass surrounding the South Pole. The shape of Antarctica is greatly distorted on a flat map of the world.

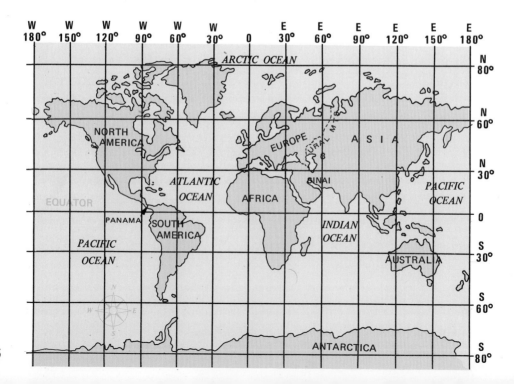

46

# What are the shapes of the continents?

Look at the map of the world shown on page 46. The names of the continents are given on the map. Notice the different shapes of the continents. It is important to be able to identify each continent by its shape.

This is the shape of the continent of North America.

This is the shape of the continent of Asia.

This is the shape of the continent of Europe.

This is the shape of the continent of Africa.

This is the shape of the continent of South America.

This is the shape of the continent of Australia.

This is the shape of the continent of Antarctica. Notice that the true shape of Antarctica is very different from the shape that is shown on a flat map. This can help you realize how much a flat map distorts shapes at the northern and southern parts of the world.

# What are the continents of the Eastern Hemisphere?

Look at the map and globe shown on this page. The north-south line on the map separates the Eastern and Western Hemispheres. The lands on the eastern portion of the map are in the Eastern Hemisphere. The globe shows the half of the world that lies within the Eastern Hemisphere.

The Eastern Hemisphere includes the continents of Europe, Asia, Africa, Australia, and part of Antarctica.

The Eastern Hemisphere also contains the waters of the Atlantic Ocean, Indian Ocean, and the Pacific Ocean.

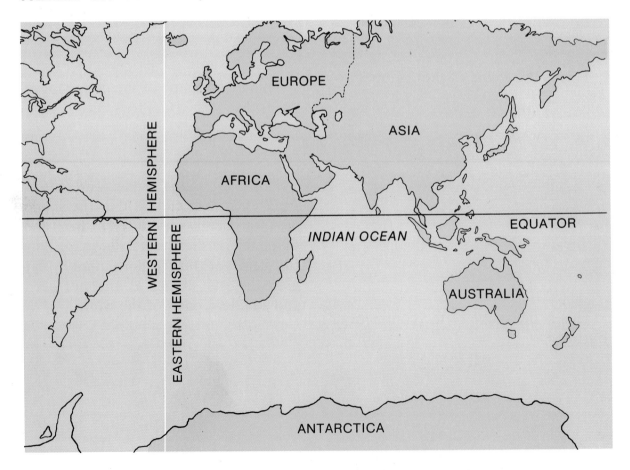

# What are the continents of the Western Hemisphere?

The map and globe on this page show the part of the earth that is the Western Hemisphere. The line from the North Pole to the South Pole on the map separates the Western Hemisphere and the Eastern Hemisphere. The lands lying to the west of the line are in the Western Hemisphere.

The Western Hemisphere includes the continents of North America, South America, and part of Antarctica. There is also a very small part of Siberia that lies within the Western Hemisphere. Siberia is part of the continent of Asia.

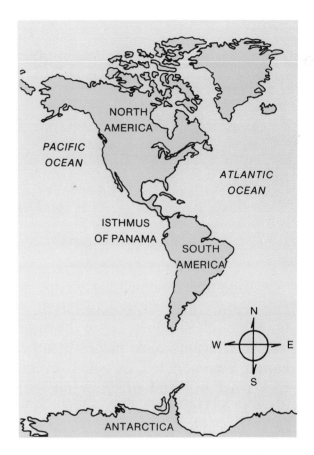

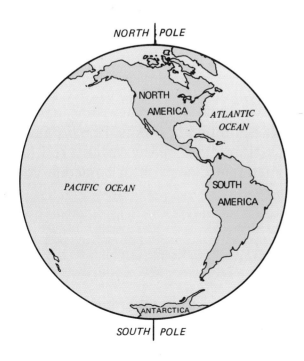

North America and South America are joined by a strip of land. This strip of land is at its narrowest at the Isthmus of Panama. An isthmus is a narrow strip of land that connects two larger bodies of land. Locate the Isthmus of Panama.

The continents in the Western Hemisphere have been called the New World. This was because the Europeans who discovered these continents regarded them as truly being a New World compared to the Old World of Europe with which they were familiar.

# What is a
# time line?

A time line is something we use to help show when events took place. A time line can also help us see the order in which events took place. In other words they can tell us which events took place first and which events took place at a later time. A time line has to be able to tell its own story. To do this, the time line must be complete. For instance, a time line like the one below is not complete and tells only part of the story.

| ANCIENT TIMES | MIDDLE AGES | MODERN TIMES |
|---|---|---|

The time line above tells us there have been three periods of time. These are the Ancient Times, which came first. It was followed by the Middle Ages, and then Modern Times. This tells us something, but we need to know more. We do not know how long ago the different periods of time began or ended.

When we use dates, we are better able to know how much time passed between different events. For instance, the time line below might tell us something about you or someone you know.

| 1970 | 1975 | 1980 |
|---|---|---|
| CHILD IS BORN | BEGINS SCHOOL | ENTERS 5TH GRADE |

The time line above tells us when this person was born, began school, and entered the 5th grade. We not only know the story of what happened, but we know when each event took place.

# What do time lines show?

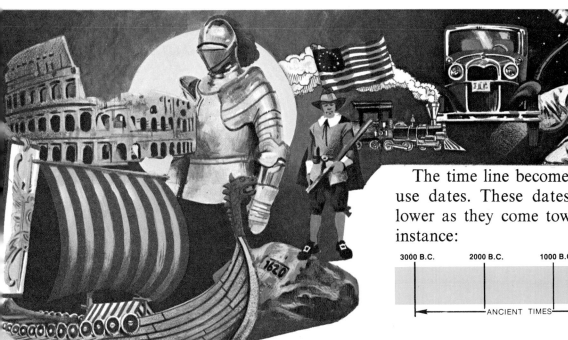

Time lines are used to show the periods of time in which events took place. Time can be divided into two periods. One period is called B.C. This is the period of the years before the birth of Christ. The other period is called A.D. The letters A.D. stand for the Latin words anno Domini. In Latin these words mean "in the year of our Lord." And they stand for the period after the birth of Christ. This is what a time line looks like when we divide it by using B.C. and A.D.

The time line becomes clearer if we use dates. These dates will become lower as they come toward A.D. For instance:

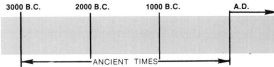

The dates will become higher during the A.D. period. For instance:

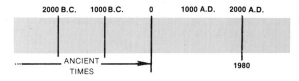

Time lines can help us see the order in which things happened. They can also point out the different periods of history.

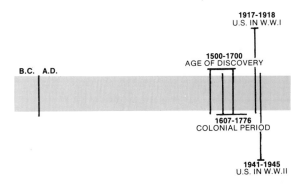

## LEARNING EXERCISES

### I. Remembering What We Have Read

Pick the best answer.

1. Panama is the boundary between
   a. Asia and Africa.
   b. Africa and Europe.
   c. North and South America.
2. The Mediterranean Sea separates
   a. Asia and Europe.
   b. Africa and Europe.
   c. Asia and North America.

3. The only continent listed below that is located in the Western Hemisphere is
   a. Asia.
   b. Africa.
   c. North America.
4. The lands where Asia and Africa join are called
   a. an isthmus.
   b. the Middle East.
   c. the Ural Mountains.

### II. The Shapes of Continents

How well do you know the shapes of the continents? Below are the outlines of the seven continents. Each has a letter upon it. Can you identify each continent?

### III. Reading a Time Line

How many years separate

1. 200 B.C. and 700 A.D.?
2. 500 B.C. and 200 B.C.?
3. 1900 A.D. and 500 B.C.?

| 500 B.C. | 200 B.C. | 0 | 400 A.D. | 700 A.D. | 1900 A.D. |

52

## IV. Learning About Maps

Can you identify the continents shown on this map? What continent is shown by the letter?

1. A
2. B
3. C
4. D
5. E
6. F
7. G

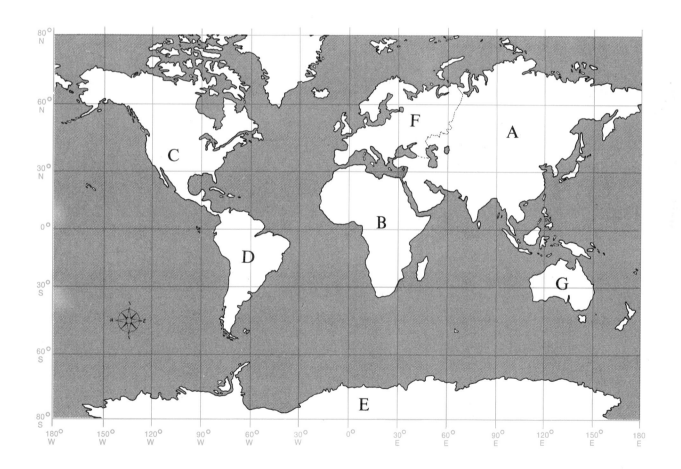

# What were the Middle Ages?

The time line on this page shows different periods of time. It shows Ancient Times, the Middle Ages, and the Age of Discovery and Exploration.

Fifteen hundred years ago, Rome was defeated by warlike tribes from northern Europe. The Fall of Rome brought many changes to Europe.

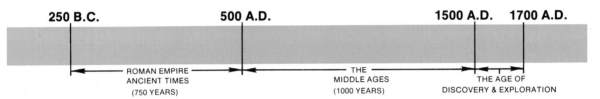

Ancient Times goes back many thousands of years. Two thousand years ago Europe lived in the Ancient Times. Most of Europe was ruled by the Roman Empire. Rome had risen from a small city-state to a mighty empire. Its emperors also ruled parts of northern Africa and the Middle East.

There is a special name for the 1,000 years following the fall of the Roman Empire. These are the years 500 A.D. to about 1500 A.D. This period of time is called the Middle Ages. The Middle Ages is the period between the end of Ancient Times and the beginning of the Modern Times in which we live.

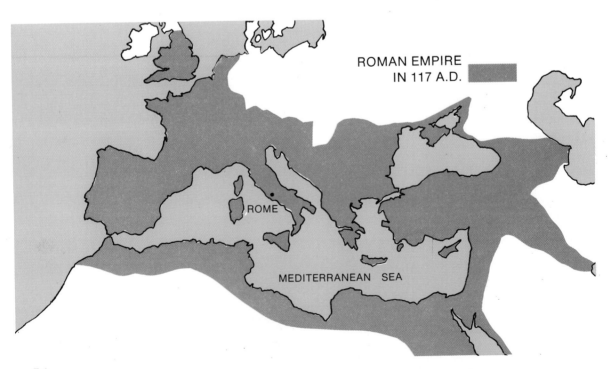

# What was life like in the Middle Ages?

Life in the Middle Ages was very different from life today. There were few big cities and almost no trade or industry. Most people lived on farms near large castles. These farms, and the lands near them, were called manors.

Each manor was ruled by a baron or other nobleman. The nobles were like kings in their own territories. Many nobles had small armies made up of knights in armor. The nobles and knights spent much of their time fighting wars. They did not do the hard work on the manors.

The work on the manors was done by poor people known as serfs and peasants. They worked as the farmers, carpenters, builders, and cloth makers. Serfs and peasants were not free to leave the land. Neither were any of their family free to leave it. They could not be bought and sold like slaves, but they were not really free.

Most manors raised their own food and made their own clothing and homes. They had little need for trade. When trade was needed, it was in the form of barter. This means they exchanged one item for another without the use of any kind of money.

The manors supplied all their own needs. This explains why there was so little trade during the Middle Ages. Because there was little trade, there was no need for big cities. Most cities were very small, walled towns. The free people of these cities were the merchants, craftsmen, and bankers. When they traded, they used gold and silver as money.

*How did life in the Middle Ages differ from today?*

*How do you suppose free people differ from serfs and peasants in the Middle Ages?*

# What were
# the Crusades?

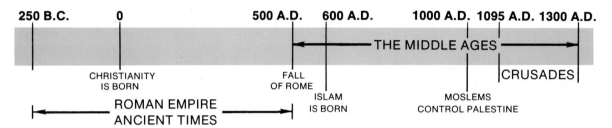

| 250 B.C. | 0 | 500 A.D. | 600 A.D. | 1000 A.D. | 1095 A.D. | 1300 A.D. |

THE MIDDLE AGES

CRUSADES

CHRISTIANITY
IS BORN

FALL
OF ROME

ISLAM
IS BORN

MOSLEMS
CONTROL PALESTINE

ROMAN EMPIRE
ANCIENT TIMES

The Crusades were an important part of the Middle Ages. The time line shows when the Crusades took place.

The Crusades were religious wars. They were wars of Christians against Moslems. The reasons for the Crusades go back to ancient times in the early Middle Ages.

A new religion was born in the land of Palestine two thousand years ago. Palestine was then a part of the Roman Empire. The founder of the new religion was Jesus Christ. This new religion is today known as Christianity.

Many Roman emperors disliked Christianity. It challenged their own religion and they felt that it was dangerous. The Romans tried to crush Christianity, but it grew stronger as time passed.

The ideas of Christianity spread rapidly after the Fall of Rome. The map on this page shows how it spread throughout Europe during the Middle Ages. After 600 A.D. Christianity was the main religion of Europe.

Christianity had first developed in the Middle East. This region had also been the birthplace of the Hebrew religion. During the 600s a third religion was born in the Middle East. Its founder was named Mohammed. His followers were known as Moslems.

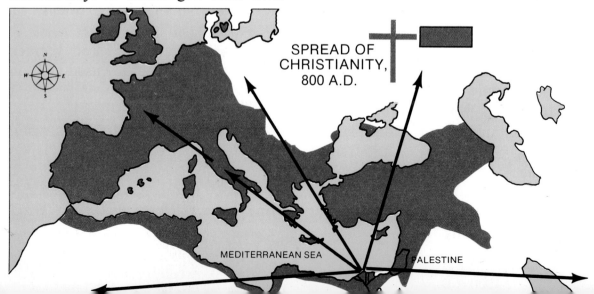

SPREAD OF
CHRISTIANITY,
800 A.D.

MEDITERRANEAN SEA

PALESTINE

The new religion was called Islam. The map shows how Islam spread throughout the Middle East and northern Africa. By the year 1000 the Moslems controlled Palestine, known also as the Holy Land. *Why do you think Palestine was called the Holy Land?*

The first Moslem conquerors had not bothered Christians living in the Middle East. However, they did try to win them over to the religion of Islam. Later a new group of Moslems took over as leaders of Islam. They made things more difficult for Christians living in the Middle East. In addition, the Moslem warriors were moving closer to the Christian city of Constantinople. Many of the Christian kings of Europe feared the spread of Islam.

By 700 A.D. the Moslem armies had invaded and conquered most of Spain. They were finally beaten in France during the early 700s. Now, four hundred years later, the Moslems were moving against Europe from another direction. Many nobles and kings in Europe were ready to fight the Moslems.

The leaders of the Christian church also feared the spread of Islam. The fall of the city of Constantinople might open all of Europe to the religion of Islam. Christian church leaders decided the Moslems must be stopped. The first step would be for Christians to win back the Holy Land.

The pope issued a call for a Holy War, or Crusade, to win back the Holy Land. The first Crusade only partly succeeded. Palestine was conquered, but was lost soon afterward. There were other Crusades during the next two hundred years. They all failed.

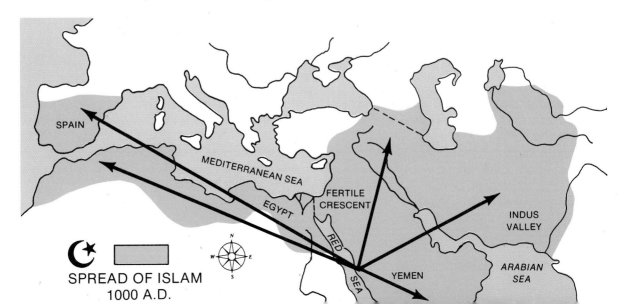

SPAIN

MEDITERRANEAN SEA

EGYPT

FERTILE CRESCENT

RED SEA

INDUS VALLEY

YEMEN

ARABIAN SEA

SPREAD OF ISLAM
1000 A.D.

# How much of the world was known to Europeans 500 years ago?

1470 A.D.  1492 A.D.                                                    1980 A.D.

DISCOVERY OF
THE NEW WORLD

A time line can show when certain things happened. For example, if we go back in time five hundred years, we are in the 1480s. This is the time just before the discovery of the New World.

The map below shows us how much of the world was known to Europeans in the 1480s, just before the New World was discovered. Most of the map is shaded. The light areas are parts of the world that were known to Europeans in the 1480s.

*Why do you think Europeans knew so little about most of the world at that time?*

It is surprising how little the Europeans knew about their own continent. Life in the Middle Ages did not involve much long-distance travel. Many people never traveled more than fifty miles from where they were born.

Europeans had never heard of the continents of North America, South America, Australia, and Antarctica. Some merchants and travelers had visited parts of northern Africa and Asia. However, most Europeans know almost nothing about either of these continents in their hemisphere.

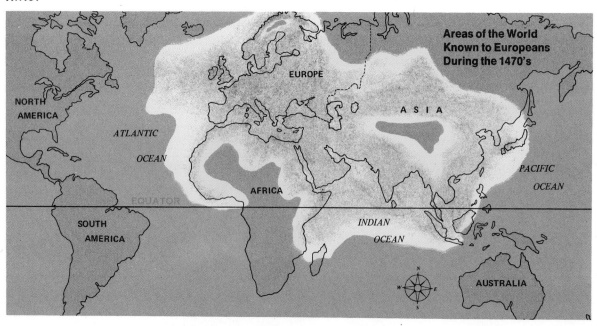

Areas of the World
Known to Europeans
During the 1470's

NORTH AMERICA
SOUTH AMERICA
ATLANTIC OCEAN
EUROPE
ASIA
AFRICA
PACIFIC OCEAN
INDIAN OCEAN
EQUATOR
AUSTRALIA

# The Vikings in the New World

About a thousand years ago the Norse people, or Vikings, lived in northern Europe. They lived in the lands known today as Norway, Sweden, and Denmark. The Norse people were known throughout Europe. They were daring sailors and fierce warriors. The Norse, or Vikings, sailed in ships to raid the coasts of England, France, Spain, and Italy. They also sailed westward into the Atlantic Ocean. Vikings started settlements on the islands of Iceland and Greenland.

Greenland was discovered and settled by a Norseman named Eric the Red. His son was named Leif Ericson, or Leif, the son of Eric. Leif was a daring sailor who did not fear the wild storms of the Atlantic Ocean.

Once long ago, Leif was returning to Greenland from Norway. His ship was blown off course in a storm. It reached a shore the Vikings had never seen before. Because the land had grapes which grew on vines, Leif called it Vineland. We now believe Vineland was on the shore of Newfoundland, a part of Canada.

When Leif and his sailors returned to Greenland, they told of the new land to the west. Later, other Vikings spent two years in Vineland. But the Vikings never settled in this new land. In time the discovery was remembered only in the stories of old people, which most of the other people did not believe and soon forgot.

The Vikings later gave up raiding other lands, settled in their own villages and engaged in fishing and farming. Only the legends of the past remained.

Today, we know that the stories of the Vikings were true. Leif Ericson and his sailors landed in the New World about five hundred years before Columbus made his voyage.

Knowing about the Vikings does not mean that we should give less credit to Columbus for his discovery. It does not matter who was actually the first to set foot in the New World. What matters is that Leif, Columbus, and many others had the courage to sail the dangerous oceans to find new lands.

Many people have compared the astronauts to Leif and Columbus. *What do you think of the comparison?*

# Why was Europe interested in new lands 500 years ago?

Europe had carried on trade with parts of Africa and Asia in Ancient Times. Most of that trade ended when the Roman Empire fell. Moslem control of the Middle East after 700 A.D. made trade even more difficult.

The Crusades failed to bring back the Holy Land for the Christians of Europe. But the Crusades opened Europe's eyes to trade. Crusaders brought back spices, rugs, fine silks, and other goods. Europeans liked these goods and wanted more of them. Kings and nobles were no longer happy on their manors. Their serfs and peasants could not produce the goods they could buy from the Middle East. The kings and nobles had to depend upon trade for these goods. *Why do you suppose the Europeans wanted spices and silks?*

An Italian traveler named Marco Polo visited far-off China in the 1200s. He brought back goods and stories of the wonders of distant lands. Soon other merchants and travelers began making the long, dangerous trip overland to China. More and more goods were brought back and traded for money.

Interest in trade grew rapidly during the 1400s. Europe wanted the riches and trade of lands never dreamed of before. But the overland routes to the Middle East and to China were long and dangerous. Some new routes had to be found.

| 700 A.D. | 1200 A.D. | 1400 A.D. |
|---|---|---|
| MOSLEMS CONTROL MIDDLE EAST | MARCO POLO VISITS CHINA | TRADE IN NEW LAND GROWS |

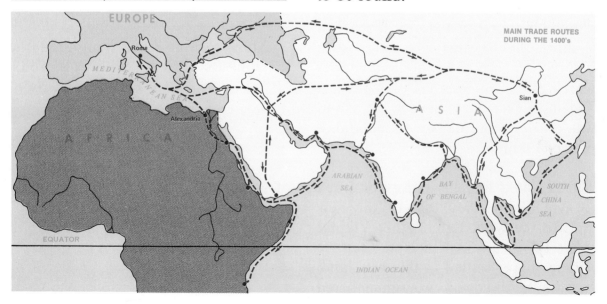

MAIN TRADE ROUTES DURING THE 1400's

# LEARNING EXERCISES

## I. Remembering What We Have Read

Pick the best answer.

1. The Middle Ages took place after
   a. the Age of Exploration.
   b. the start of modern times.
   c. the Age of Discovery.
   d. the Fall of Rome.

2. The Crusades were fought to win
   a. Constantinople.
   b. Rome.
   c. the Holy Land.
   d. new trade routes.

## II. Understanding a Time Line

Study the time line below. In which period of time did each of the following take place?

The Age of Discovery
Modern Times
The Middle Ages

| 500 A.D. | | 1500 A.D. | 1700 A.D. | 1900 A.D. |
|---|---|---|---|---|
| | A | B | C | |

## III. Thinking About Things

Can you guess the answers to these questions? The answers are not in the book. Not everyone joined the Crusades for religious reasons.

1. What might have been some other reasons people joined in the Crusades?

2. How might the world have been different if the Moslems had conquered Europe?

# Which lands did Portugal explore?

Portugal is a small country located west of Spain. In the 1400s it was interested in trade. But trade with China was in the hands of Italian merchants. The Portuguese had to look for trade and profits in Africa. There were gold mines in Africa just below the Sahara Desert. Portugal hoped to trade salt, metal goods, and cloth for this gold. Salt is scarce in Africa and Africans had long traded salt for gold.

*Why might salt be very important to Africans?*

A school for sailors was set up by Prince Henry of Portugal. The school was needed because sailors knew so little about the coast of Africa at that time. Navigators and geographers trained the Portuguese sailors. Prince Henry did not let religious prejudice stand in the way of his plans. He hired Moslems and Jews as well as Christians to teach at his school.

Prince Henry's plans worked well. During the 1450s some Portuguese captains began inching their way along the west coast of Africa. Some settlements were started along the coast and some gold was brought back. Before long the Portuguese began to wonder whether they could not sail around Africa to India.

In 1498 Vasco da Gama, a Portuguese sea captain rounded the Cape of Good Hope. He then sailed on to India. In India he picked up a rich cargo of spices and other goods. Other sea captains followed da Gama's path. Before long Portugal had set up trading stations in India. The Portuguese now controlled an all-water route to India.

Meanwhile, Portugal also became interested in America, which had been discovered by Spain. A Portuguese expedition was sent to America, led by Pedro Cabral. He landed in Brazil in 1500 and claimed it for Portugal. Brazil remained a Portuguese colony for about 300 years. Portuguese is still the language of Brazil.

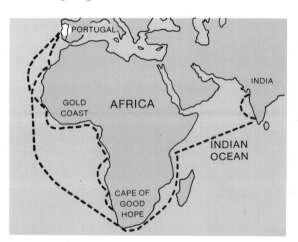

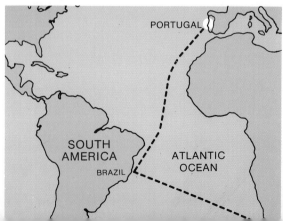

Christopher Columbus was born in northern Italy. When he was a young sailor his ship was sunk near Portugal. Columbus lived in Portugal for a time. He worked there as a sailor and map maker. During those years Columbus developed a plan to sail westward across the Atlantic Ocean to Asia. He felt that the world was round. This meant India could be reached from the west as well as from the east.

Portuguese sea captains also felt that the world was round. They agreed that anyone sailing westward would reach Asia sooner or later. But they believed that Asia was too far from Europe to be reached by sailing vessels.

Sometimes we say Columbus wanted to reach Asia. Other times we say he wanted to reach India. *Why is it correct to say either Asia or India?*

When Columbus failed to interest the Portuguese, he went to Spain. There he argued that Asia was only 2,500 miles to the west. Many sailing ships could make such a voyage without trouble. King Ferdinand and Queen Isabella of Spain agreed with Columbus. They gave him the money, ships, and crew he needed for the voyage.

We now know that Columbus was wrong in his ideas about geography. Asia is more than 2,500 miles west of Europe. Asia is actually about 11,000 miles west of Europe. But there was another body of land located about 3,000 miles from Europe. It was this land Columbus discovered in 1492. Columbus had made a mistake, but it turned out to be a lucky mistake. He did not find Asia, but he stumbled upon the New World.

Columbus never found fame and riches in his lifetime. The land he discovered was named for Amerigo Vespucci, another explorer who came later. Columbus made four voyages to this New World and died poor and lonely. But today we honor Columbus as the person whose skill and courage led to the European discovery of North and South America.

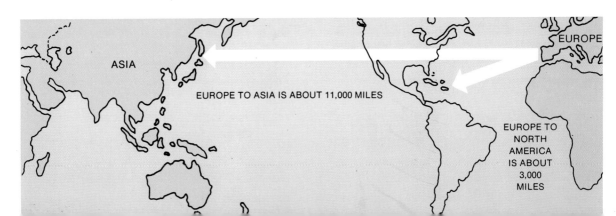

ASIA

EUROPE

EUROPE TO ASIA IS ABOUT 11,000 MILES

EUROPE TO NORTH AMERICA IS ABOUT 3,000 MILES

# Which lands did Spain explore?

Spain was ruled by Moslem conquerors for more than seven hundred years. The last Moslem armies were driven out of Spain in 1492. Spain was now able to develop its own trade and gain new lands.

Spain's search for trade routes was blocked by others. The overland trade with China was controlled by the northern Italian cities. Portugal controlled trade with western Africa. The idea of sailing around southern Africa to get to Asia seemed very dangerous.

Spain finally decided to accept the plan offered by Columbus. He proposed to sail westward across the Atlantic Ocean to reach Asia. Spain backed Columbus and he set out on his voyage. He never reached Asia. But his discovery opened the way for Spain to claim the lands of America.

Other Spanish explorers soon followed Columbus. They explored what is now Mexico, South America, and parts of the United States. Spanish trading posts and colonies were set up in many parts of the Americas. Today we often call these lands Latin America. This is because the people of Latin America speak Spanish. They also follow many of the customs of Spain. Spanish is one of the languages that developed from the Latin of Roman times.

Spain explored lands other than the Americas. Ferdinand Magellan was a Portuguese sea captain who was hired by Spain. This brave captain led his ships completely around the world. It was the first time anyone had sailed around the world. Magellan was killed during the voyage, but his discoveries gave Spain claim to Pacific lands. The map shows the lands Spain explored and claimed from 1492 to 1600.

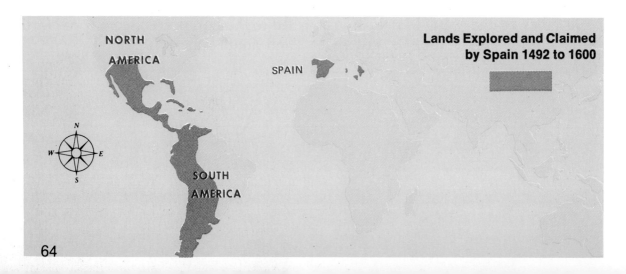

NORTH AMERICA

SPAIN

**Lands Explored and Claimed by Spain 1492 to 1600**

SOUTH AMERICA

N
W E
S

# What riches did Spain find in the New World?

When the Spaniards realized they had found a world unknown to Europeans, they were unhappy. Their goal had been the riches of Asia, not this strange new land. The Spanish explorers kept looking for ways of getting through the Western Hemisphere lands. Once past the land, they might sail on to the riches of Asia.

Not all Spanish explorers wanted only gold and other treasure. Columbus had seen that the islands of the Caribbean Sea had rich soil. He and others felt that farming could be carried on in the islands. There might be a good market for the special products that could be raised in the New World. Many new products, such as corn, tobacco, sugar, and potatoes, were brought back to Europe. Some of these products were then grown in Europe. Some European settlers raised crops on large farms called plantations. However, most Spanish settlers wanted riches. They did not want to be farmers.

For the first twenty-five years, the European discovery of America meant little to Spain. Then gold and silver were finally found. Cortes, a conquistador (kon-kees-ta-dor), crushed the Aztec Indians of Mexico. He seized their rich treasures of gold and silver. A little later, another conquistador, Pizarro, seized the treasures of the Inca Indians of Peru.

Gold and silver began to pour into Spain. Suddenly everyone was interested in the Americas. Spanish explorers called adelantados (ah-day-lahn-tah-dos), or "scouts," came looking for more treasure. The search was on for gold, silver, and other riches.

# BALBOA

Vasco Nunez de Balboa was a Spanish adventurer and explorer. He liked gold but he also liked excitement. In 1501 Balboa left Spain for Hispaniola. This is the island that is now Santo Domingo and Haiti. He found life on the island very dull. He soon began to look for excitement. In 1510 Balboa hid aboard a ship that was leaving for Panama. Once at sea, he helped the crew overthrow the captain and became their leader.

The ship reached Panama and started a new settlement called Darien.

Balboa became the governor of the new colony. The Indians in the area told Balboa about a great ocean to the west. They said gold was to be found along the shores of this ocean.

In 1513 Balboa set out to find this great ocean and the gold. With 200 Spaniards, and hundreds of Indians, he marched across Panama. The trip was only 45 miles long, but it took them three weeks. Those 45 miles were filled with swamps and jungles. Many of the men became sick and died during the trip.

Finally, Balboa and his followers reached a point from which they could see water. They were the first Europeans in America to set eyes on this giant sea. Balboa named it the South Sea. In later years, another explorer would name it the Pacific Ocean. That is the name we use today.

On September 29, 1513, Balboa walked into the water. He drew his sword and claimed the South Sea for the king of Spain. He and his party then returned to the settlement at Darien. There he found a new governor who had been sent by the king of Spain. Balboa and the new governor soon became enemies. The governor claimed that Balboa was trying to get rid of him. He had Balboa put to death.

Balboa's discovery of the Pacific Ocean was very important. He found that the Pacific and Atlantic Oceans were separated only by the Isthmus of Panama. An isthmus is a narrow strip of land that connects two larger bodies of land. The Isthmus of Panama is only 45 miles wide. It connects North America and South America.

Panama became a busy part of the Spanish empire. Ships carried gold and silver from the Philippine Islands and from Peru to Panama's Pacific coast. The gold and silver were unloaded and carried to the Atlantic side of the isthmus. The treasures were then carried by ship to Spain. The trip across Panama meant that the ships did not have to make the long and dangerous voyage around the southern tip of South America.

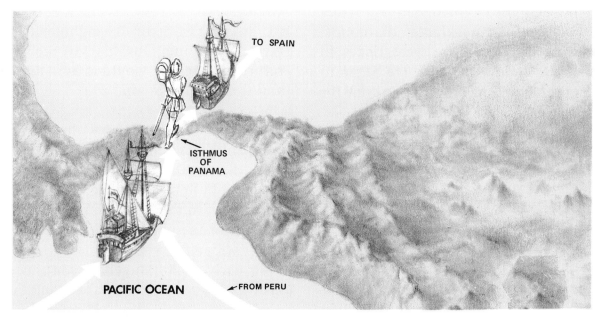

TO SPAIN

ISTHMUS OF PANAMA

PACIFIC OCEAN

FROM PERU

# MAGELLAN

In 1499 all Portugal was talking about the sea captain Vasco da Gama. He had just returned to Portugal after two years at sea. In those two years, da Gama had sailed around the southern tip of Africa to a distant port in India.

Ferdinand Magellan was excited by da Gama's trip. Magellan was a nineteen-year-old attendant at the king's court.

For five years Magellan watched Portuguese ships sail to carry on trade with India. Sea captains brought back spices, golden necklaces, diamonds, and silverware. There were riches in the new trade with India. He began to dream of winning fame and fortune for himself.

In 1502 Magellan sailed to India. Magellan spent seven years in the Far East. During this time he explored many parts of Southeast Asia.

Magellan returned to Portugal in 1511. He was now convinced India could be reached by sailing westward across the Atlantic. He knew that America was on the other side of the Atlantic Ocean. But Magellan believed he could find a passage through the American lands. Once on the other side of America, he would be in another great body of water. That body of water was then called the South Sea. Today we call it the Pacific Ocean. Magellan believed he could sail westward across the South Sea to India.

Magellan took his plan to the king of Portugal. He was turned down and left for Spain. The Spanish king agreed to give him money for his voyage. In return, Magellan would claim lands and treasure for Spain.

In 1519 Magellan, now thirty-nine years old, started his trip with five ships. Six weeks later he had reached the coast of South America. He carried on trade with the Indians and dropped anchor for the winter season.

In early 1520 Magellan continued his trip. He sailed southward along the coast of South America. At the southern tip of South America, he came to a strait. A strait is a narrow body of water between two bodies of land. He set out to sail through the strait.

The strait turned out to be over three hundred miles long. There were icebergs in the water and large rocks on both sides of the strait. The winds were strong, and ice covered the decks during most of the trip. Many of Magellan's sailors feared for their lives.

One ship captain refused to go, but the other ships followed Magellan. It took them six weeks to get through the strait. Finally, they entered a calm blue ocean. Magellan realized this was the South Sea that had been discovered earlier. He renamed it the Pacific Ocean because it was so calm and peaceful. Pacific is a Latin word that means calm and peaceful.

Magellan now sailed north toward the equator. He hoped to escape the bitter Antarctic cold. Finally he reached the Philippine Islands. There, on April 27, 1521, Magellan was killed in a battle with Indians. The sailors on the one ship that remained set sail westward from the Philippines. They moved into the Indian Ocean and sailed to the east coast of Africa. The ship then rounded the southern tip of Africa and headed north to return to Spain. On September 8, 1522, the single remaining ship of Magellan's fleet returned to Spain. Only eighteen sailors were left of the starting crew!

Magellan did not find the fortune he had sought in Asia. He did not even live to find fame for leading the first ship that sailed completely around the world. Today we hail Magellan's voyage because the brave sailors with him were the first to sail around the globe.

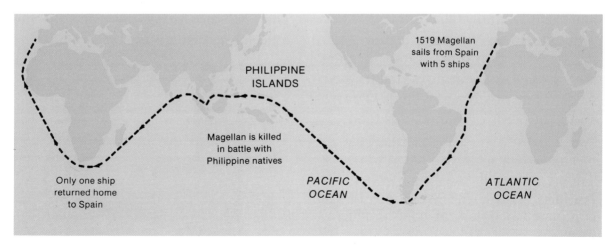

1519 Magellan sails from Spain with 5 ships

PHILIPPINE ISLANDS

Magellan is killed in battle with Philippine natives

Only one ship returned home to Spain

PACIFIC OCEAN

ATLANTIC OCEAN

# Cortes
# and the Aztecs

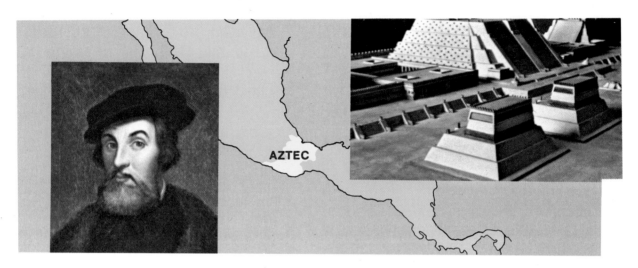

The first Spanish conquistadores came to Mexico in the 1500s. They discovered the Aztec civilization. The Aztecs were an Indian people. They had lived in Mexico for hundreds of years before the Spaniards came.

Hernando Cortes was the leader of the Spanish conquistadores in Mexico. He was amazed when he saw the Aztec civilization. The Aztecs lived in fine houses in great cities. Many of the cities were built on islands. The Aztecs had schools and courts of law. They were skilled in weaving, metal work, music, and painting. Aztec farmers used irrigation to bring water to their fields. They raised many kinds of crops and kept herds of animals for food.

The Aztecs were also fierce warriors. They conquered and ruled over other Indian tribes in Mexico. These conquered people sent gold and silver to the Aztecs. Skilled Aztec workers made jewelry and ornaments from the gold and silver. For the Aztecs, gold and silver were not valuable in themselves. They were valuable only as metals from which beautiful ornaments could be made.

When Montezuma, the ruler of the Aztecs, met Cortes, he thought Cortes was a god. He showered Cortes with gifts of jewels and gold and silver. Cortes and his men nearly went mad with greed when they saw these gifts. They set out to get the riches of the Aztecs for themselves.

Cortes soon made Montezuma a prisoner in his own palace. Then his men seized all the gold and silver they could find. When the Aztecs tried to stop them, fierce fighting broke out. Montezuma asked his people to let the Spaniards leave in peace. But Montezuma now had many enemies among his people. He was killed by an angry mob and Cortes and his men escaped.

Cortes waited a few months and then returned with his soldiers. By now he had the help of some Indian tribes who hated the Aztecs.

The Spanish force was small, but it had guns to use against the spears of the Aztecs. Cortes defeated the Aztecs and the Spanish destroyed their civilization. From then on, the Aztec Indians were ruled by their Spanish conquerors.

Cortes and his followers had found a great civilization in Mexico. They wiped out that civilization when they destroyed the Aztecs. To the Spanish conquistadores gold and silver meant more than the great civilization of the Aztec people. The greed of the Spaniards destroyed the life of the Aztecs.

# LEARNING EXERCISES

## I. Remembering What We Have Read

Pick the best answer.

1. The first Europeans to sail around Africa to India were the
   a. French.
   b. Portuguese.
   c. Spaniards.
   d. Italians.
2. The Pacific Ocean was discovered by
   a. Columbus.
   b. Cortes.
   c. Balboa.
   d. da Gama.
3. The first voyage to sail around the world was led by
   a. Cortes.
   b. Columbus.
   c. LaSalle.
   d. Magellan.
4. Spain claimed all the following except
   a. Mexico.
   b. Peru.
   c. Brazil.
   d. Hispaniola.

## II. Thinking About Things

Can you guess the answers to these questions? They are based on what you have been reading, but the answers are not in the book.

1. Were the Europeans wise in looking for gold and silver instead of settling on the land as farmers?
2. How do you suppose the Indians of the New World felt about European explorers?
3. Why might some people in Europe have been willing to move to the New World as settlers?

**FRANCISCO VASQUEZ de CORONADO**

Coronado had heard stories about seven rich cities to the north. The Indians called this land Cibola. It was said there was an endless supply of gold in these cities. Indians claimed the people of Cibola wore rings and earrings of gold. The roofs of their houses were said to be covered with sheets of gold!

In 1540 Coronado set out to find Cibola. With him were 300 Spaniards and several hundred Indians. They took along over a thousand horses, mules, and cattle. It was clear that Coronado meant to keep going until he found the gold of Cibola.

In the next two years Coronado and his men covered thousands of miles. They did not find Cibola because no such cities existed. Instead, Coronado found Indian villages in what is today Arizona and New Mexico. These were the villages of the Zuñi Indians.

The Zuñi Indians had no gold, but they led an interesting life. They lived in mud-covered homes called pueblos (poo-ehb-lohs). The pueblos were several stories high, but had no stairs. The Indians used ladders to move from one story to another.

In addition to being good home builders, the Zuñi Indians were also good farmers. The land was dry, but they used irrigation to bring water to the soil. Irrigation made it possible for them to grow corn, squash, and beans.

Coronado found the Zuñis interesting, but he still wanted to find gold. He sent groups of his men to explore the land further in many directions. One group crossed the desert and discovered the Grand Canyon in what is now Arizona.

Meantime, Coronado continued on another journey. This took him into what are today the lands of Texas, Oklahoma, and Kansas. During this trip he saw large herds of buffalo. Coronado had never seen such animals before. He also met Indian tribes on these lands. He noted that they hunted the buffalo for food and clothing. All this was very interesting, but Coronado never found the gold which he sought.

In 1542 Coronado returned to Mexico. He had not found gold, but his journey was to bring him fame in later years. Coronado is now known as one of the great early explorers of the United States.

# BARTOLOMÉ de LAS CASAS

Thousands of Spaniards came to the Americas in search of gold and silver. Bartolomé de Las Casas, a Spanish priest, came for a very different reason. His purpose was to bring the Christian religion to the Indians of America.

Las Casas first came on one of the trips made by Columbus. He spent almost all the rest of his life in America. Like most Europeans, he had thought of the Indians as savages. But, after many years in Mexico, he changed his mind. He felt that it was the Europeans who were the savages! They cared only for gold and silver. To get these treasures, they were willing to steal and kill.

This gentle priest spent years trying to win justice for the Indians. He wrote letters to the king and queen of Spain pleading for help for the Indians. In one of those letters he warned:

"We give as a real and true reckoning, that in forty years, more than twelve million persons, men, women, and children have died unjustly. . . . The reason is solely because Europeans have made gold their aim, seeking to load themselves with riches in the shortest time. . . ."

The pleas made by Las Casas were not heeded. Until his death, at the age of ninety-two, he continued to plead for justice for the Indians. Help never came. Las Casas failed because Spain cared less about people than it did about gold.

# Black explorers in the Americas

Black people lived in many parts of Europe during the 1400s and 1500s. They had been brought to Europe from Africa. Some were slaves, but many were free men and women. They earned their living as servants, merchants, craftsmen, and sailors. There were black sailors on some ships that sailed to the Americas from Europe.

It is not certain whether there was a black man in Columbus's crew. However, there were about thirty black soldiers and sailors with Balboa. He was the first European to cross Panama and reach the Pacific Ocean. Other blacks were with Cortes and Pizarro in Mexico and Peru.

A black man named Estevanico helped to discover New Mexico and Arizona in the 1500s. Estevanico, or "little Stephen," was a black sailor from Morocco in northern Africa. He was with a Spanish ship that sank in the Gulf of Mexico. The only ones left alive were Estevanico and three others. It took them seven years of overland travel to reach safety in Mexico City.

On this journey, Estevanico and his companions spoke to many Indians. The Indians told them that north of Mexico were seven cities rich in gold, silver, and jewels. They were the Seven Cities of Cibola.

Some Spanish settlers in Mexico City had also heard these stories. They decided to try to find the rich cities. They asked Estevanico to guide them. He agreed to go on ahead and send back wooden crosses to show how near he was to the cities. The larger the cross, the nearer he was to the city.

Estevanico went ahead of the others and sent back crosses that grew larger each day. Soon one of his messengers brought back a cross the size of a man. It seemed to mean he had found the cities. But when the others caught up with Estevanico, he was dead. He had been killed by the Indians. As for the famed cities, they were only the adobe villages of the Indians. There were no riches in them!

Estevanico died, and the expedition returned empty-handed, but it did open the way to the American Southwest.

# What lands did France explore and settle?

The first explorer for France, in the Americas, was an Italian named Giovanni Verrazano (Jee-o-vah-nee Veh-rah-zahno). He hoped to find a waterway from the Atlantic Ocean to the Pacific Ocean. A narrow waterway of this type is called a strait. Such a waterway would get him through to the Pacific and enable him to sail on to Asia.

Verrazano sailed to America in 1524, but he found no waterway. Nor did he find gold or silver. What he did find were the lands from Newfoundland to the Carolinas. He was the first European to set foot on the land that is now New York City. There is a bridge in New York City today that honors this explorer. It has been named the Verrazano Bridge.

Other French explorers followed Verrazano. During the 1530s and 1540s, Jacques Cartier (zhock Cahtyer) made three voyages. He, too, was looking for a strait through the Americas to Asia. Cartier found no strait, but he did explore the St. Lawrence River and the lands near it. His discoveries led France to claim parts of Canada.

In the 1600s the French journeyed farther into America. Samuel de Champlain (sham-plane) explored the St. Lawrence River area and started a number of settlements there. By this

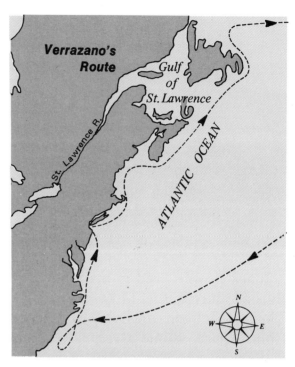

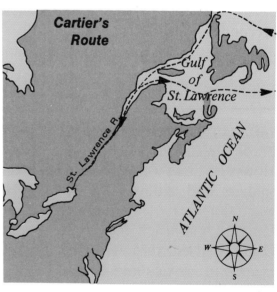

time, the eastern part of Canada was known as New France.

*Why do you suppose the eastern part of Canada was called New France?*

Two Frenchmen journeying south and west explored the area now called the Ohio River Valley. They were Father Marquette (Mar-kett), a priest, and Louis Joliet (jo-lee-yet), a trader. They were followed by the greatest French explorer in North America, Robert Cavelier de La Salle. He explored the lands from the Great Lakes to the mouth of the Mississippi River on the Gulf of Mexico.

As a result of these explorations, France claimed much of North America. This included part of Canada and the lands from the Great Lakes to the Gulf of Mexico. France also claimed the lands from the Ohio River Valley to the Rocky Mountains. These far western lands were called Louisiana by the French. The map shows the lands explored and claimed by France.

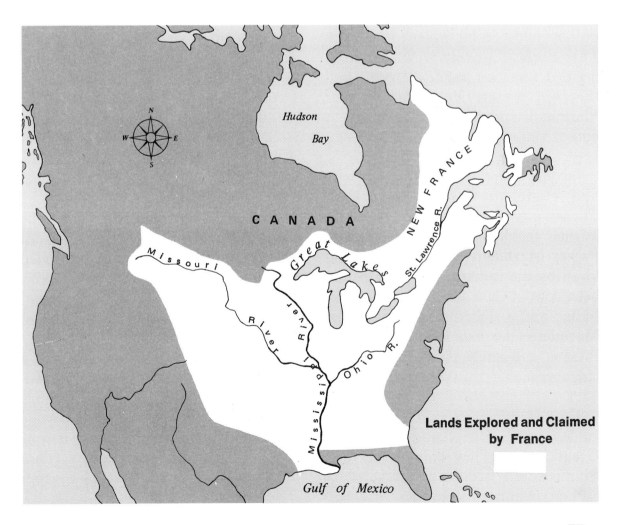

Lands Explored and Claimed by France

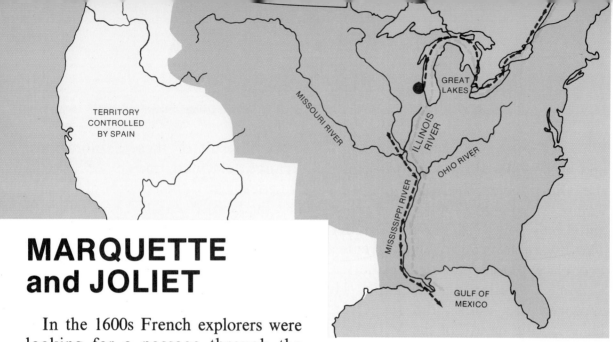

TERRITORY CONTROLLED BY SPAIN

MISSOURI RIVER

GREAT LAKES

ILLINOIS RIVER

OHIO RIVER

MISSISSIPPI RIVER

GULF OF MEXICO

# MARQUETTE and JOLIET

In the 1600s French explorers were looking for a passage through the American continent. Their main goal was to reach Asia with its rich treasures and its trading goods. The Indians told of a big water to the west. The French governor of Canada decided someone ought to try to find this big water. He asked Father Marquette and Louis Joliet to try to find it.

Jacques Marquette was a priest who had come to Canada to preach Christianity to the Indians. He had learned their customs and languages. Father Marquette was respected and loved by the Indians. Louis Joliet had been born in Canada. He was a hunter, trader, and a skilled map maker. Like Marquette, he had lived among the Indians and knew their customs and languages.

The two explorers, and their Indian guides, paddled in canoes across the Great Lakes. They came ashore in what is now Wisconsin and traveled by canoe down many streams.

After months of searching, they came upon the Mississippi River. They thought this might be the passage they were seeking. They and their guides paddled south down the river, hoping it would turn westward toward the Pacific Ocean. But the river kept flowing southward. Other rivers joined it. Still there was no sign that the river would ever lead to any ocean to the west.

Finally, the explorers realized the river must flow into the Gulf of Mexico. This area was then controlled by Spain. Disappointed and weary, Marquette and Joliet turned around and made their way back to Canada.

Marquette and Joliet did not find a passage to the Pacific Ocean. Instead, they had explored the upper portions of the Mississippi River. Their voyage lasted four months and covered four thousand miles. It gave France a claim to the vast territory of the Mississippi River Valley.

# What riches did France find in the New World?

The French explored the Americas hoping to find a strait through the land. They also hoped to find gold and silver. French explorers did not find the strait, or gold, or silver. But they did find furs and fish.

The forests of Canada have many fur-bearing animals. These include beaver, otters, and foxes. Many French settlers hunted these animals for their furs. The furs were very popular in Europe where they could be made into hats and coats.

Not all Frenchmen did their own hunting in the Americas. Some opened trading posts in Canada. They traded knives, guns, blankets, and other goods for furs which Indians brought to the trading posts. Hunting and trading became the chief work of French settlers in Canada.

Other French settlers started a fishing industry. The Grand Banks in the Atlantic Ocean near Newfoundland are rich in fish. French vessels sailed to the Grand Banks to catch the fish. They then stopped in Newfoundland to dry and cure them. Drying and curing preserved their catch of fish for the long trip to France. Dried fish from Canada was sold in many European marketplaces.

France was never able to get many people to settle in Canada as farmers. Most French settlers who came to the Americas hoped to make fortunes. Furs and fish were the chief riches that France found in the New World. These could not compare with the gold and silver of Spain's colonies. The result was that French colonies in America never attracted many people as settlers.

# LEARNING EXERCISES

## I. Remembering What We Have Read

Pick the best answer.

1. France found all the following in the New World **except**
   a. furs.
   b. fish.
   c. gold.
   d. trade.
2. Coronado was looking for
   a. Mexico.
   b. Peru.
   c. the Grand Canyon.
   d. Cibola.
3. Newfoundland was explored by
   a. Coronado.
   b. Estevanico.
   c. Verrazano.
   d. Cartier.
4. All the following were explorers for France **except**
   a. Las Casas.
   b. Verrazano.
   c. Cartier.
   d. Joliet.

## II. Thinking About Things

Can you guess the answers to these questions? They are based on what you have been reading, but the answers are not in the book.

1. What does Coronado's journey tell us about the Spanish explorers?
2. Why did Europeans keep looking for a waterway to the Pacific Ocean?
3. Why were the Grand Banks as great a treasure as the gold and silver of the Americas?

## III. True or False

1. The Zuñi Indians were good farmers.
2. Cartier's discoveries led France to claim parts of Canada.
3. Estevanico explored for France.
4. Las Casas was a priest.
5. Marquette and Joliet found the Gulf of Mexico.

## IV. Learning From Pictures

Each of the pictures tells us something about the explorers in the New World.

What does each picture mean to you?

## V. Reviewing Explorers and Hemispheres

The Eastern and Western Hemispheres are shown below. In which hemisphere did the following take place?

1. Portuguese sailors reach the Cape of Good Hope.
2. Cortes defeats the Aztecs.
3. Vasco da Gama reaches India.
4. Columbus sails from Spain.
5. French settlers fishing off the Grand Banks.

WESTERN HEMISPHERE

EASTERN HEMISPHERE

# Which lands did England explore and settle?

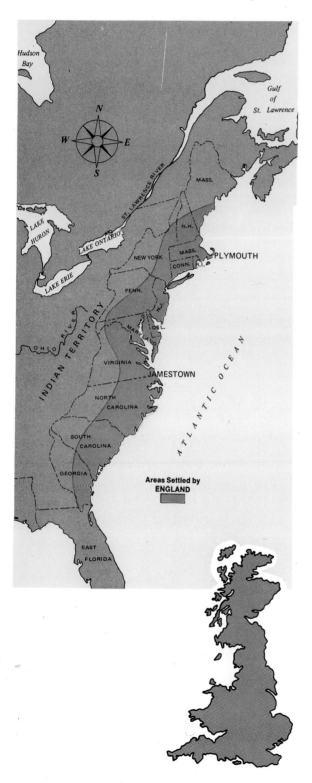

Areas Settled by
ENGLAND

England made its first claim to land in the Americas in 1497. The claim was based on the voyage of John Cabot. Cabot was an Italian who sailed to America as an explorer for England.

John Cabot probably landed in Newfoundland. He established England's first claim in America. However, England had no permanent settlement in America until 1607. That settlement was Jamestown in Virginia.

The first English settlers hoped to find gold, silver, and furs. They found none of these, but they did find rich farmland. Most of the early settlers became farmers.

*Why was England better off with farmland than Spain and France with their riches of gold, silver, furs, and fish?*

The English explored and settled the lands along the Atlantic Coast of North America. The colonies they started included Plymouth, Massachusetts Bay, Rhode Island, Pennsylvania, Maryland, and Georgia. In 1664 the English captured New Amsterdam, a colony the Dutch had started. It was renamed New York by the English. England also claimed the area around Hudson Bay in Canada. The map on this page shows the lands that the English explored and settled in America.

# What riches did England find in the New World?

Spain had found rich treasure in the Americas. England hoped to find the same, but its colonies had no gold or silver. The English settlers found other riches. These were farmland, thick forests, and good fishing waters. People came to the English colonies to make a living, not to get rich quick. They had to work hard for a living.

The colonies stretched for about one thousand miles north and south along the Atlantic coastline. Life was different in each English colony. People in the northern colonies lived differently than people in the middle colonies or southern colonies.

The map shows the locations of the northern, middle, and southern colonies. It also shows the products of these colonies.

*Which of these colonies would you have chosen for your home? Why?*

Settlers in the northern colonies found the soil rocky and not very rich. Instead of farming, they turned to fur trapping, lumbering, and fishing. Those who engaged in lumbering cut the tall trees found in the northern colonies. The timber could be used as masts on sailing ships. Those who engaged in fishing brought in catches of cod and other fish. They also hunted whales on the high seas. Whale oil was used to light the wicks of lamps in homes.

The settlers in the middle colonies were mostly farmers. They raised wheat and other grains. Some of the grain was used for food. Grains were also sold as a cash crop. Some were shipped to other parts of America and to England. The middle colonies produced so much grain that they were called the bread colonies.

The southern colonies raised rice, tobacco, indigo, and hemp. Indigo was used to dye cloth purple. Hemp was used to make rope. Southern colonies also produced tar and turpentine. The tar and hemp were used on the sailing ships of America and England.

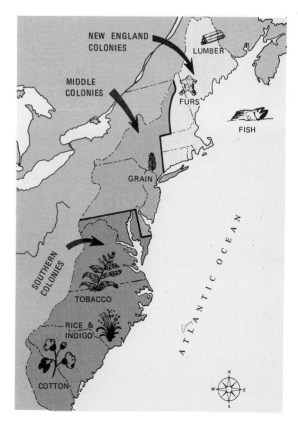

# JOHN CABOT

## Man of Mystery

John Cabot is truly a man of mystery in the exploration of America. There are no pictures of him. No letters or any other samples of his handwriting remain. There is not even a good description of this great explorer. It is as though he just walked in a door, stayed a moment, and walked out. Yet there are some things that are known about him.

The mystery about John Cabot starts with his name. He was born in northern Italy, probably in the city of Genoa. This is the same city where Columbus was born. It is probable they were both born in the same year.

His real name is believed to have been either Cabottoo, Kaboto, Bagoto, Cabuto, or something of that kind. In Italy these names were given to sailors on ships engaged in trade along the coast. From this, it would seem that Giovanni Caboto really means "John, the coastal shipping man." Later, when he sailed from England, the name Giovanni Caboto was changed by the English to John Cabot. We shall call him John Cabot.

Cabot lived in the city of Venice for fifteen years. He became a citizen of that city. He was a skilled sailor and wanted to find a sea route to India. But he felt he ought to sail north and west rather than south and west like Columbus. Cabot believed this northwestern route would lead to Cathay, or North China.

Cabot failed to win support in Spain or Portugal for his ideas. He then went to England where he hoped he could interest the king. The choice of England was a lucky one. King Henry VII of England had turned down Columbus only a few years before. He was now willing to listen to ideas for finding the Indies or China by sailing westward. Henry VII agreed to let Cabot sail under an English flag. In 1497 John Cabot and his crew set sail in a single ship, the *Matthew*. They were looking for a new northwest sea route to China.

Cabot was a fine sailor and the *Matthew* must have been an excellent ship. It made the trip from England to the land now known as Newfoundland in thirty-five days. This was very good time in those days. The sailing ships used only winds and currents to carry them across the ocean. This took great skill.

Cabot landed on an island he believed was near the Chinese mainland. He spent about a month exploring the Newfoundland area and its eastern coast. He found no humans on the land, but probably did not go very far inland. Cabot noted the thick fog in the area and also the fine fishing areas. No wonder! He had sailed into the Grand Banks area off the coast of Newfoundland. The crew caught codfish by lowering a basket into the water and raising it! This may seem a fishing story, but the Grand Banks are the world's richest fishing area.

John Cabot returned to England in less than three months. He brought back no gold, Indians, or treasures. In spite of this, the king of England was happy with the report. Both he and Cabot believed that a second trip would uncover a sea route to China. In 1498 John Cabot set out on his second voyage. This time, there were six ships making the voyage. One ship returned to port soon after the start of the voyage. John Cabot and the other five ships were never heard of again.

John Cabot, man of mystery, vanished in the most mysterious way. Whether he and the others died on the high seas is unknown. John Cabot never learned the real importance of his discoveries. He had not found a new path to India. Instead, he had discovered North America and the Grand Banks off Newfoundland. His voyage established the claim of England to North America.

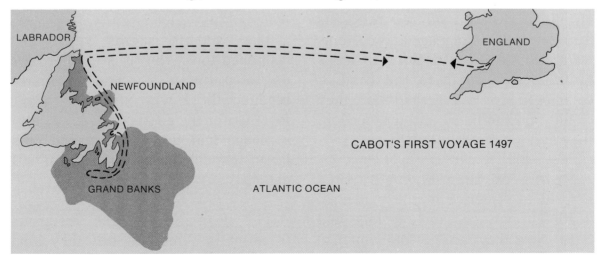

LABRADOR

ENGLAND

NEWFOUNDLAND

CABOT'S FIRST VOYAGE 1497

GRAND BANKS

ATLANTIC OCEAN

# The Mayflower Compact

People came to the New World for many reasons. Some hoped to find new trade routes to Asia. Later many came in hopes of finding gold and silver. Priests and missionaries came to bring the Christian religion to the Indians. Finally, there were those who came in search of freedom and a new way of life.

Among those seeking freedom was a small group of English people called Pilgrims. They were called Pilgrims because they left their homes to go to distant lands. The Pilgrims were searching for religious freedom. They founded the Plymouth colony in Massachusetts in 1620 as an English settlement.

The Pilgrims had been forced to leave England because of their religious beliefs. They moved to Holland where they lived for ten years. But the Pilgrims were not happy in Holland. Holland offered religious freedom, but its language and customs were strange. They decided to leave Holland and come to the English colonies in America. Perhaps here they would find the home and the freedom they had long been seeking.

Sailing on the *Mayflower,* they arrived in America in the winter of 1620. The voyage had been long and hard. Now they faced a cold winter in a strange land. They realized that they

must work together if they were to survive in their new home.

The new settlers held a meeting before they went ashore. At this meeting they drew up rules for all settlers in the new colony. The agreement they drew up is known today as the Mayflower Compact. It was the first agreement providing for self-rule in America.

The writing seems very old-fashioned today, but it is not hard for us to understand. The Compact pledged those who signed to work together for the good of all. It was also a pledge that the signers would pass laws respecting the rights of all colonists.

The Pilgrims sought religious freedom in America, but they also brought the spirit of self-rule.

# SAMOSET and SQUANTO

During the first winter in America, the Pilgrims lived aboard the *Mayflower*. Each day the men rowed ashore to build houses. At night they rowed back to the ship. Still, more than half the settlers died of cold and disease that winter.

When the winter ended, the *Mayflower* returned to England. The colonists had to face the next winter ashore in the houses they had built. Somehow they would have to learn to live in their new surroundings.

Some Pilgrims were discouraged, but others felt they could succeed. After all, the Indians were able to live by farming, hunting, and fishing. If only they could find some way of getting the help of the Indians, they might survive.

Their wish was answered by an Indian visitor named Samoset. He had learned a few words of English from visiting sailors and could speak to the settlers. The Pilgrims gave him a warm welcome. Before he left, he promised to bring a friend who might help the settlers.

Samoset returned a few days later with an Indian named Squanto. Squanto had actually lived in England for ten years! He had been kidnapped by an English explorer and taken to England. In England he had been shown as one of the strange wonders of the New World. During his stay, Squanto had learned the English customs and language. Now he was to prove a great friend to the settlers.

Squanto showed the Pilgrims how to hunt and fish in the nearby forests and streams. He also showed them how to grow corn and other crops. With his help the Pilgrims raised enough food to live through the spring and prepare for the winter ahead.

Squanto also brought Massasoit, the chief of one of the Indian tribes, to meet with the Pilgrims. Out of this meeting came a peace treaty. This treaty made it possible to develop the colony without fear of war.

# The Pilgrims and Thanksgiving

The Pilgrims worked hard all during the spring and summer of 1621. They hunted, fished, and planted crops. The previous winter half of the settlers had died of cold and disease. The Pilgrims hoped the next winter would be a better one.

The harvest that summer and autumn was good. Thanks to their Indian friends, the Pilgrims were able to raise good crops. There was plenty of corn, vegetables, and meat for the winter months. When the harvest was over, the Pilgrims wanted to give thanks to God for their good fortune.

The settlers had learned that the Indians held a ceremony each year at harvest time. At this ceremony the Indians thanked nature for the foods they had received. The Pilgrims decided to hold their own feast of thanksgiving that fall.

The governor of Plymouth invited Chief Massasoit and his tribe to the feast. This first Thanksgiving lasted three days. The Indians danced and the Pilgrims sang hymns. The Pilgrims and their guests ate deer, duck, corn, peas, puddings, and pies.

Today, more than 350 years later, we celebrate Thanksgiving. It is our national holiday in November.

*If you were an Indian at the first Thanksgiving, what might you have thought of the settlers?*

# Why did people settle in the English colonies?

Spain and France had colonies in the Americas long before the English. However, the English colonies soon had attracted more settlers than the Spanish and French colonies. There were about 300,000 people in the English colonies of America by 1700.

*What do you think were some reasons so many people settled in the English colonies?*

Many people came to the English colonies because they could have their own farmland. Most of the land in England and the rest of Europe was owned by nobles or landlords. It was every farmer's dream to own land. That dream could come true in the English colonies.

Many people came in search of religious freedom. They wanted to worship God in their own way. The Pilgrims and Puritans left England because they could not worship as they pleased. They founded the colonies of Plymouth and Massachusetts Bay. Another colony, called Pennsylvania, was founded by a religious group known as Quakers. English Catholics, who left England to escape persecution, settled in the colony of Maryland.

Many settlers were young people looking for adventure. Others came to America to start a new life. Some were convicts who had come straight to the colonies from English jails. However, not every convict was guilty of a crime. In those days people who could not pay their debts were put in jail. These convicts, and others, who agreed to settle in the colony of Georgia, were set free. Moving to the English colonies offered them a fresh start.

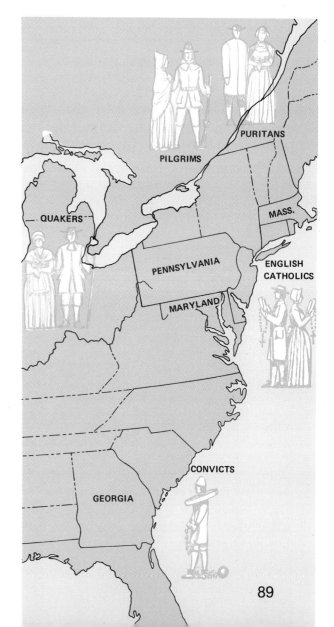

# ANNE HUTCHINSON

Freedom of religion was a new idea 350 years ago. Many settlers who came to America for this freedom would not share it with others. For example, the Puritans made their religion the only religion of their colony. Settlers who had different beliefs were punished and finally driven out of the colony.

*What do you think the Pilgrims would have thought of the person who said, "I disagree with you, but I will defend your right to say what you please"?*

Anne Hutchinson had different ideas about religious freedom. She, her husband, and their children had come to Massachusetts Bay in 1634 to find

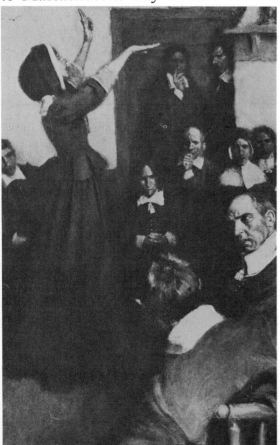

religious freedom. In those days, women were expected to make the clothes, linens, candles, and other needs of the home. They raised the children and helped grow food for the table. Anne Hutchinson not only did these things, but also was a religious leader in the colony.

Before long, she was in trouble. She, and others who disagreed with the church leaders, were forced to leave the colony. In 1638 Anne Hutchinson and her family moved to Rhode Island, a new colony. It had been founded by Roger Williams. Williams, like Anne Hutchinson, had been forced to leave Massachusetts Bay for religious reasons.

The Hutchinson family next moved to New Hampshire and founded the town of Portsmouth. A few years later, Anne Hutchinson's husband died and she moved again, this time to Long Island in New York. In 1643 Anne Hutchinson and all her family, except one daughter, were killed by Indians during a raid.

Anne Hutchinson was the first woman to become a leader in colonial government in America. She was also one of the first leaders to believe that religious freedom should be shared with others. She challenged the religious bigots of the time. Her life shows that women played an important role in early colonial life.

# JOHN PETER ZENGER

The settlers living in the English colonies thought of themselves as English people. They demanded all the rights that people living in England had. These rights included trial by jury and freedom of speech. The trial of John Peter Zenger helped make those rights include freedom of the press.

Zenger was a German who had come to the English colony of New York. He printed a newspaper called *The New York Weekly Journal.* The paper was read by many people who liked the way Zenger criticized Governor Cosby, the English governor of the city. In those days, it was against the law to criticize the government. Zenger was risking arrest by printing his stories.

In 1734 Governor Cosby had Zenger arrested. Zenger continued his charges against the governor from jail while awaiting trial. His wife printed the paper that carried criticisms of the governor.

When Zenger was finally brought to trial, everyone expected him to lose and be sentenced to jail. The governor argued that it was against the law to criticize the government for any reason. It did not matter if the charges were true or false. Zenger's lawyers argued that criticism, even of the governor, must be allowed if the charges made could be shown to be true.

The judge ordered the jury to consider only whether Zenger had criticized the governor. Zenger's lawyers asked the jury to not follow the judge and decide the matter for themselves. If they believed that Zenger had told the truth, they ought to set him free.

The jury agreed with Zenger and found him not guilty. The angry judge ordered the jury to change its decision. If they did not, he would put them all in jail! But the jury refused to be frightened and stood by their verdict. John Peter Zenger was set free.

Zenger, his wife, and the brave men of the jury established the right of a free press in America. Today that right is an important part of our system of democracy.

*How does the right to a free press play a part in your life?*

# LEARNING EXERCISES

## I. Remembering What We Have Read

Pick the best answer.

1. The first English settlement was in
   a. New York.
   b. Georgia.
   c. Virginia.
   d. Massachusetts.
2. The bread colonies were located in
   a. the southern part of America.
   b. all parts of America.
   c. the middle part of America.
   d. the northern part of America.
3. The Pilgrims settled in
   a. Georgia.
   b. Massachusetts.
   c. Virginia.
   d. New York.
4. The Mayflower Compact established the idea of
   a. freedom of the press.
   b. religious freedom.
   c. self-rule.
   d. all of the above.

## II. Headlines That Tell a Story

There are three headlines below. What is the story behind each headline?

**EDITOR JAILED FOR CRITICIZING GOVERNOR**

**VISITS BY GOOD NEIGHBORS A HELP TO THE NEW SETTLERS**

**MEMORIES OF JAIL LIFE NO PROBLEM TO NEW SETTLERS**

# FROM COLONIES
# TO INDEPENDENCE

# CONTENTS ☆ ☆ ☆ ☆ ☆ ☆ ☆ ☆ ☆ ☆ ☆ ☆ ☆ ☆ ☆ ☆ ☆ ☆

☆ ☆ ☆ ☆ ☆ ☆ ☆ ☆ ☆ ☆ ☆ ☆ ☆ ☆ ☆ ☆ ☆ ☆ ☆ ☆

**UNIT 3**

# Which nations were the main colonial powers in North America in 1750?

The map on the next page shows the colonies held by European countries in North America in 1750. It shows that Spain, England, and France were the main colonial powers.

Spain seemed to be very powerful. It held control over the lands that are today Florida, Mexico, and California. In spite of this, Spain was really very weak. Gold from the Americas had caused prices to rise in Spain. This rise in prices ruined many people in Spain. At the same time, the great Spanish fleet, or armada, had been crushed by England in 1588. Spain was never the same after that terrible defeat.

England and France were stronger than Spain in North America. France claimed most of Canada. It also claimed lands on both sides of the Mississippi River. The French hoped to control the Ohio Valley, but were being blocked by England.

The English had united all parts of their island. Together with Wales and Scotland they became Great Britain. In 1700 the British claimed the lands along the east coast of what is today the United States. They also claimed the Ohio Valley and parts of Canada.

Britain claimed less land in North America than France or Spain. However, the British had an important advantage over France or Spain. Their colonies had more people than did the Spanish and French colonies. *What might be some reasons for this?*

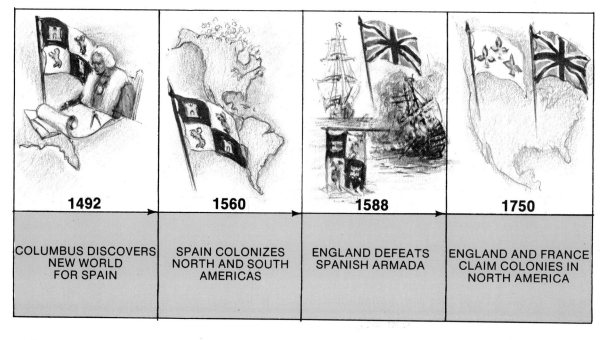

| 1492 | 1560 | 1588 | 1750 |
|------|------|------|------|
| COLUMBUS DISCOVERS NEW WORLD FOR SPAIN | SPAIN COLONIZES NORTH AND SOUTH AMERICAS | ENGLAND DEFEATS SPANISH ARMADA | ENGLAND AND FRANCE CLAIM COLONIES IN NORTH AMERICA |

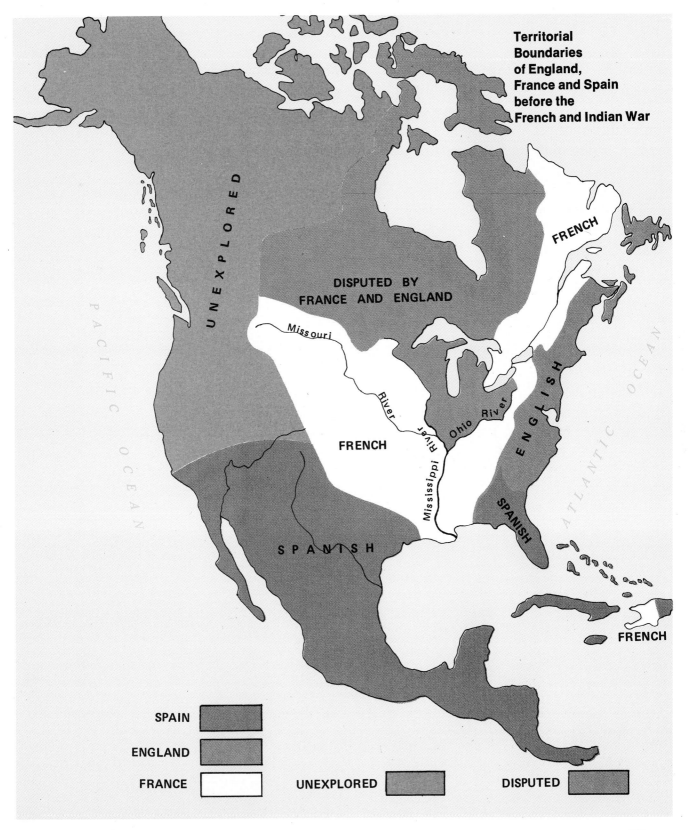

Territorial
Boundaries
of England,
France and Spain
before the
French and Indian War

UNEXPLORED

PACIFIC OCEAN

FRENCH

DISPUTED BY
FRANCE AND ENGLAND

Missouri

River

Mississippi River

Ohio River

ENGLISH

FRENCH

ATLANTIC OCEAN

SPANISH

SPANISH

FRENCH

| SPAIN | |
| --- | --- |
| ENGLAND | |
| FRANCE | |

| UNEXPLORED | | DISPUTED | |
| --- | --- | --- | --- |

# What were the causes of the French and Indian War?

In the 1700s Britain and France were the strongest countries in the world. Each wanted to be more powerful than the other. The result was a series of wars between the two countries.

In 1756 Britain and France were at war in three parts of the world. They were fighting in Europe, India, and North America. The war in North America was called the French and Indian War.

The French had many Indian allies. Great Britain had some Indian allies, but depended mainly on its colonists and on English soldiers. The fighting in North America began in 1754. It lasted until 1763.

The main causes of the French and Indian War were these:

1. Britain and France both wanted to be the most powerful country in Europe and in the world.

2. Both Britain and France claimed the lands of the Ohio Valley. These lands lie between the Great Lakes, the Ohio River, and the Mississippi River.

3. Both countries quarreled over fishing areas and territory in Canada, which both claimed.

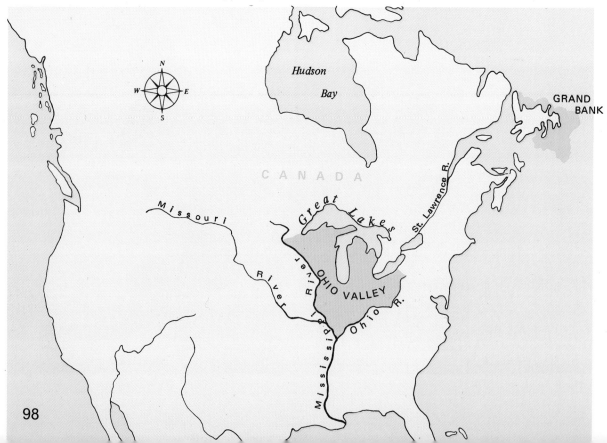

# What were the results of the French and Indian War?

The French and Indian War lasted for nine years, from 1754 to 1763. At first the French seemed to be winning. British soldiers and their American allies lost many battles to the French and their Indian allies. However, Great Britain was finally able to win the war. Its powerful fleet forced French ships to remain in port in Europe. This meant France could not bring supplies to its troops in America. Meanwhile, the American colonies served as a supply base for British soldiers. British troops scored victories in the Ohio Valley and at Quebec. These victories greatly weakened France. As a result, France was forced to sign a peace treaty in 1763. France had lost to Great Britain in Europe, India, and in North America.

The results of the French and Indian War in North America included the following:

1. France gave all its Canadian lands to Great Britain.

2. France gave all its lands east of the Mississippi River to Great Britain, except for the city of New Orleans in Louisiana.

3. France gave the city of New Orleans to Spain. The French also gave Spain the lands west of the Mississippi River. These lands were called Louisiana. Spain received these lands for helping France during the war.

4. Spain gave Florida to Great Britain.

The map shows the lands that changed hands as a result of the French and Indian War. *Why do you suppose the French so easily gave away the vast lands of Louisiana?*

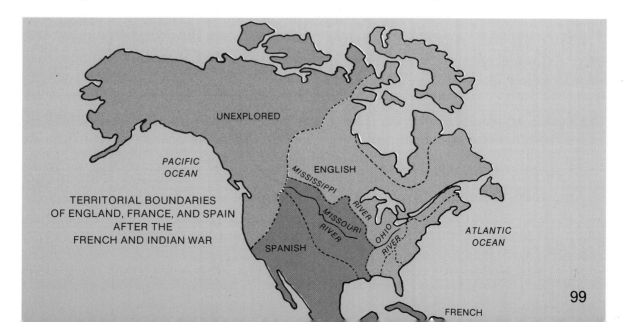

UNEXPLORED

PACIFIC OCEAN

ENGLISH

MISSISSIPPI RIVER

MISSOURI RIVER

OHIO RIVER

ATLANTIC OCEAN

TERRITORIAL BOUNDARIES OF ENGLAND, FRANCE, AND SPAIN AFTER THE FRENCH AND INDIAN WAR

SPANISH

FRENCH

# How did the British colonies change after the French and Indian war?

As a result of the war, Great Britain became the main colonial power in North America. It also became the most powerful country in the world.

Britain's new power brought many new problems. The war had been long and very costly. It left the British treasury nearly empty. The war also brought many changes in the British colonies in America.

Before the war, American colonists prided themselves on being British people living in America. They were ruled by English law and protected by the rights of English people. These rights included free speech and trial by a jury.

American colonists paid taxes to Great Britain. Before and during the war, it seemed fair to do so. The colonists had needed protection by Britain from the French and the Indians. Taxes helped to pay for this protection.

Now the war was over, and Britain needed money badly. New taxes were introduced in Britain and in the colonies. The American colonists had to pay many of the new taxes.

The colonists did not want to pay the new taxes. They felt that they had already paid their share of the war's cost by fighting in it. Besides, now that France was defeated, they no longer needed British protection. After 1763 more and more colonists thought of themselves as Americans, not as British people. They felt they ought to be given more self-rule. This meant that they wanted to be governed by other Americans, not by the British government that was three thousand miles away.

# CHIEF PONTIAC

Pontiac, the famous leader of the Ottawa Indians, was born in 1720. His tribe lived in the area that is now northern Ohio.

As a young man, Pontiac met many French traders. They came to the Northwest lands, where the Ottawas lived. The French came to trade for furs. The Ottawas, who were skilled fur trappers, enjoyed trading with the French. They found the French treated them fairly and with respect.

*Look at the map on this page and see if you can guess why the northern area was once called the Northwest.*

The Ottawas did not like the British colonists. They felt the colonists looked down on them and cheated them.

Chief Pontiac fought for the French during the French and Indian War. But the French lost the war, and control of the Ottawa lands passed to Great Britain. British settlers soon began moving into the Northwest lands. They settled in Ottawa territory.

Pontiac called on his people to drive out the British settlers. In 1763, three months after the French and Indian War, the Ottawas attacked. At first the attacks were successful, but the British were too strong. The Ottawas were finally beaten. Chief Pontiac was forced to sign a peace treaty.

For a time the Indian revolt stopped all new British settlement in the Northwest. Before long, however, more and more British settlers poured in. The lands they settled are today Ohio, Illinois, Michigan, Indiana, and Wisconsin.

Chief Pontiac failed, but he is honored today as an Indian leader. He fought to save his people's land.

# Why did Britain and its American colonies quarrel?

In 1763 Great Britain defeated France in the French and Indian War. That victory made Britain the most powerful nation in America. But in the next ten years Britain and its American colonies quarreled many times.

Many colonists felt that they had no real voice in Parliament. Parliament was the lawmaking body in Great Britain. No colonists were elected to it. This led to the colonist charge of taxation without representation. Britain did not agree. They said that the Parliament represented all people. It did not matter whether these people lived in Britain or in the colonies.

The colonists also felt that Britain was taxing them unfairly. Americans felt that Britain used colonial taxes to enrich itself. The British denied this. They pointed out that everyone, whether in Britain or in the colonies, had to pay taxes. The British also said that the taxes paid by the colonists were not very high.

The British placed taxes on such goods as molasses, tea, glass, and paint. They also passed a Stamp Act. This was a special tax in the form of a stamp. The stamp had to be placed on newspapers and legal papers. The colonists protested strongly against this tax. Britain finally dropped the Stamp Act.

The many disputes led to bad feeling on both sides. Colonists formed an organization called the Sons of Liberty. It led protests against the British. The British government then sent soldiers to enforce its laws. Many of the soldiers were housed in the homes of colonists. This led to more bad feelings.

In 1770 some colonists clashed with British troops on a Boston street. In the excitement, the soldiers fired into the crowd. Five people were killed. The Sons of Liberty charged the British soldiers had fired in cold blood. The shooting came to be known as the Boston Massacre to the colonists.

The Boston fighting was soon shown to have been an accident. In spite of this, the colonists grew steadily angrier. Colonial leaders organized stronger protests against British rule.

# The Boston Massacre

Boston was a trouble spot for the British government. The people of Boston did not want British soldiers living in their houses. They were angered by the soldiers marching in the Boston streets. Colonists called the soldiers lobster-backs. This was because of the red-coated uniforms they wore.

Trouble broke out in March 1770. A small squad of British soldiers was drilling in a Boston street. About fifty colonists gathered and began shouting insults at the soldiers. Suddenly someone knocked one of the lobster-backs down. The frightened soldiers fired into the crowd and killed five colonists. Those killed included a sailor, a ropemaker, an apprentice, a newly arrived Irishman, and a black workman named Crispus Attucks.

Samuel Adams was a leader of the Sons of Liberty. He demanded that British troops be withdrawn from Boston. This was done. Soon after, the British soldiers involved in the shooting were put on trial. They were found not guilty.

The incident in Boston was really only a street fight between soldiers and some colonists. The soldiers had fired in self-defense. But the people of Boston would not believe it. Too angry to be fair, they called the incident the Boston Massacre.

# CRISPUS ATTUCKS

Crispus Attucks was born a slave in a town near Boston. He escaped from slavery and became a sailor. In 1770, the year he was killed, he was forty-seven years old.

Crispus Attucks was well-known along the Boston dock area. He was called the Mulatto because he was a black man with some Indian blood. He was six feet tall and was the sort of person who stands out in a crowd. By 1770 Crispus Attucks no longer went to sea. He worked at odd jobs near the Boston docks. Much of his time was spent with those who protested against the British.

Crispus Attucks had been born a slave. He knew how precious freedom was and was ready to fight for it. When a crowd of colonists began shouting at a group of British soldiers, he was soon involved. He urged the colonists not to be frightened off the streets by the soldiers. The shouting in the streets grew louder and it seemed the soldiers might be in danger. Suddenly the nervous soldiers fired off a volley of shots. Five colonists, including Crispus Attucks, were killed by the shots. Crispus Attucks, was one of the first Americans to die in the protests against British rule.

# John Adams defends British soldiers

Five colonists had been killed in the streets of Boston by British soldiers! "Massacred" was how Samuel Adams and other colonial leaders put it. The city was afire with anger. Demands were made for all the soldiers to be removed from Boston. This was done. Colonists also demanded that the soldiers be put on trial. A trial was set and it seemed they would all be found guilty.

The six British soldiers and their commander, Captain Preston, were in serious trouble. The best lawyers in Boston would not defend them. A good lawyer had to be found. Otherwise the soldiers would be found guilty and punished severely by the court.

Friends of Captain Preston went to John Adams for help. They asked him to defend the soldiers. It was a hard thing for Adams to decide. He believed as strongly in liberty and the colonial cause as his cousin Samuel Adams. But he also believed in justice and a fair trial. He felt he must defend the soldiers who had fired in self-defense. John Adams agreed to take the case. He was joined by Josiah Quincy, another young Boston lawyer.

In spite of criticism by many colonists, the two young lawyers did their best and won! Captain Preston and the soldiers were found not guilty.

The Boston Massacre, as it came to be known, was a great tragedy. But it would have been a greater tragedy if innocent British soldiers had been punished unfairly.

*Do you think John Adams was right in defending British soldiers who had killed colonial patriots?*

105

# The Boston Tea Party

Great Britain was left nearly bankrupt by the French and Indian War. The only way to fill the treasury was to raise money by taxes.

Since colonists fought against the new taxes, Britain finally dropped most of them. However, the British kept the tax on tea. Some merchants smuggled in tea to avoid paying the tax. They were able to sell it below the price of tea shipped from Britain. Some smugglers were also part of the colonial protest movement.

In 1773 Parliament passed a new law lowering the tax on tea. British tea, even with a tax, was now cheaper than the tea being smuggled in. This should have made the colonists happy, but it did not. Some merchants feared that they would lose the profits they made by smuggling tea. Other Americans felt Britain was trying to control all colonial trade.

John Hancock and Samuel Adams led the Boston protest against the new tax on tea. Late in December 1773, a number of the colonists took action. Disguised as Indians, they boarded a British ship. They then dumped the cargo of tea into the harbor.

The story of the Boston Tea Party, as the incident was called, spread to all the colonies. People said that Hancock, Adams, and Paul Revere had led the raid. However, no one could prove them guilty. Britain was angered and decided to punish the entire city by closing the port to ships. The Boston Tea Party proved to be one of the events that started the Revolution in 1775.

# Who were the leaders of the colonial protest movement?

There were differences among the leaders of the protest movement in the colonies. Some of the leaders were willing to fight. Others were against the use of violence. They said that Great Britain could be talked into making changes.

Boston and Virginia were the two main centers of protest in the colonies. Samuel Adams was the outstanding colonial leader in Boston. His cousin, John Adams, who would later be the second president of the United States, was another leader. Two others were a young merchant named John Hancock and a skilled silversmith named Paul Revere. The Virginia protest leaders were Thomas Jefferson and Patrick Henry. Jefferson would later be the third president of the United States.

The Virginia colonists also had the support of George Washington. He had fought bravely in the French and Indian War and was greatly respected. Washington would later become the first president of the United States.

In 1772 these leaders, and others such as Benjamin Franklin of Philadelphia, joined together. They organized a Committee of Correspondence. Its purpose was to help them keep in touch with one another. In 1774 after the closing of Boston harbor, they organized the First Continental Congress. It sought to unite the colonists in future dealings with the British. Its first action was to send a message to the British king. The message was a last effort to try to prevent violence. It failed.

Samuel Adams

John Adams

John Hancock

*Leaders from Boston*

Paul Revere

Thomas Jefferson

Patrick Henry

*Leaders from Virginia*

George Washington

*Leader from Philadelphia*

Benjamin Franklin

# LEARNING EXERCISES

## I. Remembering What We Have Read

Pick the best answer.

1. Britain and France fought for world power in
   a. India.
   b. North America.
   c. Europe.
   d. all of the above.
2. During the French and Indian War the American colonists helped the
   a. French.
   b. British.
   c. Indians.
   d. Canadians.
3. "Taxation without representation" was a charge made by
   a. England against France.
   b. England against the Americans.
   c. Americans against France.
   d. Americans against England.
4. A leader of the colonial protest movement in Virginia was
   a. John Adams.
   b. Benjamin Franklin.
   c. Patrick Henry.
   d. John Hancock.

## II. Thinking About Things

Can you guess the answers to these questions?
The answers are not entirely in the book.

1. How might the fighting in the French and Indian War have led Americans to have less respect for the British?
2. If you were a colonial merchant, how would you have felt about the Boston Tea Party?

## III. Learning From Maps

Look at the map of
North America. Look
for the letters on it.
Answer these questions.

1. Which letter stands for
   Florida?
2. Which letter stands for
   Canada?
3. Which letter stands for New
   Orleans?
4. Which letter stands for
   Louisiana?

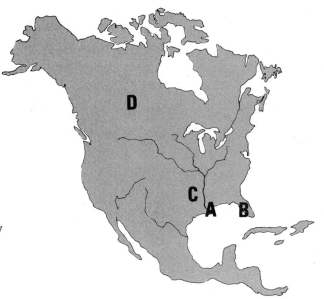

## IV. Learning From Pictures

What is the story behind each of the pictures below?

# How did fighting break out between Great Britain and the colonists?

The disputes between Britain and the colonists grew worse after the Boston Tea Party. Some colonists, known as minutemen, stored weapons near Boston. British troops were sent to seize these weapons. They were also to arrest John Hancock and Samuel Adams.

The British troops marched out of Boston hoping to surprise the colonists. But word of their approach was spread by Paul Revere and William Dawes. The minutemen gathered to stop the British troops. Fighting broke out at Lexington and Concord, two villages near Boston. These battles on April 19, 1775, mark the start of the American Revolution.

More fighting took place a month later. A small band of Americans, led by Ethan Allen, captured the British forts in upstate New York. Americans could now march into Canada, the British colony to the north. The Continental Congress ordered a colonial force to invade Canada. It was hoped that the Canadians would help the Americans.

At about the same time, American colonists occupied the hills around Boston. The British decided the hills must be cleared. They sent more than two thousand British troops to attack the three thousand colonists holding the hills. The result was the Battle of Bunker Hill in June 1775. The British troops seized the hills, but suffered terrible losses.

The battles around Boston and in upstate New York showed that the colonists were willing to fight. The efforts of the Continental Congress to settle differences peacefully had failed. The American Revolution had begun.

# Lexington and Concord

On April 19, 1775, seven hundred British soldiers marched toward Concord, Massachusetts. Their aim was to seize weapons and ammunition stored by colonists. They also wanted to arrest John Hancock and Samuel Adams.

Paul Revere and Will Dawes rode by horse to warn the colonists the redcoats were coming. They were not able to reach Concord, but the warning was spread by another colonist, Dr. Prescott.

Minutemen were ready when the British reached Lexington. This is a village on the way to Concord. About seventy minutemen were waiting, commanded by Captain Parker. The British commander, Major Pitcairn, ordered the minutemen to leave the area. Captain Parker also told his men

to leave, but ordered them not to drop their weapons.

Both sides were nervous. The British commander warned his men not to fire, but a shot rang out. Then the British troops fired upon the Americans killing eight men. The rest of the Americans retreated from Lexington and the British advanced.

*Why is the firing at Lexington sometimes called "the shot heard 'round the world"?*

The British marched on from Lexington to Concord. By this time, word of the shooting had spread ahead of them. Hundreds of colonists moved toward Concord carrying their guns. They hid in barns, trees, and behind fences. These colonists were ready to fight when the British troops returned on the way back to Boston.

The British soldiers did not find Adams and Hancock in Concord. Nor did they find any stores of arms or ammunition. When they began the march back to Boston, they ran into gunfire from the hidden colonists. About four thousand Americans fired on the British troops. British losses were about 250 killed and wounded. The Americans lost about ninety men. The weary British troops barely made it back to Boston and safety that evening.

# Patrick Henry asks for "Liberty or Death"

The fighting at Lexington and Concord shocked the members of the Continental Congress. They had been meeting in Philadelphia to decide on a plan of action. The use of guns had not been part of their plans up to then.

Many members of the Congress wanted to help Massachusetts. Some wanted to send troops to that colony. Others felt it was useless to fight against the well-armed, trained British soldiers. For a time it seemed that nothing would be decided by the Congress.

Among the delegates was a tall, red-haired lawyer from Virginia named Patrick Henry. He believed strongly in self-rule for the colonies. Patrick Henry had made many speeches before the Virginia Assembly. Once he had warned King George that other rulers had been removed in the past. He pointed out that it could happen again if the king did not listen to colonial protests. That speech had nearly led to Patrick Henry's arrest on the charge of treason. Now he was ready to make another fiery speech. It was one that would be long remembered.

The delegates were quiet as Patrick Henry spoke. He declared that the time called for action, not for words. They cheered wildly as he said:

" . . . The war must come, and let it come! . . . Our brothers are already in the field. . . . Why stand we here idle? . . . Is life so dear or peace so sweet as to be bought at the price of liberty? . . . I know not what course others may take, but as for me, give me liberty or give me death!"

# Why did the colonists declare their independence?

Fighting had begun at Lexington and Concord in 1775. Soon afterward, George Washington took command of the colonial army. It was known as the Continental Army for the rest of the Revolution. At the start, it numbered 15,000 troops.

The Continental Army was willing to fight. However, its main purpose was to win self-rule, not independence. Its early flag showed the British Union Jack in the upper left-hand corner and thirteen stripes for the thirteen colonies. In 1775 most of the colonists in the Continental Army still thought of themselves as British people.

Many people in Britain and in the colonies did not want war. Colonial leaders sent a petition to King George III of Britain. In it, the king was asked to unite Great Britain and the colonies in a peaceful way. But the king refused to read the petition. He declared that the colonial protesters were rebels. The king ordered his generals to crush Washington and the rebel army.

The king's action helped make many colonists favor independence. The British would not listen to their complaints. Maybe it would be better to be free of British rule. Americans were helped in their views by the writings of Thomas Paine. He wrote a little pamphlet called *Common Sense.* It convinced many colonists that they

ought to seek independence. One of those won over to the idea of independence was George Washington.

On July 4, 1776, the Continental Congress approved the Declaration of Independence. The colonists were no longer asking for reforms from the British government. They were now declaring they were free!

113

# The Declaration of Independence

The American Revolution began in 1775. At that time the colonists were not seeking independence. They wanted more self-rule and changes in the British tax laws. Most colonists thought of themselves as loyal British citizens.

A year of fighting changed the minds of many colonists. They were no longer interested in changes, or reforms. Many colonists now wanted to separate from Britain. They wanted to set up their own government in America. This feeling was not held by all the colonists. However, it was a strong feeling in many parts of the American colonies.

On July 4, 1776, the Continental Congress approved the Declaration of Independence. The most important part of the Declaration of Independence says:

"We hold these truths to be self-evident, that all men are created equal, that they are endowed by their Creator with certain inalienable rights, that among these are life, liberty, and the pursuit of happiness."

What do these words mean? They

mean that the signers of the Declaration believed that all people are created equal. Though the Declaration speaks of all men, the use of that word really means all people. The Declaration meant that all people have rights that can not be taken from them by any government. All people should therefore be treated as equals before the law. That is, the laws should be the same for all American people.

These words do not seem unusual to us today. When they were written in 1776 they were very daring. They were the words of revolutionists.

The Declaration of Independence is part of our history. It has shaped many of our ideas about democratic government. But we must remember that when it was written in 1776, the Declaration did not apply to all people. It did not apply to the more than 700,000 black people, who were held as slaves by Americans. It did not apply to women. In 1776 women had no right to vote or even to own property.

In spite of these shortcomings, the Declaration of Independence was a great step forward. Today we know the Declaration of Independence means even more than it did in 1776. All people, blacks as well as whites, women as well as men, are entitled to the rights that it mentions.

There were thousands of Americans who fought in the Revolution. They risked their lives in battles against the well-trained British armies. It must have often seemed to them that they had no hope of winning. Yet they fought and suffered and refused to give up. Today we might wonder why they risked everything in what seemed a hopeless effort.

# Why did the Americans win the War of Independence?

The American Revolution lasted from 1775 to 1783. Only about one-third of the colonists supported the Revolution. One-third of the colonists favored the British. Another third of the colonists did not take sides during the Revolution.

Some Americans favored the Revolution for economic reasons. They wanted no new taxes and less control by Britain of their trade. Other colonists favored the Revolution for political reasons. They wanted to be ruled by their own assemblies, not by the British Parliament. Still other Americans supported the Revolution for personal reasons. Many felt a sense of loyalty to their fellow colonists. They wanted to help them.

The colonists had little money, few skilled generals, and almost no navy. In spite of this they managed to win.

Why? The reasons why the Americans were able to win their independence include the following:

1. The British were directing the war far from the scene of the battles. The fighting was going on in America, but the British were directing the war from London. This often led to mistakes by the generals. Many people in Britain also felt the king was wrong.

They wanted him to change the policies that had angered the American colonies.

2. The British had to use foreign troops, mostly Hessians from Germany. The Hessians were called mercenaries because they were paid to fight. Soldiers fight better when they believe in a cause. The Hessians were not fighting for a cause, but the Americans were.

3. After 1778 Britain had to fight France, Spain, and Holland as well as the colonists. France gave money, ships, and soldiers to help the Americans.

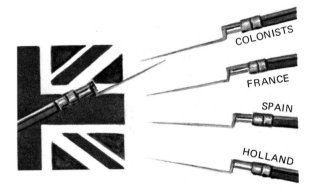

COLONISTS

FRANCE

SPAIN

HOLLAND

4. George Washington proved to be a great military leader. He also received much help from foreign volunteers including Lafayette, Pulaski, von Steuben, DeKalb. They helped to train Continental Army soldiers to become better fighters.

5. The British did not understand the fighting spirit of the colonists. They did not think that colonial farmers could fight as well as trained British and Hessian soldiers. They were wrong.

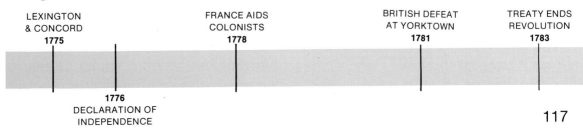

LEXINGTON & CONCORD 1775

FRANCE AIDS COLONISTS 1778

BRITISH DEFEAT AT YORKTOWN 1781

TREATY ENDS REVOLUTION 1783

1776 DECLARATION OF INDEPENDENCE

117

During most of the war, American troops were very near to defeat. At times Washington's army consisted of only a few thousand men.

The worst time of the war was the winter of 1777-1778. Washington and his soldiers spent that winter at Valley Forge, Pennsylvania. The bitter cold and lack of food and clothing caused great suffering. The letters of some of the soldiers tell how much suffering there was.

One colonel wrote that many soldiers were barefooted. They were forced to live in tents in spite of the cold weather. A general wrote that there was little food for the troops. Even the horses were dying for lack of food. Some soldiers had been without meat or bread for four days. One soldier wrote that he could follow hundreds of his fellow soldiers by the bloody tracks they left on the snow.

That winter at Valley Forge was the closest the Americans came to defeat. But this was an army that meant to hang on and win. They were helped by the strength of General Washington. Somehow, they felt, he would find a way to victory. The courage they showed that terrible winter is one of the great stories of our history.

## LEARNING EXERCISES

### I. Remembering What We Have Read

Pick the best answer.

1. The minutemen were
   a. English soldiers.
   b. tax collectors.
   c. American colonists.
   d. Indians.
2. The American Revolution was supported by about
   a. one-half of the colonists.
   b. two-thirds of the colonists.
   c. one-third of the colonists.
3. The Continental Army was made up of
   a. Hessian mercenaries.
   b. soldiers called redcoats.
   c. Indian allies.
   d. American colonists.
4. The problems of the colonists during the Revolution included
   a. lack of skilled generals.
   b. lack of a real navy.
   c. lack of money.
   d. all of the above.

### II. Learning From Pictures

What do these pictures tell us about the Revolutionary War?

# "I have not yet begun to fight"

Captain John Paul Jones

On September 23, 1779, thirty-nine British merchant ships were sailing off the coast of England. They were protected by two British warships. Suddenly, a force of American and French warships appeared. They were led by the ship *Bonhomme Richard,* commanded by Captain John Paul Jones. Both sides opened fire.

The flagship of the British was called the *Serapis.* It was newer, bigger, and better armed than the *Bonhomme Richard.* Nevertheless, Captain Jones directed his sailors to attack the *Serapis.* Deadly cannon fire from the British vessels smashed the American ship's sides and wrecked many of its cannons. A frightened sailor tried to haul down the American flag as a sign of surrender. Captain Jones stopped the sailor by hurling a pistol at him. The *Bonhomme Richard* moved closer. The firing went on.

At one point the captain of the *Serapis* called out to the Americans to surrender. John Paul Jones shouted back, "I have not yet begun to fight!"

The crew cheered its captain's words and fought on. Finally, the *Bonhomme Richard* drew alongside the *Serapis.* The crew threw out hooks to bring the vessels together. Fierce fighting now went on with guns firing at point-blank range. When the smoke cleared, it was the British ship that was forced to surrender.

Most Americans don't remember the details of the battle very well today. But the ringing words of Captain Jones "I have not yet begun to fight" have never been forgotten.

# Black men in the Revolution

Crispus Attucks, a black man, was killed in the Boston Massacre. That fight took place in 1770, five years before the start of the American Revolution.

Black men were also present in the early battles of the Revolution. Peter Salem, Samuel Craft, and Isaish Barjonah were black men who fought at Lexington. Peter Salem was also at Bunker Hill with Cuff Hayes, Prince Hall, Pomp Fisk, and others. They fought side by side with the white colonists.

The leaders of the Revolution did not try to get blacks to enlist. General Washington, a slave owner, was fearful of using blacks. He felt black slaves who fought might demand their freedom after the war.

The British tried to enlist slaves. They offered to free any slaves who ran away to serve in the British Army. Many slaves in the South did run away. However few of them actually fought for the British.

The British offer to free runaway slaves made General Washington change his mind. Black men were accepted as soldiers in the Continental Army. By the end of the war, about 5,000 had served.

Those who had been slaves before the war were given their freedom for their brave service. Although General Washington remained a slave owner, he expressed his thanks and admiration for their loyalty and courage.

# Foreigners fight for American freedom

The American Revolution was fought for liberty. This appealed to many Europeans. Some of them came to America to help the colonists.

One European who joined the Continental Army was the Marquis de Lafayette. This twenty-year-old French nobleman believed in liberty and freedom. He hoped the ideas of the American Revolution would spread. They might some day help to bring changes to his own country. Lafayette fought in many battles and was wounded in action. He was at Yorktown when the British surrendered to Washington.

Count Casimir Pulaski had helped lead a revolt in Poland as a young man. The revolt failed and he had to flee to France for safety. He heard about the American Revolution and decided to join the Continental Army. Pulaski fought bravely as a cavalry leader. He died leading a cavalry charge in Georgia in 1779. This brave Polish leader was only thirty-one years old when he died. There is a monument to his memory near Savannah, Georgia.

Johann Kalb was born in one of the German states in 1721. He took the title Baron de Kalb because it helped his military career. The title may have been false, but de Kalb was a brave soldier. He had fought for France at one time and joined the Continental Army in 1776. He was with Washington at Valley Forge. De Kalb died in battle in 1780 after being wounded eleven times.

Thaddeus Kosciusko (kos-ee-us-koh) was a Polish patriot and general. He hoped to win freedom for his own country some day. In the meantime, he fought for the colonial cause. General Kosciusko fought in many Revolutionary War battles with great skill and bravery.

Baron Friedrich von Steuben was an experienced army officer. He had been in charge of training and drilling soldiers in Prussia. This was one of the German kingdoms. In 1777 he accepted an offer to train the Continental Army. His skill in training soldiers proved a great help to General Washington. Von Steuben also commanded troops in battle and was brave and calm under fire.

# HAYM SALOMON

Born in
POLAND

fought for
its freedom

PRUSSIA

RUSSIA

AUSTRIA

Haym Salomon was born in Poland in 1740. He grew up with a deep love for freedom because he was both a Pole and a Jew. As a Pole, he saw his own country lose its freedom to its powerful neighbors. As a Jew, he was often the victim of prejudice.

When Poland was attacked, Haym Salomon joined the Polish fight for freedom. He was later forced to flee to the Netherlands. In 1772 he came to America, settling in New York. He soon became wealthy as a businessman.

Haym Salomon did not have to take sides in the Revolution. The British who captured New York wanted to do business with him. Instead, Haym

Salomon chose to help the colonists.

He first served as a spy for the Americans. This led to his arrest by the British who put him in jail. He escaped after two years and fled to Philadelphia for safety. For the rest of the war he raised money for the colonial army. He is supposed to have raised $700,000, much of it from his own fortune. The money helped supply goods, clothing, and guns for the Continental Army.

Haym Salomon lived to see the final victory of the United States. However, it had cost him everything. When he moved back to New York after 1783, he was almost penniless. He died in 1785, two years after independence was won.

# GEORGE WASHINGTON

During the French and Indian War many colonists fought for the British. Young George Washington fought as an officer in the British Army. He barely escaped being killed while fighting for the British. The war taught Washington much about how battles should be fought.

When the war ended, Washington returned to his Virginia plantation. He soon found that he was against many of the new British rules for the colonies. He became a leader of the protest movement in Virginia. He was greatly respected by his neighbors.

In 1775 George Washington went to Philadelphia as a delegate to the Continental Congress. News of the fighting at Lexington and Concord reached the Congress. It appointed Washington commander-in-chief of the colonial army. He served in that post for the next eight years.

The colonial army was never very large. It often lacked guns, ammunition, clothing, and food. At first, the soldiers were poorly trained. They were scared of the trained, well-armed British and Hessian soldiers. In spite of all this, the colonists held together. They learned to be soldiers and they fought for eight long years. Much of the credit must go to George Washington.

Washington was the perfect leader for the colonial army. Knowing his soldier's weaknesses, he planned his battles carefully. When he saw his soldiers would be beaten, he retreated. But he also won battles by daring moves that caught the enemy by complete surprise.

The story of how the small, poorly trained colonists defeated the British is almost a miracle. George Washington was one of the leaders who helped make the miracle possible.

# What were some results of the American Revolution?

The American Revolution lasted from 1775 to 1783. At first the colonists had only wanted lower taxes and more self-rule. After 1776 they also wanted independence from Great Britain.

In the first year of the war the Americans suffered many defeats. However, they gained two important victories in late 1776 and early 1777. These were at Trenton and Princeton in New Jersey. They also won an important victory in 1777 at the Battle of Saratoga. For the next six years, however, the American forces were often beaten in battle.

Finally the British had a major defeat at Yorktown, Virginia in 1781. There, more than eight thousand British troops laid down their arms. The Revolution went on for another two years, but no more big battles were fought. The British defeat at Yorktown left them too weak to fight on.

King George III of Britain finally

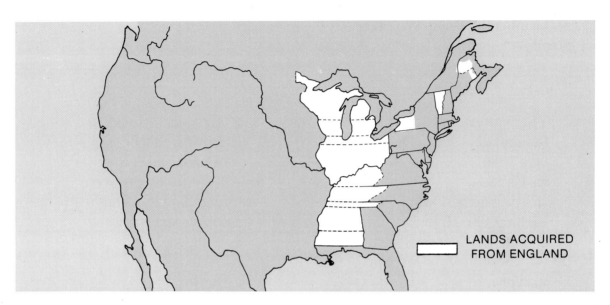

LANDS ACQUIRED FROM ENGLAND

admitted the war was lost. He agreed to peace talks with the American and French representatives in Paris. A peace treaty was signed in 1783. The Treaty of Paris, as it was called, included these terms:

1. Britain recognized that the United States was independent.

2. Britain gave the new nation all the land west to the Mississippi River, north to Canada, and south to the border of Florida.

The map on this page shows the boundaries of the new nation in 1783.

The treaty that ended the war granted independence to a new nation.

But there were other important results of the American Revolution. The political results were shown when the thirteen colonies became thirteen states. They were joined together in the United States of America. There were also economic results of the American Revolution. The Revolution ended the British trade controls upon the colonists. American trade was now free to develop on its own.

The American Revolution also brought important social results. There was no aristocracy, or nobility, in the new United States. This meant the new nation would have no kings, princes, or other nobles.

Finally, an important result of the American Revolution was the spread of its ideas. The ideas put forward in the Declaration of Independence became known and accepted in many parts of Europe.

# LEARNING EXERCISES

## I. Remembering What We Have Read

Pick the best answer.

1. The western border of the independent United States was
   a. Canada.
   b. the Pacific Ocean.
   c. the Ohio River.
   d. the Mississippi River.

2. All the following are true **except**
   1. George Washington was fearful of using blacks as soldiers.
   b. Black men were present at the battle of Bunker Hill.
   c. The English did not want to enlist slaves.
   d. Crispus Attucks was killed during the Boston Massacre.

3. All the following were foreigners who fought for the colonists **except**
   a. Pulaski.
   b. Attucks.
   c. Kalb.
   d. Lafayette.

4. The Continental Army won victories at
   a. Yorktown.
   b. Princeton.
   c. Saratoga.
   d. all of the above.

## II. Using Time Lines To Remember What We Have Learned

Look at the time line below. It shows four dates. Each date also has a letter.

1. Which date and letter stand for the fighting at Lexington and Concord?

2. Which date and letter stand for the end of the Revolutionary War?

3. Which date and letter stand for the end of the French and Indian War?

4. Which date and letter stand for the signing of the Declaration of Independence?

| 1763 | 1775 1776 | 1783 |
| A | B C | D |

## III. True or False

1. Foreigners came to America to help the colonists in the Revolution.
2. Haym Salomon came to America as a child.
3. George Washington fought for the French in the French and Indian War.
4. The Treaty of Paris ended the American Revolution.
5. The ideas of the Declaration of Independence were not accepted by the rest of the world.

## IV. Matching Words and Events

Match the words in Box A with the pictures shown in Box B.

### BOX A

1. "Give me liberty or give me death."

2. "I have not yet begun to fight."

3. ". . . all men are created equal."

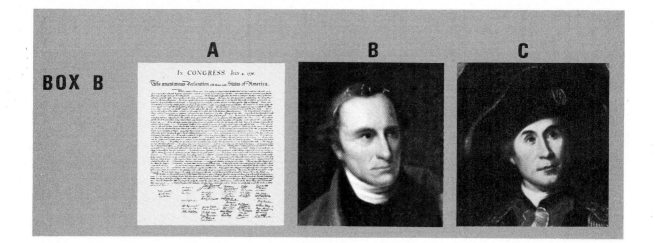

BOX B

A     B     C

## V. Learning From Maps

Look at the map below.
There are letters on that map.

1. Which letter stands for the Ohio Valley?
2. Which letter stands for the Great Lakes?
3. Which letter stands for Louisiana?
4. The Treaty of Paris established the boundaries of the new United States. Which letters on the map stand for those boundaries?

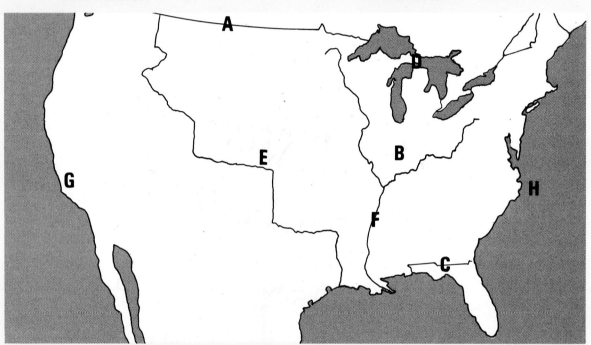

## VI. Thinking About Things

Can you guess the answers to these questions? They are based on what you have been reading, but the answers are not in the book.

1. How might the British have been more successful in their fight against the American colonists?
2. Why were some people in England on the side of the American colonists?

# A NEW NATION IS FOUNDED

# CONTENTS ☆ ☆ ☆ ☆ ☆ ☆ ☆ ☆ ☆ ☆ ☆ ☆ ☆ ☆ ☆

☆ ☆ ☆ ☆ ☆ ☆ ☆ ☆ ☆ ☆ ☆ ☆ ☆ ☆ ☆ ☆ ☆ ☆

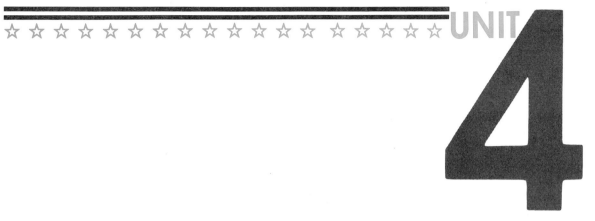

UNIT

4

# How was the United States governed under the Articles of Confederation?

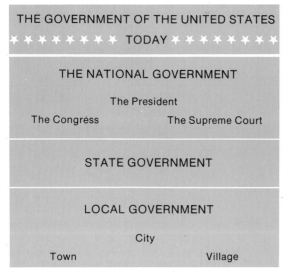

THE GOVERNMENT OF THE UNITED STATES
★ ★ ★ ★ ★ ★ ★ ★ TODAY ★ ★ ★ ★ ★ ★ ★ ★

THE NATIONAL GOVERNMENT

The President

The Congress        The Supreme Court

STATE GOVERNMENT

LOCAL GOVERNMENT

City

Town                        Village

Today we have three different kinds of government in the United States. These are the local governments, the state governments, and the national or federal government. Each of these governments has certain powers. However, the federal government is the most powerful.

From 1781 to 1789 the new United States had a very different form of government. At that time the nation was governed under the Articles of Confederation. The Articles served as the first constitution of the new United States.

A confederation is a loose union of independent states. Each state has its own laws, its own soldiers, and its own form of money. The national government has little power. Most of the power remains with the states making up the confederation.

Today we are accustomed to a strong national government. We are likely to wonder why the colonists set up a national government that was weak. Part of the answer was that most of the American people had grown up as citizens of a colony. They had no experience with a national power except that of Great Britain. In addition, most colonists had little chance to travel to the other colonies. Roads were poor and travel was slow and dangerous. The result was that most people stayed within their own colony. They thought of themselves as Virginians or New Yorkers rather than as Americans.

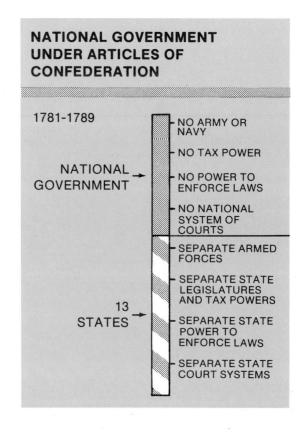

**NATIONAL GOVERNMENT UNDER ARTICLES OF CONFEDERATION**

1781-1789

NATIONAL GOVERNMENT →
- NO ARMY OR NAVY
- NO TAX POWER
- NO POWER TO ENFORCE LAWS
- NO NATIONAL SYSTEM OF COURTS

13 STATES →
- SEPARATE ARMED FORCES
- SEPARATE STATE LEGISLATURES AND TAX POWERS
- SEPARATE STATE POWER TO ENFORCE LAWS
- SEPARATE STATE COURT SYSTEMS

NEW YORK

VIRGINIA

The colonists also feared the power of a strong national government. They had just fought against the power of the British rulers. The British government had tried to make laws for all the colonies. These had often proved harmful and costly. Many Americans felt a strong national government might repeat the British mistakes. This led them to accept the idea of the confederation form of government.

Colonists also felt a strong central government would bring interference in their lives. They believed that the best kind of government was one that did as little as possible. The confederation system of government gave local people greater control over the rulers. Many Americans liked such a form of government. They were strongly against any idea of a central government.

# Why did some Americans want a new Constitution?

In spite of many weaknesses, the Congress under the Articles did two important things. First, the Congress worked out the peace treaty with Britain in 1783. The treaty gave independence to the colonies. From then on, the United States was truly an independent nation.

The second thing was the settlement of the land claims in the northwest.

These lands, shown on the map, are known as the Northwest Territory. They were claimed by several states after they became part of the new United States. In 1787 the states gave up their claims. The Northwest Territory became the property of the national government.

*Which states were later formed from the lands of the Northwest Territory?*

In spite of these successes, the first government under the Articles did not please many Americans. The reasons included the following:

1. Congress had no power to raise money through taxes. It had to ask the states for money. Congress had no means to force the states to make such payments. The result was that Congress could not even pay its debts.

2. Congress had no army or navy of its own. It had to ask the states for troops when they were needed.

3. Congress could only pass laws with the approval of nine of the thirteen states. Once the laws were passed, Congress had no way to enforce them.

4. All changes, or amendments, in the Articles of Confederation had to be approved by all thirteen states.

These and other weaknesses of the Articles led to a demand for change. Such change would make the national government stronger.

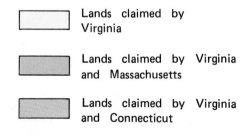

Lands claimed by Virginia

Lands claimed by Virginia and Massachusetts

Lands claimed by Virginia and Connecticut

# The Constitutional Convention

The many weaknesses of the Articles of Confederation led to a demand for change. Something had to be done to settle the disputes between the states. Some Americans felt that the answer was a stronger national government.

Some efforts had been made to settle certain problems. Virginia and Maryland met in 1785 to discuss a problem they were having. George Washington, now a private citizen of Virginia, led the meeting. It was held in his Mount Vernon, Virginia home. To everyone's surprise the Mount Vernon meeting was a success. It worked out a system for control of navigation on the Potomac River. This river ran between Virginia and Maryland.

The success at Mount Vernon led to a call for a meeting of all thirteen states. This was to be held in 1786 at Annapolis, Maryland. Its purpose was to encourage the states to work together. The Annapolis meeting was a failure. However, it did send out a call for another meeting. This meeting was to be held in Philadelphia in 1787. Its purpose was to change the Articles of Confederation.

In May 1787, forty-five delegates met in Philadelphia. The oldest of the delegates was eighty-one-year-old Benjamin Franklin. The youngest was twenty-six-year-old Jonathan Dayton of New Jersey. George Washington served as president of the convention. Also present were Alexander Hamilton and James Madison. Madison's notes tell us the most about what went on in the secret convention meetings. Madison would later be known as the father of the Constitution. *Can you guess why?*

The delegates soon saw that they could not change the Articles. Such a change would need the approval of all thirteen states. The delegates knew that would be impossible. They decided, instead, to write a new constitution.

# Why is the Constitution sometimes called "A Bundle of Compromises"?

The delegates in Philadelphia had decided on a bold move. Instead of trying to change the Articles of Confederation, they were going to write a new constitution. They worked at this task for four months in 1787. There were many times when it seemed they must fail.

Writing a new constitution was difficult. This was because each of the thirteen states had special interests. Large states like Virginia wanted more representatives in Congress than smaller states. Small states like Connecticut felt all states should have an equal number of representatives in Congress.

The representation issue was finally settled by the Great Compromise. This compromise provided for two houses of Congress in the national government.

The House of Representatives, or lower house, was to be based on population. Each state would be entitled to a number of representatives in this house. That number would be based on the population of the state. This compromise favored the larger states.

The Senate, or upper house, was to have an equal number of members from each state. Two senators would be elected by each state, regardless of its size or population. This compromise favored the smaller states.

The Great Compromise helped to settle the issue of representation. Large states and small states each gained part of what they wanted by this compromise.

A second important compromise concerned the issue of slavery. Southern states had thousands of black slaves. The slaves were not allowed to vote and they had no rights of citizenship. But the southern states wanted all slaves counted for

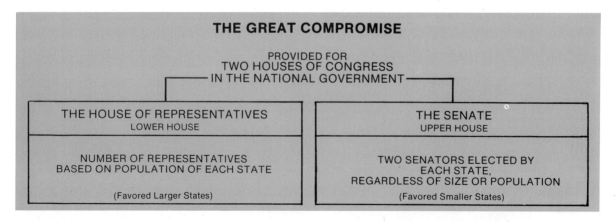

THE GREAT COMPROMISE

PROVIDED FOR
TWO HOUSES OF CONGRESS
IN THE NATIONAL GOVERNMENT

THE HOUSE OF REPRESENTATIVES
LOWER HOUSE

NUMBER OF REPRESENTATIVES
BASED ON POPULATION OF EACH STATE

(Favored Larger States)

THE SENATE
UPPER HOUSE

TWO SENATORS ELECTED BY
EACH STATE,
REGARDLESS OF SIZE OR POPULATION

(Favored Smaller States)

representation in Congress. This would give southern states many more members of Congress in the House of Representatives.

The free states were those with no slaves, or very few slaves. These states were mainly located in the North. Free states did not want slaves counted as part of the population. If the slaves were not counted, the northern states would have greater power.

In the arguments over whether to count slaves, there was no discussion of slavery itself. Both North and South seemed willing at the time to accept the idea of slavery. What was being discussed was the question of power. Would the southern states or northern states have the greatest power in Congress? That was the real problem.

The issue was finally settled by the Three-Fifths Compromise. This allowed southern states to count every five slaves as three persons for representation.

It has been said that the United States made racism and prejudice a part of its Constitution. *How does the Three-Fifths Compromise affect this idea? Why do you suppose the Three-Fifths Compromise is no longer in effect?*

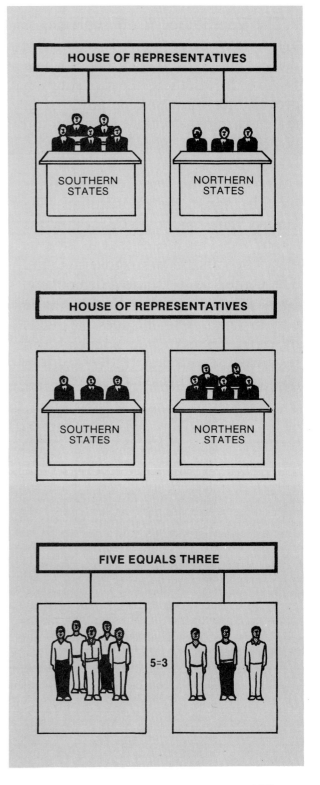

# What system of government did the Constitution establish?

The Constitution is the supreme, or highest, law of our land. It establishes the system of government under which we live. In addition, the Constitution provides for ways to keep any part of the government from becoming too powerful.

Let's look at some of the things provided for in the Constitution. The United States under the Constitution is a republic. This means that its citizens elect the officials who govern them. The United States is also a democracy. In a democracy the citizens have certain rights. This includes the rights of a free press, free speech, and freedom of religion. Citizens of a democracy also have the right to a fair and speedy trial if they are accused of crimes. The rights of citizens in a democracy are known as civil rights. The Constitution provides for the civil rights of the citizens of the United States.

The Constitution also provides for a federal system of government. This is a system in which power is divided between the states and the national, or federal, government. The division of power keeps either the states or the federal government from having too much power.

Certain powers are given only to the federal government. These include the power to make war and peace, to print

money, and to regulate, or control, trade between the states. The powers of the national government are listed in the Constitution.

FEDERAL AND STATE GOVERNMENT SHARE POWER

FEDERAL GOVERNMENT ONLY HAS THE POWER TO

Make War or Peace,
Print Money,
Regulate or Control Trade
Between the States

The powers not given to the federal government remain with the states. This means that the states actually control such things as education, marriage and divorce, and elections.

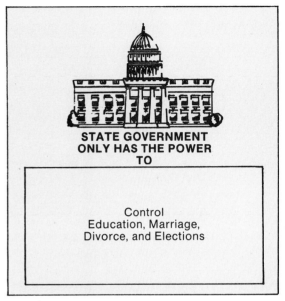

STATE GOVERNMENT ONLY HAS THE POWER TO

Control
Education, Marriage,
Divorce, and Elections

The Constitution provides that certain powers are shared by the national government and the states. These powers include the right to pass tax laws, to borrow money, build roads, and try lawbreakers.

FEDERAL AND STATE GOVERNMENTS BOTH SHARE THE POWER TO

Pass Tax Laws,
Borrow Money, Build Roads,
Try Law Breakers

*Which seems to have more power, the national government or the states?*

# LEARNING EXERCISES

## I. Remembering What We Have Read

Pick the best answer.

1. Under the Articles of Confederation most of the power was held by
   a. the Congress.
   b. the courts.
   c. the states.
   d. the president.
2. The original purpose of the meeting in Philadelphia was to
   a. write the Northwest Ordinance.
   b. make changes in the Articles of Confederation.
   c. write a new Constitution.
   d. write the Articles of Confederation.
3. The three-fifths compromise dealt with the matter of
   a. amending the Constitution.
   b. the powers of Congress.
   c. slavery.
   d. approving the Constitution.
4. Only the federal government has the power to
   a. pass tax laws.
   b. borrow money.
   c. build roads.
   d. declare war.

## II. Thinking About Things

Can you guess the answers to these questions? They are based on what you have been reading, but the answers are not in the book.

1. What might be the reason that the House of Representatives is called the Lower House while the Senate is the Upper House?
2. The colonists had feared a central government might have too much power. Why might that be bad for the country?

## III. Learning About Maps

The map below, of the Northwest Territory, has five letters on it.
Each letter stands for a state.

1. Which letter stands for the state of Michigan?
2. Which letter stands for the state of Illinois?
3. Which letter stands for the state of Indiana?
4. Which letter stands for the state of Ohio?

## IV. Understanding Our Government

There are four headlines shown below.
Look at each headline and tell if it applies to action by the federal government or by a state government.
Explain your answers.

**NEW POSTAGE STAMPS
TO BE PRINTED**

**FOUR STATE SHIPPING
RULES NOW IN FORCE**

**SPECIAL ELECTION SET
FOR MAY 8TH**

**MARRIAGE AGE
DROPPED TO 18**

# How is the United States governed under the Constitution?

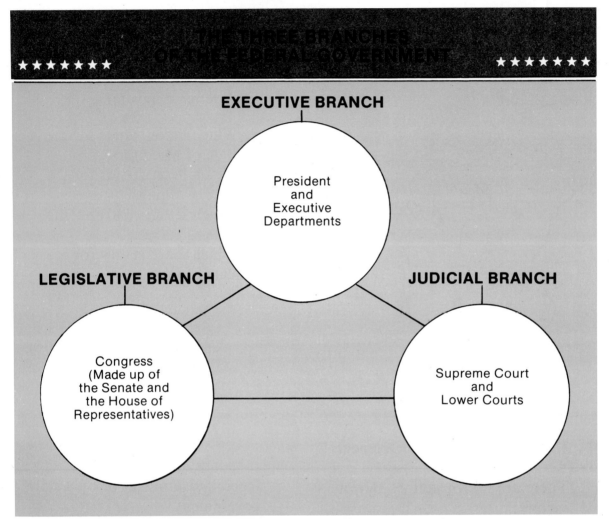

THE THREE BRANCHES
OF THE FEDERAL GOVERNMENT

★ ★ ★ ★ ★ ★ ★ ★ ★ ★ ★ ★ ★ ★

**EXECUTIVE BRANCH**

President
and
Executive
Departments

**LEGISLATIVE BRANCH**

Congress
(Made up of
the Senate and
the House of
Representatives)

**JUDICIAL BRANCH**

Supreme Court
and
Lower Courts

The power of the national government is shared by its three branches. These are the legislative, the executive, and the judicial branches. Each of these branches has certain important powers. The separation of power keeps any branch from becoming too powerful. Those who wrote the Constitution took care to provide for this separation of power.

Each branch of the national government has a certain job to do. In addition, each checks, or controls, the power of the other branches. The Constitution provides for a balance of power within the government. The system of checks and balances makes sure that no branch of government will ever become too powerful. Let us examine the powers of each branch and see how they check and balance each other. Let's see how checks and balances work.

# What are the powers of the legislative branch?

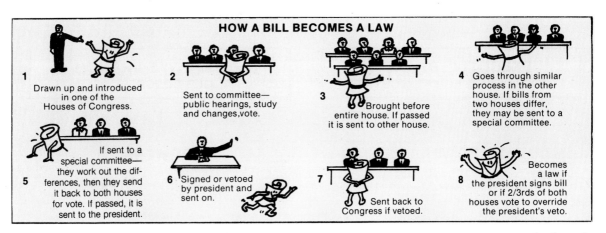

**HOW A BILL BECOMES A LAW**

1 Drawn up and introduced in one of the Houses of Congress.

2 Sent to committee—public hearings, study and changes, vote.

3 Brought before entire house. If passed it is sent to other house.

4 Goes through similar process in the other house. If bills from two houses differ, they may be sent to a special committee.

5 If sent to a special committee—they work out the differences, then they send it back to both houses for vote. If passed, it is sent to the president.

6 Signed or vetoed by president and sent on.

7 Sent back to Congress if vetoed.

8 Becomes a law if the president signs bill or if 2/3rds of both houses vote to override the president's veto.

The legislative branch is the name given to the Congress. It is made up of the House of Representatives and the Senate.

The legislative branch makes laws for the country. A law must pass by a majority vote of both houses of the Congress. It must also be approved by the president. The president can check the power of Congress by refusing to approve a law. This refusal is known as a veto. It is one of the checks the president has over the legislative branch.

If the president does not approve a law, Congress can still overcome the veto. They can pass the law over the veto by a two-thirds vote of both houses of Congress. It is generally very difficult to do this. However, it has been done many times in the past.

The Congress can also check the power of the president in other ways. Sometimes the Senate refuses to approve an appointment made by the president. There have also been times when the Congress has refused to pass money bills. This leaves the president without the money needed to carry out certain programs that the president wants.

*We sometimes say Congress has the power of the purse. What does that mean?*

The Congress also has the power to remove a president from office. This can only be done if the president has committed serious acts of wrongdoing. In such cases the House of Representatives must first vote to impeach the president. A trial is then held in the Senate with the chief justice of the Supreme Court presiding. If two-thirds of the Senate find the impeached president guilty, the president is removed from office. Only one president has ever been impeached, and none has ever been found guilty.

# What are the powers of the executive branch?

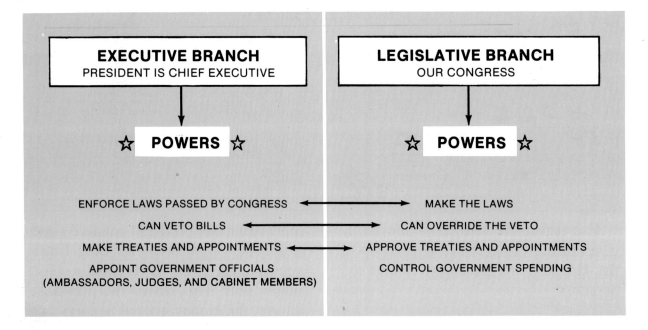

| EXECUTIVE BRANCH | LEGISLATIVE BRANCH |
|---|---|
| PRESIDENT IS CHIEF EXECUTIVE | OUR CONGRESS |

☆ POWERS ☆      ☆ POWERS ☆

| | |
|---|---|
| ENFORCE LAWS PASSED BY CONGRESS ⟷ | MAKE THE LAWS |
| CAN VETO BILLS ⟷ | CAN OVERRIDE THE VETO |
| MAKE TREATIES AND APPOINTMENTS ⟷ | APPROVE TREATIES AND APPOINTMENTS |
| APPOINT GOVERNMENT OFFICIALS (AMBASSADORS, JUDGES, AND CABINET MEMBERS) | CONTROL GOVERNMENT SPENDING |

The executive branch enforces the laws that are passed by Congress. The president is the head of the executive branch. This branch sees that the laws are carried out equally everywhere in the United States. A law cannot be enforced one way in the North and another way in the South or in the West.

The president is elected to office by all the voters in the nation. Many other executive officials are appointed by the president. These appointments must receive the approval of the Senate. For example, the president appoints the secretary of defense, the secretary of state, and all other members of the Cabinet. The president also appoints all ambassadors, and all army, navy, and air force officers. All of these appointments must be approved by the Senate. This is one important check the legislative branch has over the executive branch. The president is also in charge of making treaties with other nations. However, those treaties must be approved by the Senate. This is an important check of the legislative branch over the executive branch.

The president, as leader of the executive branch, has great power. The president has to approve all laws passed by the Congress. The president's veto can "kill" most bills that Congress may want. The president also has the power of the executive office. A president is the leader of the entire nation, not of a city or a state. The president speaks in the name of all the people of the United States.

# What are the powers of the judicial branch?

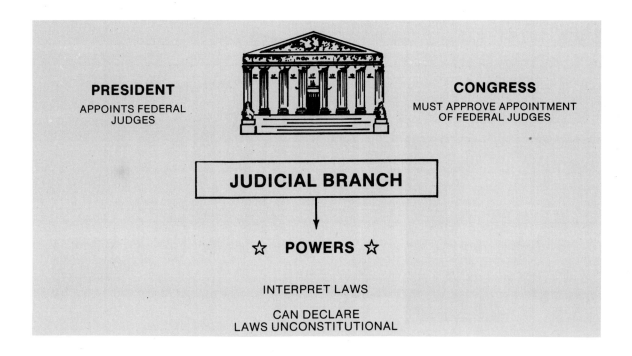

PRESIDENT
APPOINTS FEDERAL JUDGES

CONGRESS
MUST APPROVE APPOINTMENT OF FEDERAL JUDGES

JUDICIAL BRANCH

☆ POWERS ☆

INTERPRET LAWS

CAN DECLARE LAWS UNCONSTITUTIONAL

The judicial branch decides the meaning of laws that come before it in court cases. The federal courts and the Supreme Court study these laws. They decide if the laws are proper under the terms of the Constitution. If they decide the law is not proper or unconstitutional, that law is dropped.

The judicial branch has the power to declare laws unconstitutional. This is a powerful check over the legislative and executive branches. But these two branches can also check the judicial branch. For example, all federal judges are appointed for life by the president. This gives the executive branch the power to name the judges of the judicial branch.

A federal judge appointed by the president must be approved by the Senate. This gives the legislative branch a check over the judicial and executive branches.

The system of checks and balances is part of the separation of power. The people who wrote the Constitution wanted a national government. However, they made sure the national government would never be able to destroy the liberties of the people.

*Do you think the president, the Congress, or the Supreme Court is the most powerful part of the national government?*

# JOHN MARSHALL

In 1801 John Marshall was forty-six years old. He had fought in the Revolution and was also well-known as a lawyer and a politician. Now he was about to begin a new career which would bring him his place in history. In 1801 John Marshall was appointed chief justice of the United States Supreme Court. He was to spend the next thirty-four years as chief justice.

Marshall was the third chief justice, but he was different from the others. He made the Supreme Court an equal partner with the executive branch and legislative branch. Marshall was a leader of the Supreme Court in every way.

Thomas Jefferson, a Democratic-Republican, had been elected president in 1801. The Federalists had been the political party in office. But the Federalists lost their control of Congress and the presidency in the election of 1800. They now feared that the newly elected Democratic-Republicans would make too many changes. The Federalists decided they must keep control of the federal courts. President John Adams, a Federalist, appointed John Marshall as chief justice just before Adams left office. He hoped that Marshall, a Federalist, would strengthen the judicial branch against the powers of the new president.

During the years that Marshall was chief justice, others were appointed to the Supreme Court. Some of these justices were Democratic-Republicans, but they soon began to agree with John Marshall. It was Marshall's idea that the Supreme Court had the right to decide if laws were constitutional. No such power was given by the Constitution. However, Marshall believed that such power was taken for granted by those who had written the Constitution.

Marshall and the Supreme Court held many state laws to be unconstitutional. Then, in 1803, the Supreme Court held a law, passed by Congress, to be unconstitutional. By this action, Marshall declared the right of the Supreme Court to rule on federal as well as state laws. It gave great power to the federal court system.

The action taken against a federal law in 1803 created much bitterness. The Democratic-Republicans thought the Supreme Court was going too far. However, there was no challenge made to the power of the Supreme Court.

John Marshall established the right of the Supreme Court to review laws passed by Congress. No use was made of that right for the next fifty-four years. It was not until 1857 that a Supreme Court again declared an act of Congress to be unconstitutional. Since then, the Supreme Court has used that power many times.

It was John Marshall who strengthened the federal judicial system. He made it an equal partner with the other branches of government.

# Why does the Constitution have a Bill of Rights?

After four months of discussion and compromise, the Constitution was written. The delegates to the Constitutional Convention agreed it should go into effect when nine of the thirteen states had ratified, or accepted, it. Almost at once, Americans began taking sides.

Some Americans, known as the Federalists, favored the Constitution. They felt it would bring about a strong central government. The Federalists were led by Alexander Hamilton and James Madison.

**JAMES MADISON**

**ALEXANDER HAMILTON**

**THOMAS JEFFERSON**

Thomas Jefferson was the leader of the anti-Federalists. They were against adoption of the Constitution. Anti-Federalists felt a strong central government was a danger to liberty. They wanted a Bill of Rights to be added to the Constitution. This would help protect the rights for which the Revolution had been fought.

The Federalists had to give in. They promised to add a Bill of Rights if the Constitution was ratified. This promise was kept. In 1791 two years after the Constitution went into effect, the Bill of Rights was adopted.

## What does the Bill of Rights say?

The Bill of Rights protects most of our democratic rights. It is the name given to the first ten additions, or amendments, to the Constitution. Here are just a few of the rights it guarantees:

• Freedom of religion, speech, press, and assembly.

• Protection against searches by police, except when they have a lawful right to make such searches.

• The right to a fair and speedy trial. The right to a trial by a jury.

• Protection against being forced to testify against oneself.

• Protection against being tried twice for the same crime. Also, protection against unfair fines or cruel punishment.

The people who wrote the Constitution did not believe in democracy as we know it. Hamilton did not trust the people and wanted to limit their power and liberty. He and his followers did not favor a Bill of Rights.

Jefferson and his followers disagreed with Hamilton and the Federalists. Jefferson believed strongly in the rights of common people. He sought to protect those rights. Jefferson's belief

resulted in the Bill of Rights. It has helped democracy to grow in the United States.

It has been said that it is hard to live with the Bill of Rights. This is because we are not always willing to let others have the rights we want for ourselves. Look at the guarantees given by the Bill of Rights. Now ask yourself these questions:

*1. Do you favor freedom of speech for everyone?*

*2. Do you believe that police ought to only make lawful searches?*

*3. Do you believe that no one ought to be forced to testify against himself or herself?*

151

# Why is our Constitution a "living" Constitution?

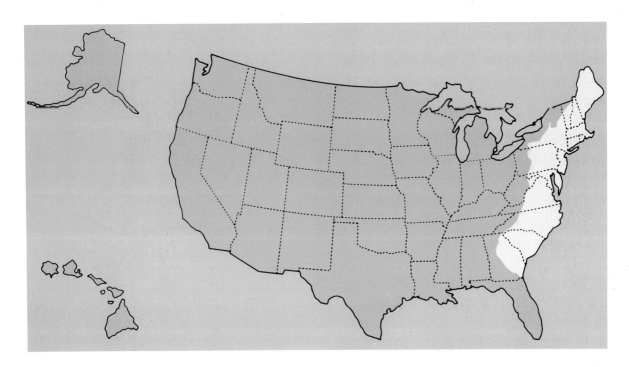

When the Constitution was written, the United States was different from what it is today. In 1787 there were only thirteen states. Today there are fifty states. But the United States has changed in more ways than in size.

In 1787 there were no automobiles, jet airplanes, television, or telephones. There was no electricity, atomic energy, or space ships. There were no large factories or billion-dollar industries. All of these things have happened since 1787. They have made the United States a very different country. Yet the country is still governed by the Constitution. We have to ask ourselves why the Constitution is still useful. *What has kept the*

*Constitution from becoming useless or old-fashioned after so many years?*

The answer is that the Constitution has changed in many ways. Some of the change is the result of additions, or amendments. Since 1787 there have been twenty-six amendments to the Constitution. An amendment must first be approved by a two-thirds vote of both houses of Congress. Then it must be approved by three-fourths of all the states. It is not easy to change the Constitution by an amendment. However, such changes have taken place.

Still another way of changing the Constitution is through court decisions. Many cases come before the federal courts and the Supreme Court. The cases often arise because of laws passed by Congress. The courts, in deciding the cases, have to see if the laws are proper and constitutional. The decisions of the federal courts, especially the Supreme Court, are important. They are part of the "unwritten Constitution" of the United States.

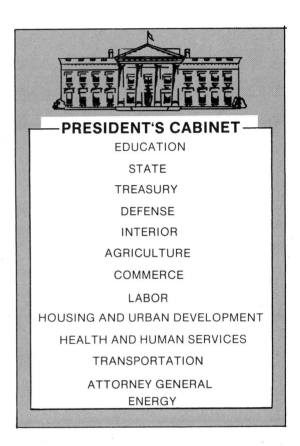

**PRESIDENT'S CABINET**

EDUCATION

STATE

TREASURY

DEFENSE

INTERIOR

AGRICULTURE

COMMERCE

LABOR

HOUSING AND URBAN DEVELOPMENT

HEALTH AND HUMAN SERVICES

TRANSPORTATION

ATTORNEY GENERAL

ENERGY

**Warren Burger is the Chief Justice of the Supreme Court. It is the job of the Supreme Court to interpret the Constitution.**

Another part of the unwritten Constitution results from customs. These customs have developed over the years. For example, the Constitution says nothing about political parties or a presidential Cabinet. But these are accepted today as though they were part of the Constitution.

Amendments, court decisions, and customs have kept the Constitution from becoming old-fashioned. They have helped it to grow and to remain up-to-date. That is why we speak of our living Constitution.

# What were the problems of the new government?

The first problem of the new government in 1789 was how to organize itself. It was doing things for the first time. What it did, and how it was done, would be important for the future. Other presidents, Congresses, and federal judges would be following the examples of the first government.

President Washington divided the executive branch into departments. Each was headed by a secretary who met with the president and advised him. These advisers became known as the president's Cabinet. Other presidents followed Washington's example in appointing a Cabinet. Today the Cabinet is part of our unwritten Constitution.

President Washington and his Cabinet members faced many problems. These included money problems, relations with foreign nations, and making the new nation strong.

Alexander Hamilton was the secretary of the treasury. He had to solve the money problems. Thomas Jefferson was secretary of state. He was in charge of relations with foreign countries. Henry Knox was the secretary of war. He had to build up the country's army and navy.

Hamilton had the most difficult job in the Cabinet. The Congress, under the Articles of Confederation, had borrowed large sums of money. This money had to be paid back if the new government was to last. In addition, some of the states also owed money. Some way had to be found to raise money to pay off all these debts. Such payment would establish the good credit of the United States.

Hamilton decided upon a strong step. He asked the national government to take over all debts owed. This included debts owed by the states. To pay for them, Hamilton asked Congress to pass a number of new tax laws. These taxes raised enough money to gradually pay off all the debts. Hamilton's plan helped to establish the credit of the United States. It also gave strength to the new national government.

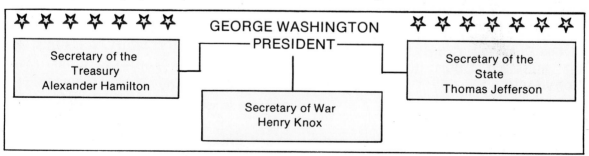

GEORGE WASHINGTON — PRESIDENT

Secretary of the Treasury
Alexander Hamilton

Secretary of the State
Thomas Jefferson

Secretary of War
Henry Knox

# LEARNING EXERCISES

## I. Remembering What We Have Read

Pick the best answer.

1. The power to declare a law unconstitutional belongs to the
   a. executive branch.
   b. judicial branch.
   c. legislative branch.
   d. states.
2. A proposed amendment to the Constitution must be approved by a two-thirds vote of both Houses and by
   a. the Supreme Court.
   b. the president.
   c. all of the states.
   d. three-fourths of the states.
3. The president's Cabinet must be
   a. members of Congress.
   b. elected to the office.
   c. approved by both Houses.
   d. approved by the Senate.
4. Our presidents are chosen by the
   a. Congress.
   b. people.
   c. states.

## II. Can You Guess the Answers to These Questions?

The answers are not in the book.

1. Which of the guarantees in the Bill of Rights do you think most important?
2. Are political parties useful to our country?
3. Today our country owes hundreds of billions of dollars. How can you lend money to the United States?

## III. Fact or Opinion

Is each of the following a Fact or an Opinion?

1. The federal government has three branches.
2. The executive branch has more power than the other branches.
3. The best judges are in the federal courts.
4. The first ten amendments are called the Bill of Rights.
5. John Marshall helped to strengthen the power of the federal courts.

# GEORGE WASHINGTON

## Our First President

George Washington had a very strong sense of duty. As an officer during the French and Indian War, he served the British loyally for four years. After the war, he served as a member of the House of Burgesses. This was the name for the Virginia colonial legislature. Later, when Virginia joined the colonial revolt, Washington led the Continental Army. He left his family and lands for eight long years to lead that army to victory. His soldiers loved and respected him for his honesty and sense of duty.

When the war ended, Washington returned to Virginia. He hoped to lead a quiet life as a well-to-do farmer. But he was called to serve his country again. Under his strong leadership the Constitutional Convention met in Philadelphia. Out of this meeting a new Constitution was born.

National elections were held in 1789, after the states had adopted the Constitution. The first Congress was elected to office. At the same time the voters selected the people who would choose a president. These people are known as the Electoral College. The members of the Electoral College met in 1789 and chose George Washington to be the first president. He was their unanimous choice.

George Washington had hoped to go back to private life. He did not seek any more positions of power and leadership. But his sense of duty led him to take on the hard work of leading the new government. Of all the American presidents, only George Washington was the unanimous choice of the Electoral College. He was truly the "father of his country."

# ALEXANDER HAMILTON

The date was July 11, 1804. The place was Weehawken, New Jersey. Two men faced each other in a duel with pistols that day. One was Aaron Burr, the vice-president of the United States. The other was Alexander Hamilton who had been secretary of the treasury under Washington. The two men had long been enemies and Hamilton had kept Burr from winning the presidency in 1800. Now Burr wanted revenge.

He had forced Hamilton to accept a challenge to a duel. Hamilton did not believe in duels, but he did not wish to be thought a coward. When the order to fire was given, Hamilton aimed and fired over Burr's head. Burr did not do the same thing. Burr's bullet struck home. Within minutes, Hamilton was dead. His death was a great loss to the United States.

Hamilton had come to the colonies from the West Indies at the age of sixteen. Four year later, he was serving as an officer with General Washington in the American Revolution.

After the Revolution, Hamilton married and practiced law. He also continued to serve his country. Because he felt there ought to be a strong national government, he served as a delegate to the Constitutional Convention in 1787. Later he worked hard to win the ratification of the Constitution by the states. He succeeded.

When Washington became president, he appointed Hamilton as secretary of the treasury. It was Hamilton who developed a plan to solve the money problems of the new government.

Hamilton had many differences with Thomas Jefferson. In spite of these differences, Hamilton had great respect for Jefferson. He showed that respect in the election of 1800. The anti-Federalists, now called Democratic-Republicans, won the election. However, it was not clear whether the Electoral College would select Jefferson or Aaron Burr as President. Alexander Hamilton urged the Federalists on the Electoral College to vote for Jefferson. He believed Jefferson was a better person than Burr even though he often disagreed with Jefferson. This decision to help Jefferson made Burr an enemy of Hamilton. Four years later it led to the duel in New Jersey.

# BENJAMIN FRANKLIN

In 1787 fifty-five delegates met in Philadelphia to write the American Constitution. Among those present was eighty-one-year-old Benjamin Franklin. He was an old man, but the delegates respected his wisdom and ability.

Benjamin Franklin was no ordinary person. He lived at a time when people were expected to be able to do many things. A person could be a farmer and also be a writer or a political leader. People were expected to do many things. But, even then, Franklin was a man of outstanding abilities.

Benjamin Franklin was born in Boston in 1706. He learned to be a printer and moved to Philadelphia when he was seventeen years old. Franklin owned his own newspaper and also printed a famous almanac. An almanac is a book that is filled with all sorts of information. Science, hints to housewives, notes on farming, and hundreds of small jokes were all included in Franklin's *Poor Richard's Almanac*.

Franklin had so many interests, it is hard to imagine how he found time for all of them. He founded a library, a school, and a fire-fighting company. He also interested himself in science and invention. One of his inventions was the Franklin stove. This stove was widely used in the Philadelphia area for many years. Franklin also used a kite, with a key attached to it, to attract lightning to the metal in the key. In this way he helped prove that lightning contained electricity. While he was doing all these things and more, Franklin was also busy in politics. He served in the Pennsylvania Colonial Assembly and was postmaster general for the colonies.

Franklin's fame spread to Great Britain and to France. He went to Britain where he represented Pennsylvania and other colonies before the king. Franklin proposed a plan under which Britain would have given more rights to its American colonies. That plan was never accepted. However, a plan very much like it was accepted by Britain a hundred years later.

When the differences between the colonies and Britain grew worse, Franklin sided with the colonists. He returned to Philadelphia and was a member of the Continental Congress. Franklin was also one of the authors of the Declaration of Independence.

By this time Franklin was an old man. However, he agreed to serve the colonial cause in France. He traveled to France and lived there from 1776 to 1785. During those years Franklin was very popular in France. He was able to win loans from France for the colonists. Franklin also arranged for a treaty between France and the colonists. As a result, France declared war on Britain. France sent troops and warships to America. They helped General Washington defeat the British at Yorktown.

Franklin helped draw up the treaty of peace that won American independence. When he returned to the United States in 1785, he expected to live quietly. But he was soon needed to help draw up the Constitution of the United States. Benjamin Franklin, at the age of eighty-one, became one of the leaders at the Constitutional Convention. He lived to the age of eighty-four and was honored as a kindly figure who was both wise and brave.

# How did the United States grow in size?

Look at the map on this page labeled United States in 1801. It shows the boundaries of the United States at that time. The western border was the Mississippi River. That river was of great importance to many Americans.

American farmers in the western lands shipped their goods to market on the Mississippi River. Flatboats carried the farm goods down the river to New Orleans. This city was held by Spain. In New Orleans the goods were stored, then loaded for shipment aboard ocean-going vessels. These vessels sailed from New Orleans to the eastern United States and to European ports.

In 1800 Spain controlled New Orleans and the Louisiana Territory. The Spanish government allowed American farm goods to be stored in the city of New Orleans at low cost. This was important to the western farmers. Without it, they could not afford to send their goods to market. They would be ruined.

During 1800 New Orleans and the Louisiana Territory were given to France by Spain. The American

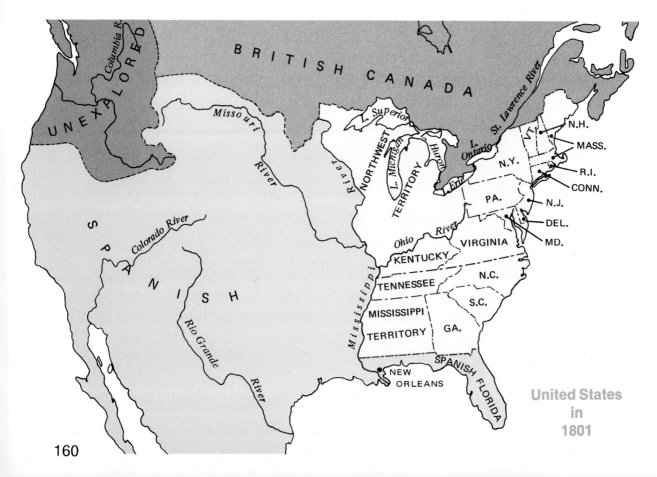

United States in 1801

160

people were alarmed when they learned of this action. The ruler of France was Napoleon Bonaparte. He dreamed of setting up a new French empire in America. New Orleans was to be his food storehouse. It would supply French troops that were to be kept on the part of the island of Santo Domingo called Haiti.

President Jefferson decided that the United States must control New Orleans. American representatives were sent to France to offer to buy the city. To their surprise, Napoleon offered to sell more than the city of New Orleans. He also offered the rest of the Louisiana Territory. His plans for a new empire had been overturned by a revolt of black people in Haiti. Napoleon now wanted to get rid of the lands.

Napoleon's change of plans led to the Louisiana Purchase by the United States in 1803. The map labeled United States in 1803 shows the new boundaries of the United States after the purchase. At a price of only fifteen million dollars, President Jefferson had doubled the nation's size!

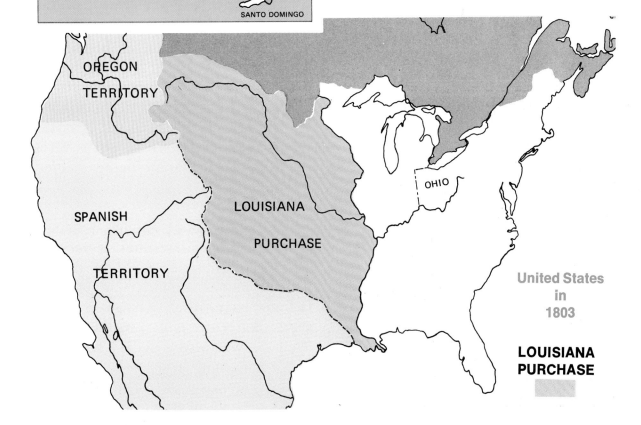

NEW ORLEANS

ATLANTIC OCEAN

HAITI

SANTO DOMINGO

OREGON TERRITORY

SPANISH

TERRITORY

LOUISIANA

PURCHASE

OHIO

United States in 1803

LOUISIANA PURCHASE

# PRESIDENT THOMAS JEFFERSON

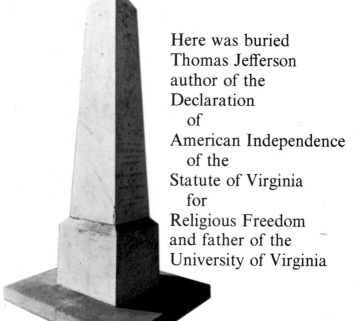

Here was buried
Thomas Jefferson
author of the
Declaration
of
American Independence
of the
Statute of Virginia
for
Religious Freedom
and father of the
University of Virginia

These words are written on the tombstone of Thomas Jefferson. He wrote them himself before he died. It may seem strange that he did not even mention that he had also been president of the United States. Jefferson may well have felt that the things he listed were in some ways more important than being elected president.

Everything about Thomas Jefferson was unusual. Sometimes it seemed there was nothing he could not do. He was a lawyer, scientist, diplomat, farmer, architect, inventor, and statesman. *Does that seem like a lot?* Well, he was also a skilled horseman and a musician.

Jefferson, the architect, designed his own home in Virginia. He called it Monticello (mon-ti-chello). It still stands today and thousands of Americans visit it each year.

Young Thomas Jefferson wrote the Declaration of Independence. In it he declared "all men are created equal" and have the right to "life, liberty, and the pursuit of happiness."

Jefferson also wrote the *Statute of Virginia for Religious Freedom*. This law put an end to the taxes Virginians paid to support a state church, even if they did not belong to it. He helped to make church support voluntary rather than something forced upon people. The *Statute* was a great victory for religious freedom.

Jefferson was a strong believer in the importance of education. He felt education and knowledge could help people overcome ignorance, superstition, and prejudice. Jefferson often felt that founding the University of Virginia was as important as being president of the United States.

Jefferson's ideas about democracy were not shared by many other people. President John Adams, a Federalist, lost reelection to Jefferson in 1800. These one-time friends were political enemies for many years. But they put aside their differences in later years. When the ninety-one-year-old Adams died on July 4, 1826, his last words were "Tom Jefferson lives." He did not know that the eighty-three-year-old Jefferson had died earlier the same day.

163

WASHINGTON

COLUMBIA R.

ROCKY MOUNTAINS

Portage around Missouri Falls

MISSOURI R.

Reach the
Pacific Ocean
November, 1805

SNAKE

RIVER

COLUMBIA RIVER

MONTANA

OREGON

Meet Shoshone Indians
and Sacajawea's brother.

WYOMING

# LEWIS and CLARK

IDAHO

"Great joy in camp. We
are in view of the ocian. . .
this great Pacific Octean
which we been so long
anxious to see, and the
roreing or noise made by
the waves brakeing on the
rock shores (as I suppose)
may be heard distictly."

William Clark

Meriwether Lewis

These words, including the poor
spelling, were written on November 7,
1805. They were written by William
Clark in his journal, or diary. He had
been keeping that journal for the past
year and a half. In it he told of the
day-to-day happenings on the
expedition he and his partner,
Meriwether Lewis, were leading.

William Clark and Meriwether
Lewis had been sent on their famous
expedition by President Jefferson. The
Louisiana Purchase of 1803 had
doubled the size of the United States.
However, almost nothing was known
about the territory. President Jefferson
sent Lewis and Clark to explore this
vast new part of the United States.

The expedition started out from St.
Louis in May 1804 with about forty
people. Lewis and Clark planned to
follow the Missouri River upstream to
its source. Then they planned to
journey westward to the Pacific Ocean.

The explorers found it hard to move
against the river currents. By winter,

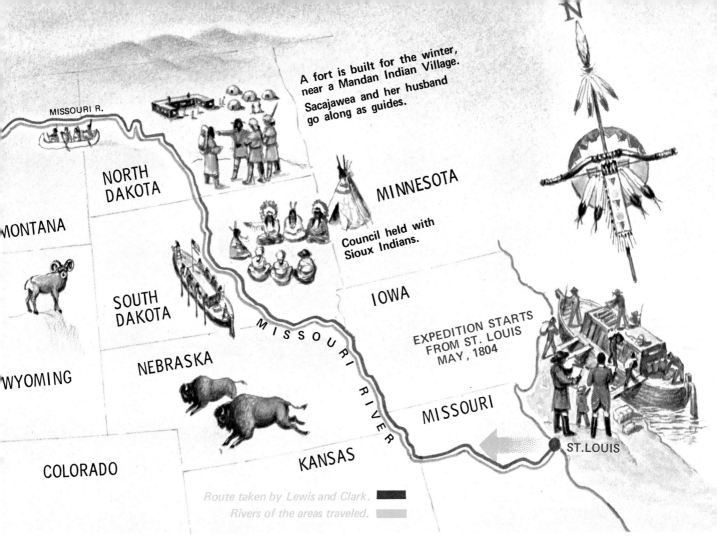

MISSOURI R.

NORTH DAKOTA

A fort is built for the winter, near a Mandan Indian Village. Sacajawea and her husband go along as guides.

MINNESOTA

MONTANA

Council held with Sioux Indians.

SOUTH DAKOTA

M I S S O U R I   R I V E R

IOWA

WYOMING

NEBRASKA

EXPEDITION STARTS FROM ST. LOUIS MAY, 1804

MISSOURI

ST. LOUIS

COLORADO

KANSAS

Route taken by Lewis and Clark.
Rivers of the areas traveled.

however, they reached a Mandan Indian village in what is now North Dakota. There they met Sacajawea, or "bird woman." She had been born a Shoshone, a tribe that lived in the Rocky Mountains. Her husband was a French fur trapper and had brought her east to the lands of the Mandan Indians. Lewis and Clark realized that Sacajawea could be a great help on the journey ahead. She and her husband agreed to lead the expedition westward.

When the expedition reached the land of the Shoshones, it had more good luck. The chief turned out to be a brother of Sacajawea. He told Lewis and Clark how to reach the Pacific Ocean.

Lewis and Clark followed the route given them by the Shoshone Indians. They journeyed down the Columbia River through beautiful mountain lands. Then, on November 7, 1805, they came to the mouth of the Columbia River. In front of them lay the Pacific Ocean which they had "been so long anxious to see." No wonder there was "great joy in camp." Lewis and Clark had opened a whole new territory to settlement in the future.

# LEARNING EXERCISES

## I. Remembering What We Have Read

Pick the best answer.

1. The United States bought the Louisiana Territory from
   a. Spain.
   b. Britain.
   c. France.
   d. the Indians.
2. Alexander Hamilton served as
   a. secretary of state.
   b. vice-president.
   c. secretary of the treasury.
   d. none of the above.
3. The United States bought Louisiana in order to get
   a. Haiti.
   b. New Orleans.
   c. Florida.
   d. the Northwest Territory.
4. Benjamin Franklin was all of the following **except** a
   a. printer.
   b. general.
   c. colonial representative to Britain.
   d. member of the Continental Congress.

## II. Who Might Have Said?

Here are three sentences. They might have been said by Alexander Hamilton, Thomas Jefferson, or Lewis and Clark. Who might have said:

1. "Aaron Burr is not fit to be president."
2. "We have seen this new land with our own eyes."
3. "All men are created equal."

## III. Learning From Pictures

Each of the pictures tells us something about an event in American history. What are the events shown in the pictures?

1.

2.

3.

4.

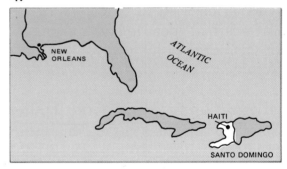

## IV. Thinking About Things

Can you guess the answers to these questions? The answers are not in the book.

1. How did the Louisiana Purchase help keep foreign powers from American borders?

2. How might American history have been different if the Louisiana Territory had not been bought?

3. Why did Americans fear French control of Louisiana more than they feared Spanish control?

# What were the causes of the War of 1812?

The United States doubled its size after 1803. However, it was still weaker than many European nations. Because of its weakness, the United States wanted to keep out of disputes and wars.

President Washington had warned the American people against taking sides in European wars. Great Britain and France fought a series of wars after 1792. The United States was three thousand miles away, but it could still be involved. Some Americans sided with Britain, others with France. In addition, American ships carried goods to both nations. All of this might easily involve the United States.

Washington wanted the United States to remain neutral. This meant favoring neither Britain nor France. However, the Federalists sided with Britain. The anti-Federalists favored France, though they did not like Napoleon, the French leader.

President John Adams took office in 1797. He continued Washington's policy of neutrality, but barely avoided a war with France. The danger of war grew greater after 1801 when Jefferson became President.

Britain and France each tried to cut off the other's trade. Britain, which had the stronger navy, placed a blockade upon the lands controlled by France. British warships seized vessels that tried to enter ports in those lands. Some of those vessels belonged to Americans.

President Jefferson felt he could avoid trouble by stopping trade. But this proved very harmful to American trade and shipping. Many Americans were thrown out of work and the plan was finally dropped.

Once again British warships stopped American vessels on the high seas. They searched the vessels and seized sailors whom they claimed were deserters from British ships. This impressment of American sailors, as it was called, angered many Americans. It seemed Britain did not respect American rights to freedom of the seas. This was one of the important causes of the War of 1812.

Many Americans were also angry because Britain still held trading posts in the Northwest Territory. The British were supposed to have left that area when the United States received its independence. Americans also believed that Britain encouraged Indians to attack Americans in the Northwest Territory. This was another cause of the War of 1812.

There were also Americans who wanted to take Canada away from Britain. These War Hawks, as they were called, were mainly southerners and westerners. They were willing to go to war against Britain to make Canada a part of the United States. This was another cause of the War of 1812.

There were people in Britain who still acted as if the United States was a British colony. There were also Americans who felt that Britain wanted to retake the United States as a colony. These attitudes helped to bring on the War of 1812.

*The War of 1812 is sometimes called the Second War of Independence. Can you explain why it has this name?*

# "The Star-Spangled Banner" is written

"Oh say, can you see, by the
    dawn's early light
What so proudly we hailed at the
    twilight's last gleaming? . . ."

These are the opening lines of our national anthem, "The Star-Spangled Banner." Do you know how this song came to be written? It is a very interesting story and it happened during the War of 1812.

During the War of 1812 an American force captured the city of York in Canada. They burned it to the ground. The British were angry and swore to get revenge. In August 1814, the British captured and burned the city of Washington, D.C. They next moved to seize the city of Baltimore. But first they had to destroy Fort McHenry, which guarded the city. A fleet of British ships dropped anchor near the fort. Aboard the British flagship was an American prisoner of war, Dr. William Beanes.

Dr. Beanes had a friend in Baltimore, a young lawyer named Francis Scott Key. On September 13, 1814, Francis Scott Key rowed out to the British ships. He wanted to win freedom for his friend, Dr. Beanes. The British commander agreed to free the prisoner. However, he told Key that he and Dr. Beanes must remain aboard until morning. The British ships were going to attack Fort McHenry that night. The British expected the fort to surrender by morning. They promised to free their prisoner at that time.

Francis Scott Key did not sleep that night as the British guns pounded Fort McHenry. The American gunners in the fort fired back bravely. From the deck of the warship, Key could see the flash of guns firing away.

Could the Americans hold out against the British attack? During the long night, Francis Scott Key asked himself that question many times. The night finally gave way to the light of dawn. Key peered anxiously through the haze and smoke. When the air cleared, he saw the stars and stripes flying over the fort. The British had failed to capture Fort McHenry. Baltimore was saved.

Francis Scott Key quickly wrote down his experience in a poem. That morning, after the British released him and Dr. Beanes, he went to Baltimore. He read his poem to friends and it was soon put to the music of an old song. Today we know that song as "The Star-Spangled Banner." It is our national anthem. *Do you know the words of "The Star-Spangled Banner?"*

# The battle of New Orleans

We live in a world of fast communication. We hear about important events in other parts of the world almost as soon as they happen. The telephone, radio, and television carry the news quickly across oceans and continents. This was not true in 1815. Communication depended on slow sailing vessels, stagecoaches, and horseback riders. It took many weeks to send a message from Europe to the United States.

During Christmas week of 1814 an important message was sent from Europe to America. The message was addressed to the United States government, then in New York City.

It took weeks for that message to get to a vessel sailing to America. More weeks passed while the ship was at sea. The message did not reach New York until February 1815. That was about six weeks after it began its journey from Europe.

Three weeks before the message arrived in New York, a great battle was fought. On January 8, 1815, British troops fought the Americans in the Battle of New Orleans. The British hoped to smash the American defenses

## A TIME LINE OF THE IMPORTANT MESSAGE

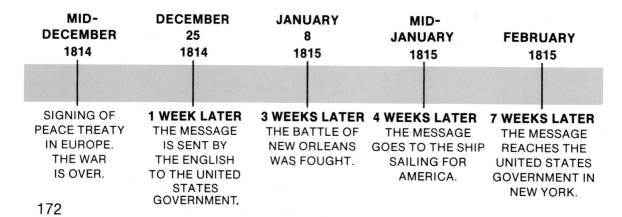

| MID-DECEMBER 1814 | DECEMBER 25 1814 | JANUARY 8 1815 | MID-JANUARY 1815 | FEBRUARY 1815 |
|---|---|---|---|---|
| SIGNING OF PEACE TREATY IN EUROPE. THE WAR IS OVER. | **1 WEEK LATER** THE MESSAGE IS SENT BY THE ENGLISH TO THE UNITED STATES GOVERNMENT. | **3 WEEKS LATER** THE BATTLE OF NEW ORLEANS WAS FOUGHT. | **4 WEEKS LATER** THE MESSAGE GOES TO THE SHIP SAILING FOR AMERICA. | **7 WEEKS LATER** THE MESSAGE REACHES THE UNITED STATES GOVERNMENT IN NEW YORK. |

in front of the city. General Andrew Jackson, who commanded the American Army, made preparations to stop the British. Jackson's troops included backwoods sharpshooters, black volunteers, and some people suspected of being pirates. They joined General Jackson to defend the city of New Orleans.

The British tried to charge the American lines. They ran into deadly gunfire from the Americans. More than 2,000 British soldiers were killed or wounded. Only seventy-one Americans were killed or wounded in the battle. The Battle of New Orleans was a terrible defeat for Britain.

But the real story is that this battle need never have been fought. The lives of those who died were wasted because of the lack of faster communication.

The War of 1812 had actually ended in December 1814. The message that took six weeks to arrive in America told of the signing of the peace treaty in Europe. But that message did not arrive until six weeks later, in February 1815. The war had ended, but those who were fighting in America did not know this. The Battle of New Orleans was fought three weeks after the peace treaty ended the war. In New Orleans soldiers had died and there was no reason for their dying.

# What were some results of the War of 1812?

The War of 1812 lasted for about two years. At the start, the British were stronger than the Americans. Britain's fleet was the most powerful in the world. Its soldiers were well-armed and well-trained. The United States had almost no trained army or navy.

the plan of the War Hawks to make Canada part of the United States. The American troops were also defeated by the British who captured Washington, D.C. The White House was burned and President Madison barely escaped capture.

In spite of this, the United States managed to avoid a complete defeat for two reasons:

First, Britain had to send ships, supplies, and troops 3,000 miles across the Atlantic Ocean.

Second, Britain was at the same time fighting a war with France in Europe.

American troops failed in their efforts to invade Canada. This ended

The American Navy did not do as badly as the Army. Although most of the fleet was forced off the high seas, a few warships won victories. The most famous American ship of the war was the *U.S.S. Constitution,* known as Old Ironsides. American ships also won victories on Lake Erie and Lake Champlain. It was these victories that made Britain agree to a peace treaty in 1814. The greatest American Army victory, the Battle of New Orleans, came after the war ended.

Who won the War of 1812? It would seem that neither side really won. No territory changed hands. Britain did not even agree to stop the impressment of sailors, though this was one reason for the war. Impressment ended, however, because Britain defeated France in the European wars. This made it unnecessary for Britain to seek sailors for their vessels.

But the War of 1812 did have some important results. The United States gained respect at home and in Europe. British influence in the Northwest Territory was ended. Americans

awakened to a sense of patriotism and pride in their nation. A new feeling ran through the land—a feeling that Americans were a united people, a nation. This feeling of nationalism was one of the most important results of the War of 1812.

Imagine living in a world in which there was no writing. There would be no books, no newspapers, no letters, and nothing to write on blackboards! Suppose you wanted to communicate, or pass ideas to other people. You could only do this by speaking or by using signs.

There are ways of writing by using pictures. Picture words were used by the Egyptians 3,000 years ago. A form of picture writing is used in China to this day. But suppose you had neither an alphabet nor a system of picture writing. How would you communicate? Without an alphabet it is hard for people to communicate.

This problem of how to communicate troubled an Indian more than 150 years ago. That Indian's name was Sequoya (See-kwoy-uh). He was a member of the Cherokee tribe in the southeastern part of the United States. Sequoya had time to think of such problems. He was crippled in one leg and spent his time as a craftsman and silversmith.

In 1812 Sequoya was about forty years old. Though he was lame, he helped the Americans in the War of 1812. Sequoya noticed the way the Americans wrote messages on paper and read them. He wondered about the mystery of the "talking leaves." That was what the Indians called the paper. Sequoya wondered if his own people could learn to use talking leaves.

Finding a way for the Cherokee people to read and write became Sequoya's life work. But the Cherokees had no system of writing, and they had no alphabet. Sequoya had to find a way to get around that.

Picture writing seemed a way to

make the leaves talk. Sequoya had never heard of Egyptians or Chinese, but thought of the idea of using pictures. He spent years creating pictures for words. Then he gave each of those pictures a sound to match the Cherokee language. But all his work was destroyed in one day by his angry wife. Sequoya left home and traveled west with his daughter. He began again the long work of creating a Cherokee system of writing.

Luckily, Sequoya now decided to try to create an alphabet for the Cherokee language. He hoped to make it something like the English alphabet. However, there are only twenty-six letters in the English alphabet. Sequoya had to create eighty-six letters, each standing for a sound in the Cherokee alphabet.

Years passed before Sequoya was ready to prove he could produce talking leaves for his people. He and his young daughter presented the system to a council meeting of the Cherokees. Sequoya sent his daughter into the room where the council was meeting. He remained outside, unable to hear what was being said. The council members gave his daughter a message which she wrote on paper in the new Cherokee alphabet. The marks she made on the paper meant nothing to the tribal members. Sequoya was then called into the room. The paper was put before him. To the surprise of the council, he could read it easily. This proved that he had developed an alphabet for the Cherokee language.

The greatness of Sequoya is not only that he created an alphabet. It must be remembered he spoke no non-Indian language. He had never attended school and was not trained in the science of languages. Sequoya had used his brain to create a new alphabet. By this action he brought the talking leaves to the Cherokee people. They could now learn to read and write in their own language.

# LEARNING EXERCISES

## I. Remembering What We Have Read

Pick the best answer.

1. The seizure of American sailors by the British was known as
   a. a blockade.
   b. impressment.
   c. neutrality.
   d. the right of deposit.

2. The War Hawks were
   a. Canadians.
   b. British naval officers.
   c. Indians in the Northwest Territory.
   d. Americans who wanted to seize Canada.

3. All the following are true of the War of 1812 **except**
   a. The British seized the White House.
   b. France helped the United States in America.
   c. The Battle of New Orleans was not fought after the end of the war.
   d. Neither the British nor the Americans really won the war.

4. During the wars between Britain and France
   a. the Federalists favored France.
   b. all Americans favored Britain.
   c. the anti-Federalists favored Britain.
   d. the anti-Federalists favored France.

## II. Who Might Have Said?

Below are three sentences. They might have been said by Andrew Jackson, Francis Scott Key, or Sequoya. Who might have said:

1. "Is the flag still flying?"
2. "The leaves will talk for us."
3. "My sharpshooters and volunteers can stop the British soldiers."

## III. Learning From Pictures

Each of the pictures tells us something about an event in American history. What are the events shown in the pictures?

1.

2.

3.

## IV. Thinking About Things

Can you guess the answers to these questions? The answers are not in the book.

1. How might the British have tried to avoid war with the United States in 1812?
2. Why was it hard for Americans to be neutral in the wars in Europe between Britain and France?

# Why did different sections of the United States disagree with each other?

Look at the time line on this page. It shows some events of the first fifty years of United States history. These events led to the growth of a national spirit in the United States.

Nationalism was a force that united the American people. But this did not mean that all Americans thought alike. Then, as today, Americans disagreed on many things. Some disagreements divided the nation on a sectional basis.

A section is a part of the nation that has common interests. The interests of one section are often different from

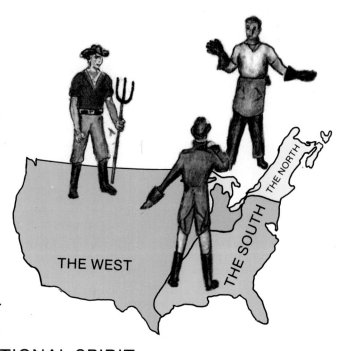

THE WEST

THE SOUTH

THE NORTH

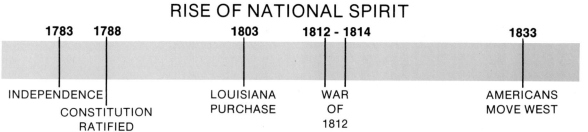

RISE OF NATIONAL SPIRIT

| 1783 | 1788 | 1803 | 1812 - 1814 | 1833 |
|------|------|------|-------------|------|
| INDEPENDENCE | CONSTITUTION RATIFIED | LOUISIANA PURCHASE | WAR OF 1812 | AMERICANS MOVE WEST |

those of another section. By 1833 there were three main sections in the United States. These sections were the North, the South, and the West. The map shows where these sections were located. Each section had its own ways of looking at things and its own special interests. The sectional interests of different parts of the United States often opposed a single, national spirit.

The sections disagreed on some things. These included slavery, taxes on goods coming into the country, and

road and canal building. Sectional disagreements prevented a single, national policy that would have the support of all the people. Let us examine the issues on which sections differed during the early 1800s.

**Internal Improvements**

Internal improvements mean roads and canals. The West wanted roads and canals to be built by the federal government. Roads and canals would help western farmers ship their crops

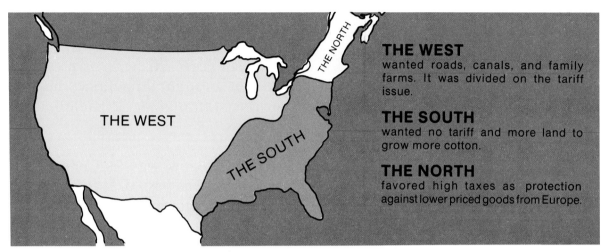

**THE WEST**
wanted roads, canals, and family farms. It was divided on the tariff issue.

**THE SOUTH**
wanted no tariff and more land to grow more cotton.

**THE NORTH**
favored high taxes as protection against lower priced goods from Europe.

to markets. The South was against the national government spending money on roads and canals. Most southern cotton farms were near rivers or close to ocean inlets on the coast. The South did not need internal improvements to ship its cotton. The North was divided on the issue.

### Tariffs

The North favored high taxes on goods coming into the country. These taxes on incoming goods are known as import tariffs. The new industries of the North needed the tariffs as protection against lower-priced goods from Europe. High tariffs would help to protect the "infant industries" of the North. The South was against high protective tariffs. These tariffs raised the cost of goods. Southerners wanted to buy the cheaper goods from Europe. The West was divided on the issue of high tariffs.

### Slavery

The South favored slavery. After the invention of the cotton gin in 1793, slavery had expanded rapidly. The South depended upon black slaves to plant and harvest the rich cotton crops. Southerners also wanted new lands on which to grow more cotton. They wanted to expand their slave holdings to the western territories. Americans who lived in the West and North did not need slavery. Their life was built around small family farms. The people of the West and North were against the southern plan for expanding slave holdings in the new western lands. They wanted the new lands for their own family farms.

Sectionalism still divides the American people on some issues. *Can you think of any present-day issues that divide the North and South or that divide the West and the East?*

# JOHN QUINCY ADAMS

John Quincy Adams knew that much was expected of him. The Adams family was one of the most famous in New England. His father, John Adams, had been a leader in the American Revolution. Later, John Adams became the second president of the United States. Samuel Adams, a cousin, had organized the Boston Tea Party. John Quincy Adams never forgot it was his duty to serve the United States.

In 1825 John Quincy Adams became president of the United States. It was a proud day for the family. His father, John Adams, watched his son take the oath of office. This is the only time that a father and son served as presidents of the United States.

In 1828 John Quincy Adams failed to win reelection. He retired to Boston. It seemed that his life in American politics was at an end. But, to everyone's surprise, he began a new political life. In 1830 John Quincy Adams was elected to the House of Representatives.

Many friends felt that being a congressman was beneath an ex-president. Adams disagreed with them.

To Adams, no office of public service was beneath any American. Adams served in Congress for the next seventeen years. His term as president had not brought him fame, but he became famous as a member of Congress.

While Adams was in Congress, a special rule was passed. It tried to stop debate on anti-slavery petitions. This gag rule, as it was called, had been put forward by pro-slavery congressmen. They wanted to end discussion of slavery in the Congress.

John Quincy Adams believed the gag rule was wrong. He felt it was against the right of petition and free speech. These rights are guaranteed by the Constitution. Adams felt he must uphold the Constitution.

From 1836 to 1844 John Quincy Adams fought the gag rule. Time and again he would start a debate on anti-slavery petitions. He was always ruled out of order and forced to stop speaking. Somehow, he always managed to say a few words against slavery and the gag rule. The country admired his courage and his efforts. He soon became known as Old Man Eloquent. Finally, in 1844, Congress put aside the gag rule. John Quincy Adams had defeated an attempt to limit constitutional rights of petition and free speech.

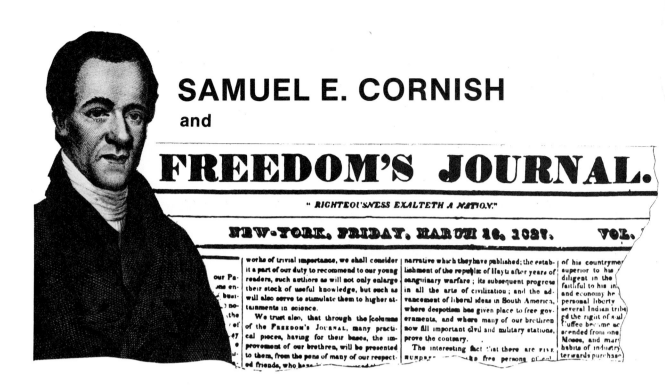

SAMUEL E. CORNISH

and

FREEDOM'S JOURNAL.

" RIGHTEOUSNESS EXALTETH A NATION."

NEW-YORK, FRIDAY, MARCH 16, 1827. VOL.

Slavery was one of the great sectional issues after 1820. About 4,000,000 black people were held as slaves. Most of the slaves were on farms or plantations in the South. Many people in the North and the West wanted to stop the spread of slavery to the new lands west of the Mississippi. These Americans did not really care about ending slavery or freeing the black slaves. They wanted to keep southern slave owners from taking over the rich western lands.

There were, of course, other people who wanted to put an end to slavery anywhere. These people felt slavery was evil. They spoke out against it and printed newspapers urging freedom for the slaves.

Not all black people in the United States were slaves. Nearly 400,000 black people were free men and women. These free blacks were active in the anti-slavery movement for many years. Samuel E. Cornish was one of these free black people. In 1827 he and another black man, John B. Russwurm, founded the newpaper, *Freedom's Journal.* It was the first newspaper printed by black people in the United States. In the first issue, Mr. Cornish declared:

"We wish to plead our own cause. Too long have others spoken for us . . . we intend to lay our case before the public . . . we must be firm. . . ."

Samuel E. Cornish and *Freedom's Journal* brought a new voice into the fight against slavery. This was the voice of the millions of black people, slave and free. *Freedom's Journal* wanted black people to speak for themselves in the fight for freedom and justice.

# ANDREW JACKSON

was made a general. He won a great victory at New Orleans. After the war, Jackson fought against the Seminole Indians in Florida. By 1824 he was a national hero and he entered politics.

Jackson was a candidate for the presidency in 1824, but was not elected. His admirers felt he had been robbed of the presidency by rich politicians in the North. The result was the forming of new political parties by 1828. Jackson and his followers were the Democratic-Republicans. His opponents called themselves the National Republicans.

In 1828 Jackson ran again for president and won. He was reelected to a second term and his party changed its name to the Democratic party. This is the same Democratic party that exists today, more than one hundred fifty years later.

President Jackson wanted to make the national government stronger. Although he received most of his votes from the South and West, Jackson opposed many southern ideas. Most southerners did not want a strong national government. They favored putting the rights of the states above those of the national government. Jackson disagreed. His famous words, "Our Federal Union, it must be preserved," were the words of a great national leader and a patriot.

On March 4, 1829, Andrew Jackson was inaugurated as the seventh president of the United States. A huge crowd jammed into the White House and spilled out on the lawn. They grabbed plates of ice cream, cake, and cups of punch. It was a great day for the common people, for Jackson was their president. He was born in a log cabin and had worked his way to fame and success. To the people he was "Old Hickory." They felt he was as strong and tough as hickory wood.

At the age of thirteen, Jackson fought in the Revolution. He was captured by the British. Jackson is said to have quarreled with an English officer who slashed him with a sword. He carried the scars on his arm and head all his life. Jackson never forgave the British.

Later, Jackson became a lawyer, landowner, and a congressman from Tennessee. During the War of 1812 he

# "Our federal union, it must be preserved"

On April 13, 1830, the leaders of the Democratic party held a banquet. It was in honor of Thomas Jefferson's birthday. Jefferson had died four years before, but he was remembered for his service to the country. The Democrats also honored Jefferson as the founder of the anti-Federalists. That party became known as the Democratic-Republican party. By 1830 this was shortened to the Democratic party.

President Jackson, as the head of the party, was the honored guest at the banquet. What he would say was very important to the party and to the country. Americans were badly divided by many sectional issues. The question of tariffs on goods coming into the country was a big issue. Such tariffs were a help to the North with its many new industries. But the South felt the high protective tariffs were costly to their section. Was it fair to ask the South to pay the extra cost of goods? The South said "No."

Many southerners wanted to limit the federal government. They argued for states' rights. This meant the right of a state to decide many issues for itself. Southerners felt they did not have to obey laws that interfered with the rights of the state. The Tariff of 1828 especially annoyed most of the South. They proposed to disobey this high, protective tariff which harmed the interests of many southern states.

The Jefferson birthday celebration had been planned by southern Democrats. They wanted to use it to present their states' rights arguments. Southerners hoped to win President Jackson's support for their side. After all, he was a southerner and a slave owner. Jackson had not yet spoken out on states' rights. The southerners wanted him to take a stand. They felt he might help them.

During the banquet, speeches and toasts were offered. All were in favor of states' rights. At last, the time came for President Jackson to give the main toast. All eyes were upon him. In a loud, clear voice he said, "Our Federal Union, it must be preserved." With those few words he boldly declared that the national government, not the states, must come first.

# Pioneer women

Thousands of women went west to live in the new lands of the nation. These pioneer women, like the pioneer men, faced hard work and dangers. They worked in the fields and in the homes. Pioneer women also raised families, taught school, and helped to build the churches. They brought a sense of civilization to the pioneer lands.

There were other women who were pioneers, but did not go west. They were pioneers in ideas and social concerns.

Dorothea Dix was a teacher in a girls' school. In 1841, the thirty-nine year-old Dorothea agreed to teach a Sunday school class in a nearby Massachusetts jail. What she saw in the jail shocked her and changed her life. She devoted herself to bringing better conditions to prisons, poorhouses, and insane asylums. Dorothea Dix spoke at hundreds of meetings and wrote to legislatures in many states. Her efforts led to improvements in poorhouses and asylums. During the Civil War she was appointed the superintendent of women nurses for the Union Army.

Dorothea Dix was a pioneer in working to help the poor and the helpless.

Elizabeth Blackwell was born in England. She came to the United States in 1832, at the age of eleven. Blackwell was a teacher for a while, but was determined to become a doctor. In 1849 she received her medical degree. She was the first female medical doctor in the United States. In 1857 Dr. Blackwell founded the New York Infirmary for women and children. In 1868 she started a women's medical college.

Elizabeth Blackwell was a pioneer in the field of women's medicine.

Sojourner Truth was a black slave born in New York in 1797. At that time slavery was still legal in New York. Her name as a slave was Tabella. She fled from slavery in 1827 and took the name of Sojourner Truth. Her new name meant "a traveler for the truth." The truth in her life was the need to end slavery.

Sojourner Truth spent many years writing and speaking against slavery. Her deeply religious nature had a great effect upon those who heard her. She was a pioneer in the effort to end slavery in the United States.

# LEARNING EXERCISES

## I. Remembering What We Have Read

Pick the best answer.

1. The southern section favored
   a. high tariffs.
   b. extending slavery.
   c. building new roads.
   d. protection of new industries.

2. All the following are true about Andrew Jackson **except**
   a. He wanted a stronger national government.
   b. Most of his votes came from the West and South.
   c. He put states' rights before national rights.
   d. He led the Democratic party.

3. In what sense was the United States lucky in the War of 1812?

4. What might have happened if the United States had lost to Britain in the War of 1812?

## II. Using Time Lines To Remember What We Have Learned

Look at the time line below. Answer these questions:

1. In which period of time was the Constitution approved?

2. In which period of time did the Battle of New Orleans take place?

3. In which period of time was the Louisiana Territory purchased?

| 1770 | 1790 | 1810 | 1830 |
|---|---|---|---|
| A | B | C | D |

## III. Learning From Pictures

Each of the pictures tells us something about life in the United States. What does each picture mean to you?

**FREEDOM'S JOURNAL.**

1.

2.

# Why did Americans move west?

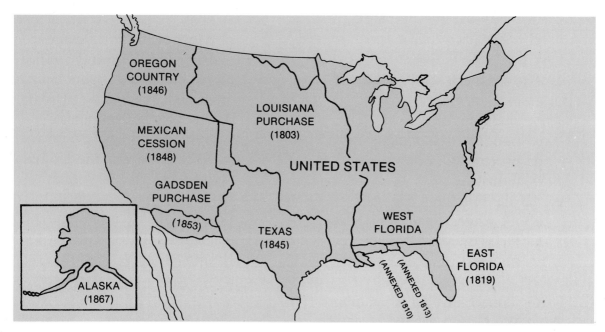

Look at the map on this page. It shows the lands added to the United States after 1800. These include the Louisiana Purchase, Florida, the Oregon Territory, Texas, and the Mexican Cession lands. Other lands were added as the United States adjusted its boundaries with Canada and Mexico.

Now look at the map that shows where Americans lived in 1810 and in 1850. The maps show that many people moved west during these years. *Why would people leave their homes, friends, and families to move to distant lands?*

There are many reasons why people move from one place to another. One reason can be economic. This means a desire for jobs, cheap farmland, or the hope of finding gold. Another reason is social. They may hope to get a new start in life. A third reason is political. Some people may be looking for a freer form of government. Still another reason is religious. There may be a desire to find religious freedom.

Large-scale movements of people involve some or all of these reasons. The early settlers to America came for many of these reasons. At first they hoped to find new trade routes to Asia, or to find gold and silver. No new trade routes were found and only the Spaniards discovered a source of gold and silver. But before long others were coming to America. They were coming for the treasure of cheap farmland. Farmland was as good as gold.

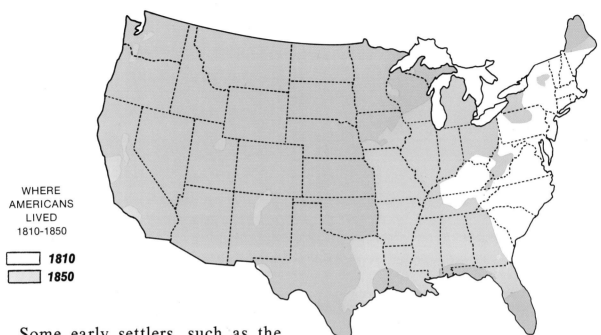

WHERE
AMERICANS
LIVED
1810-1850

☐ *1810*
▨ *1850*

Some early settlers, such as the Pilgrims and Catholics, moved to America for religious freedom. Still others wanted a freer system of government than existed in Spain, France, or in Britain. Many others came seeking a fresh start in life.

We know about the many reasons why early settlers came to America. But what about the Americans who moved westward during the 1800s? What were they seeking? In the years from the 1800s to the 1840s there were very few looking for gold. Most people moving west sought cheap farmland and a new start in life. Tens of thousands of immigrants came to America from Europe. Many settled in the West. The cheap farmland of the United States was a dream come true for them. The same was true of

Americans who left the small, rocky farms of New England. They found treasure in the larger farmlands and the rich soil of the western lands.

Few Americans moved west for religious and political freedom. These generally existed in all parts of the United States. But religious and political freedom did attract many people from Europe. These new Americans moved west for freedom as well as for economic and social reasons. They found that freedom.

Each year thousands of immigrants move to the United States. *What do you think are their reasons for moving today? How do their reasons compare with those of Americans who moved west in the 1800s?*

189

# Why did the United States go to war with Mexico?

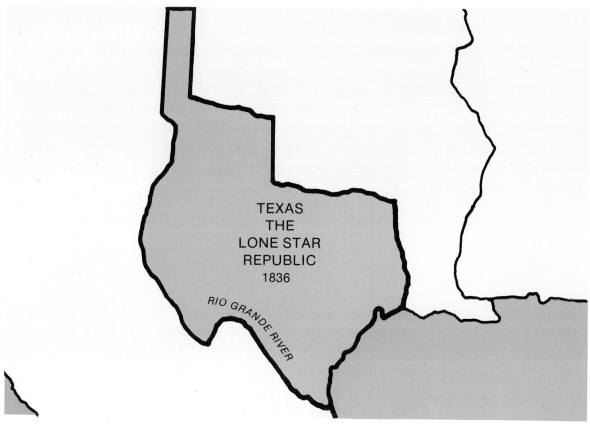

TEXAS
THE
LONE STAR
REPUBLIC
1836

RIO GRANDE RIVER

Many Americans moved westward after 1810. During the 1820s Americans also pushed southwest across the border into Texas. Texas was part of Mexico at that time.

Mexico had won its independence from Spain in 1821. Its leaders wanted to make the country stronger. To do this, they invited Americans into Texas as ranchers and farmers. They believed the new settlers would become Mexican citizens in time.

By 1830 there were about twenty thousand Americans living in Texas.

Many of them refused to become Mexican citizens. They also kept slaves, though slavery was not allowed by the Mexican government. This led to disputes between the American settlers and the Mexican government.

Civil war broke out in Texas in 1835. An American, Sam Houston, led the Texans against the Mexican government. Texas won its independence in 1836 and became the Lone Star Republic.

The new republic then asked to become a part of the United States.

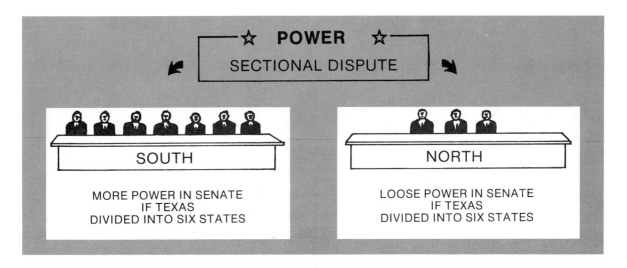

☆ **POWER** ☆
SECTIONAL DISPUTE

**SOUTH**

MORE POWER IN SENATE
IF TEXAS
DIVIDED INTO SIX STATES

**NORTH**

LOOSE POWER IN SENATE
IF TEXAS
DIVIDED INTO SIX STATES

The request touched off a great sectional dispute in the United States. The North and West did not want to admit Texas because of slavery. They also feared that Texas would be broken into as many as six states. This would give greater power to the South in Congress, especially in the Senate. Northern states already controlled the House of Representatives because of their greater population. But the Senate was still evenly divided between slave states and free states. If the huge area of Texas was broken into six states, southerners would control the Senate.

Texas was refused admission as a state. It remained an independent republic until 1845. In 1845 Texas was finally admitted as a state. The Mexican government was angered by this action. They felt the United States had helped the Texas revolt. In addition, Mexico disagreed with the boundary claims made by Texas and the United States. Mexico declared that the southern boundary of Texas should be the Nueces River. The United States declared the southern boundary to be the Rio Grande River.

Shooting broke out in the boundary area. The fighting became the direct cause of the Mexican War in 1846. An indirect cause of the war was the growing nationalist spirit in the United States. Many Americans wanted the United States boundaries to extend from coast to coast. They wanted Texas and all the Mexican lands as far west as the coast of California. These Americans declared it was the destiny of the United States to extend from the Atlantic Ocean to the Pacific Ocean. They were willing to go to war with Mexico to achieve that destiny.

# SAM HOUSTON

Soon after Andrew Jackson became president, he received a visitor. The visitor, dressed in Indian clothing, had come to speak for the Cherokee Indians. The United States owed money to the Cherokees for land it had taken from them. The visitor asked Jackson to make good the government's many promises to pay the Cherokees.

Andrew Jackson's visitor was not a Cherokee. He was Sam Houston, a long-time friend of President Jackson. Houston had fought with Jackson's army at New Orleans. Later he became a congressman from Tennessee, and then governor of the state. Small wonder that President Jackson warmly embraced Sam Houston, though he did not approve of his Indian clothing. Jackson, like most westerners, did not like Indians. He probably thought it odd that Houston should wear Indian clothing.

Sam Houston did not think it unusual to dress as a Cherokee. He ran away from home at the age of fifteen. Houston had lived with the Cherokee Indians for three years. All his life he remained loyal to the tribe which had adopted him as a son. Now he spoke for them. He had come to plead their case with the president. Houston did not change Jackson's mind in this matter. Little was done for the Indians by the government.

After the meeting, Sam Houston left for the Mexican lands of Texas. He commanded the Texas forces in the revolt against Mexico. When Texas won its independence, Sam Houston became president of the Lone Star Republic. As president he worked to gain the admission of Texas as a state in the United States. When this was done, he became a senator from Texas.

Later he served as governor of the state. His many services to Texas are remembered to this day. Houston, the largest city in Texas, is named for this great American.

# LOS NIÑOS

Every nation has its heroes. These are the men and women who offer their lives to help their country. Although we are familiar with our country's heroes, we usually know little about the heroes of other countries. Among the heroes of Mexico are a group of teen-age boys who fought in the Mexican War. They are known in Mexican history as los niños, or "the boys."

The niños of Mexico were all military cadets. They were studying to be army officers at a school near Mexico City. As American troops, led by General Scott, marched toward Mexico City, a call went out for volunteers to fight the Americans. The niños of the school rushed to the defense of their city.

The fighting that day was among the hardest of the war. It did not end until almost all the teen-age niños were killed. Then the Mexican flag was hauled down in surrender.

The bravery of those young men is honored in Mexican history. Today Americans join the Mexican people in saluting the bravery of los niños. They believed their country was right and they fought to the end to defend their land.

The Mexican troops were unable to stop the Americans. As the Mexican soldiers fell back, the Americans came face to face with the young boys. To their surprise the niños would not give up or run away. Instead, they fought back fiercely.

# What were the results of the war with Mexico?

The Mexican War was very one-sided. The Mexican Army was brave, but had no chance to win. It was no match for the much larger, better equipped American Army.

After fighting broke out in 1846, an American force moved speedily into California. The American settlers in California prepared the way by rising in revolt against Mexican rule. The revolt was a success and the settlers set up the Bear Flag Republic. It asked admission to the United States.

Meanwhile, two American forces moved into Mexico. One army crossed the border and pushed south. It met and defeated a Mexican Army at Buena Vista. Another American force landed at Vera Cruz, on the east coast of Mexico. It moved inland to the capital, Mexico City. In spite of the bravery of Mexican troops, the Americans captured Mexico City. The Mexican government was forced to sign a peace treaty in 1848.

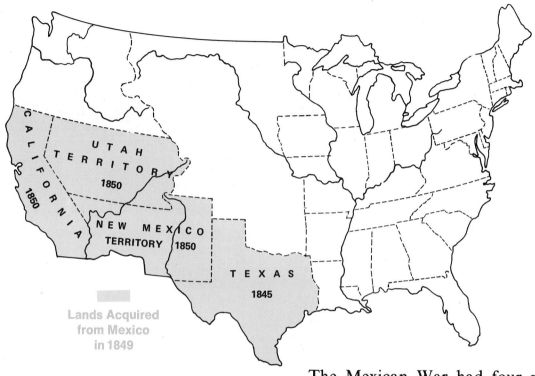

CALIFORNIA
1850

UTAH TERRITORY
1850

NEW MEXICO TERRITORY
1850

TEXAS
1845

Lands Acquired
from Mexico
in 1849

The map shows the territorial changes resulting from the Mexican War.

Mexico recognized Texas as a part of the United States. It accepted the Rio Grande River as the southern boundary of Texas. This had long been the claim of the Americans. It meant that Mexico lost many miles of land south of the Nueces River. In addition, Mexico gave up California and the lands that today make up New Mexico and Arizona. This territory is known as the Mexican Cession. In return for this land, the United States paid Mexico about eighteen million dollars.

The Mexican War had four main results:

One result was that Mexico bitterly resented the loss of vast territory. Some of that bitterness exists to this day in the relations between Mexico and the United States. A second result was the growth of sectional feeling in the United States. The South hoped to extend slavery to the new lands. This was strongly opposed by the North and the West. A third result was the growth in nationalist and patriotic feeling. The fourth result was the increased power of the United States. The victory over Mexico made the United States one of the great powers in the world.

# Gold is discovered in California

SUTTER'S MILL CALIFORNIA

"Gold! The hills are filled with gold!" These words, spoken in California in 1848, spread swiftly across all of America. Before long thousands of people poured into California. Men, women, and children traveled thousands of miles in ships, wagons, and on foot. They dreamed of the riches of the "golden West."

The story of the discovery of gold in California starts with John Sutter. He decided to build a sawmill on the American River near Sutter's Fort. This was a settlement he had founded. Sutter hired a mechanic, James Marshall, to start the work. Marshall never finished the sawmill. While digging a ditch, he found a sparkling stone. It turned out to be gold. The news spread like wildfire across the United States.

In the next year people swarmed into California by the thousands. Those who came in search of gold were known as the 49ers. *Can you guess how they got this name?* Not all the 49ers were Americans. Some came from as far away as Europe, China, and Australia. Only a few found the riches they dreamed of. Most of them settled on farms or in towns in California and nearby states.

But what about John Sutter, the man on whose property gold was found? Did he become rich? Unfortunately, he did not. His fields and his sawmill were destroyed by the rush of new settlers. John Sutter was ruined by the cry of "Gold."

# What were the boundaries of the United States in 1853?

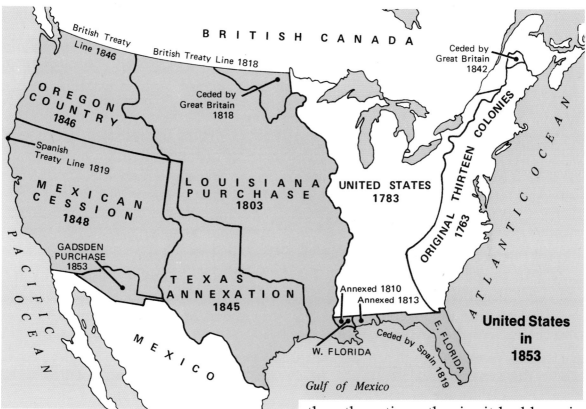

The United States won its independence in 1783. It celebrated its seventieth anniversary in 1853. Those seventy years had brought many changes in American life. During those seventy years the United States had grown in size and population. In 1783 there were only about four million people living in the United States. By 1853 the population had increased to about twenty-three million people.

The United States also greatly expanded its boundaries during those years. The map shows the boundaries of the United States in 1783 and in 1853. By 1853 the country was more than three times the size it had been in 1783. The United States now stretched from the Atlantic Ocean to the Pacific Ocean.

During these years the United States had purchased the Louisiana Territory from France. It had also gained the lands of Florida from Spain. Later, the British agreed to give up lands on the Canadian border. They also gave up the Oregon lands in a compromise. The Mexican War had ended with Texas and the lands of the Mexican Cession part of the United States. The Gadsden Purchase of lands from Mexico in 1853 rounded out the American borders.

197

# LEARNING EXERCISES

## I. Remembering What We Have Read

Pick the best answer.

1. Americans moved into Mexico's territory of Texas
   a. against the wishes of Mexico.
   b. at the invitation of Mexico.
   c. after Texas became a republic.
   d. to settle boundary disputes.

2. The Bear Flag Republic is connected with the area of
   a. Mexico.
   b. Texas.
   c. California.
   d. Oregon.

3. All of the following were part of the United States in 1853 **except**
   a. Oregon.
   b. Alaska.
   c. New Mexico.
   d. Florida.

4. The boundary settlements of the United States involved
   a. Spain and Portugal.
   b. France, England, and Germany.
   c. England and Portugal.
   d. Spain, France, and England.

## II. Thinking About Things

Can you guess the answers to these questions? They are based on what you have been reading, but the answers are not in the book.

1. How might the settlement of the West have been different if gold had not been discovered?

2. Do you suppose the Mexican War would have ever taken place if the United States had not bought Louisiana?

3. How do you imagine the Mexican War is taught in Mexican schools? How might it be taught differently than in American schools?

## III. Learning From Maps

Look at the map of the United States below.
The letters on the map stand for areas that were added to the original boundaries.

1. Which letter stands for the Oregon Territory?
2. Which letter stands for the Mexican Cession?
3. Which letter stands for the Louisiana Purchase?
4. Which letter stands for Florida?

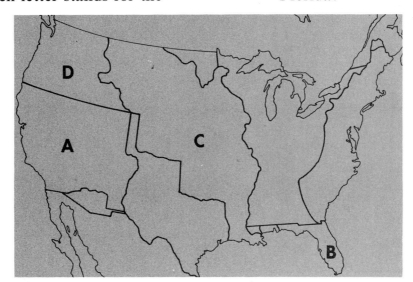

## IV. Headlines That Tell a Story

What events in American history are told by each of the headlines below?

**REMEMBER
THE ALAMO**

**SUTTER'S MILL
OR BUST**

**ON WHAT 'SPOT'
WAS BLOOD SHED?**

**FREE LAND
FOR FREE PEOPLE**

## V. Reviewing People and Events

How well do you remember the people and events appearing in this unit?
Below are the names of five people listed in Column A. Next to these names are five events listed in Column B.
On a separate sheet of paper, match the events in Column B with the names that are in Column A.

COLUMN A
People
1. Sam Houston
2. Thomas Jefferson
3. The 49ers
4. Samuel Cornish
5. Andrew Jackson

COLUMN B
Events
a. first black newspaper published
b. Texas wins independence
c. American victory at New Orleans
d. United States buys Louisiana
e. gold in California

## VI. Reviewing the Spirit of Nationalism

This unit has told of the rise of an American national spirit. How well do you understand this national spirit? Below are some words that might appear on banners. Which banners would show a spirit of nationalism? Explain why.

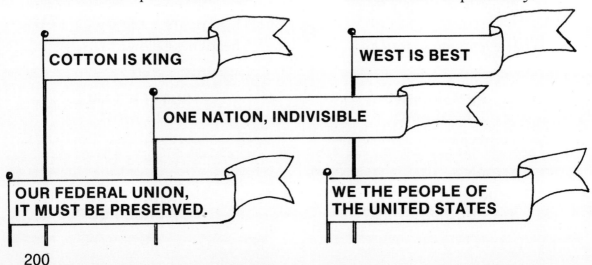

COTTON IS KING

WEST IS BEST

ONE NATION, INDIVISIBLE

OUR FEDERAL UNION, IT MUST BE PRESERVED.

WE THE PEOPLE OF THE UNITED STATES

# AMERICANS FIGHT FOR HUMAN RIGHTS

# CONTENTS ☆☆☆☆☆☆☆☆☆☆☆☆☆☆☆☆

☆☆☆☆☆☆☆☆☆☆☆☆☆☆☆☆☆☆☆☆☆☆

# UNIT 5

# What is meant by human rights?

The United States is a democracy. Its citizens elect their leaders to run the government. Those leaders defend the rights of all the American people. The government leaders are guided by the Constitution of the United States. The Constitution protects all citizens of the United States.

American citizens have property rights that are protected by the Constitution. Property—the goods or land we own—may not be taken from us except for a special reason. For example, the government may take our property to build a highway or a school. But if the property is taken, we must be paid for it. This is one way our property rights are protected.

LEAVE THE POINTER DOWN

Americans also have human rights. Many of these rights are written down in the Constitution. They include the right of all people to life and liberty. This means we cannot be arrested or jailed unless we are charged with breaking a law. That charge must be proved in a court of law. Those accused and put on trial are entitled to a speedy trial. They are also entitled to a lawyer and trial by jury. These are some of the human and legal rights with which we are familiar.

Some human rights are not tied to laws. Human rights also include the right to be treated with dignity, fairness, and respect. No person ought to suffer from prejudice because of religion or skin color. Nor should people be treated unfairly because they are poor. The expression "Do unto others as you would have them do unto you" is a good guide for upholding human rights.

The law upholds our right to fair treatment. The United States has laws to stop acts of discrimination against blacks, Chicanos, women, and others. These are often known as equal rights laws.

Laws can help protect human rights, but they are not the only answer. Our human rights depend upon all of us trusting our fellow Americans.

*Why do you think human rights are important? How can we protect our human rights?* The answers to these questions are important in our daily lives.

The United States has done more than protect the human rights of its own citizens. The government has also shown its concern for the human rights of people in all parts of the world. This means concern for the rights of people to be free to practice their own religion. It also means the right of all people to be protected from unfair arrest and trial, and cruel punishment. *Do you think the United States is right in acting on behalf of the human rights of people in other parts of the world? In what ways can the United States try to protect the human rights of those who are not American citizens?*

# How has the United States treated the human rights of the American Indians?

TLINGIT

MANDAN

BLACKFEET

SIOUX

CHUMASH

CHEYENNE

ILLINOIS

HOPI

APACHE

ALGONQUINS

IROQUOIS

MOHEGANS
DELAWARES

CHEROKEE

SEMINOLE

People lived in America long before Columbus landed in the New World in 1492. Columbus called these people Indians. This was because he thought he had landed in the Indies islands of Asia. That name is still widely used. However, the American Indians are not related to India or to the people of the Indies. We sometimes use the name Amerindian when speaking of the Indians of America. Today we also use the term Native Americans for the people that have been called Indians.

In 1492 there were about 800,000 Indians in what is now the United States. The map names some of the Indian tribes and shows where they lived. We sometimes forget that not all the Indians of America were alike. The many tribes had different customs and languages. They lived and worked in many different ways.

*How might the tribal differences have made it easier for Europeans to defeat the Indians?*

The first settlers paid little attention to the rights of Indians. Many settlers used force to take Indian lands. Sometimes they bought the land from the chiefs. The United States continued the policy of taking land from the Indians. Many Americans treated the Indians as inferiors.

The Declaration of Independence says all people have a right to "life, liberty, and the pursuit of happiness." But the United States did not believe Indians had these rights. As Americans moved westward, the Indians were forced off more and more lands. If the Indians refused, the government sent soldiers to put them down. Special

lands, called reservations, were set aside. Indians were forced to live on these lands. The reservations were often too poor for use for farming or raising animals.

The United States paid little attention to the human rights of Indians in the past. This is changing as Indians demand the right to full citizenship. Today there are more than 500,000 Indians. Some still live on reservations, but many others live in cities and on farms. The American Indians can never return to the life that their ancestors lived. But they are working to regain the dignity and respect which was nearly taken from them.

# Hiawatha and his dream of Indian unity

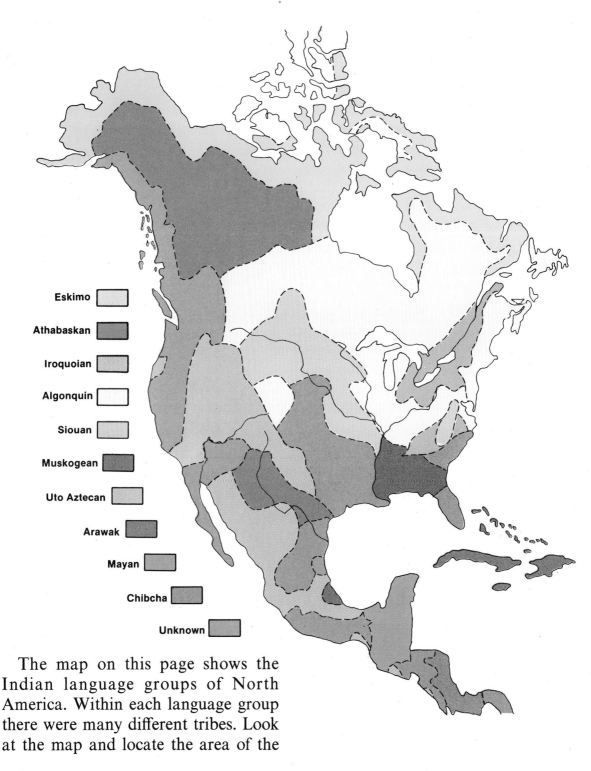

Eskimo

Athabaskan

Iroquoian

Algonquin

Siouan

Muskogean

Uto Aztecan

Arawak

Mayan

Chibcha

Unknown

The map on this page shows the Indian language groups of North America. Within each language group there were many different tribes. Look at the map and locate the area of the

Iroquois-speaking tribes. You will see that the Iroquois were surrounded by the larger, more powerful, Algonquin-speaking tribes. *What effect do you think this might have had upon the Iroquois?*

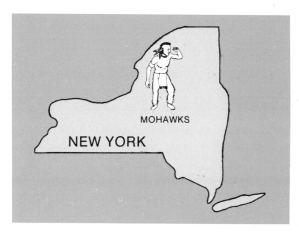

Hiawatha was a leader of the Mohawk tribe which lived in northern New York. The Mohawks and the nearby Cayuga, Oneida, Seneca, and Onondaga were all Iroquois-speaking peoples. Yet they often were at war with one another. Sometime during the 1500s, Hiawatha put forward the idea of a League of the Iroquois people. He felt that a league would put an end to wars among these people. It would also make them strong enough to keep other tribes from attacking them.

Hiawatha's idea was not accepted by his own tribe. In fact, it was considered so dangerous that he was ordered to leave his home. Most Indians were not yet ready for the idea of uniting into larger groups.

Hiawatha did not give up. He traveled up and down the Mohawk Valley and talked about the need for Indian unity. Slowly the idea of an Iroquois League took hold. The Mohawk, Cayuga, Oneida, Seneca, and Onondaga tribes formed a confederation. It was known at first as the Five Nations. Years later the Tuscarora tribe joined. It then became known as the Six Nations or the League of Iroquois.

Hiawatha hoped to unite all the Indians and end wars. He did not succeed. After he died, fighting broke out again. Had he succeeded, the history of the Indian people, and of our country, might have been different.

*How might Indian unity have affected the European effort to take over North America?*

THE FIVE NATIONS

CAYUGA    MOHAWK    ONEIDA

SENECA    ONONDAGA

A CONFEDERATION

# Why was slavery brought to America?

Slavery was once very common in many parts of the world. In ancient times the Greeks and Romans made slaves of the people they conquered.

There was also a form of slavery in many parts of Africa. The Arabs, too, had slaves. However, among the Arabs and Africans it was often the custom to make slaves part of the family.

In most parts of the world the slaves had few rights. They were the property of their masters. Slaves were bought and sold, like pieces of property. Slave owners could punish slaves. Sometimes they killed them, though this meant losing the value of the property.

Slavery had almost disappeared in Europe by the 1500s. However, Spain and Portugal quickly introduced slavery in their American colonies. Slaves provided cheap labor for the gold and silver mines and for the plantations.

At first the Europeans used Indians as slaves. This did not work out well. Most of the Indians could not be trained to do the sort of work needed.

Great numbers of the Indians died in slavery. The European settlers began looking for other slaves to work for them.

Before long the Europeans started using black people from Africa as slaves. Spain and Portugal sent ships to Africa to seize black people. The Africans were then shipped to South America and Mexico as slaves. More than fourteen million black Africans may have been sent to the New World as slaves between 1600 and 1800. Many millions of black Africans died on the way. They died because of

terrible conditions on the slave ships.

The first black people were brought to North America in 1619. They were not slaves. These black people came to Jamestown, Virginia, as indentured servants. Indentured servants worked without wages for about seven years. After that time they were set free and started out on their own. Many poor white Europeans came to America as indentured servants. Indentured servants had few rights, but were not slaves.

In time the use of indentured servants stopped. White Europeans came to the New World as free men and women. They came of their own free will. This was not true of black Africans. They were taken by force and brought to North and South America as slaves. Slaves were a source of cheap labor for the white colonists. Slavery became important because it was economically profitable.

# How did slavery affect the American people?

The chart shows how the population of the United States grew in seventy years. It also shows that slavery grew rapidly in those years.

| DATES | TOTAL U.S. POPULATION (approximate) | TOTAL SLAVE POPULATION (approximate) |
|---|---|---|
| 1790 | 4,000,000 | 700,000 |
| 1810 | 7,200,000 | 1,200,000 |
| 1830 | 13,000,000 | 2,000,000 |
| 1850 | 23,200,000 | 3,200,000 |
| 1860 | 31,500,000 | 4,000,000 |

There were nearly 750,000 black Americans in 1790. Almost all of these blacks were slaves. Seventy years later, in 1860, there were more than 4,000,000 black slaves. There were also about 400,000 free blacks. Nine in every ten black Americans were slaves in 1860.

At first slavery had existed in almost all the states. It soon died out in northern states, but grew rapidly in the South. *Why do you think slavery died out in the North? Why did it grow in the South?*

Slavery affected black people in many ways. Slaves had no rights and were often mistreated. They worked hard and received no wages. They could be bought and sold by their masters. Slave families were often broken up and sold to different owners. Slaves received no education. It was a crime to teach a slave to read and write. Most states had strict runaway laws. This helped masters catch and punish slaves who tried to escape to freedom.

Black people who were not slaves were treated as inferior people. They faced discrimination in finding jobs, housing, and education. Free blacks could not own property, vote, or hold office in many states.

THE NORTH

THE WEST

THE SOUTH

LAND ACQUIRED
FROM MEXICO

Slavery also affected white Americans. The Southern slave owners tried to have the government protect their slavery interests. They especially wanted to expand slavery into the new territories. The southerners hoped to bring slavery into the new lands won from Mexico. But Americans in the North and West did not want slavery to expand. They wanted to start farms and businesses in the new territories. This might not be possible if slavery were allowed to spread.

At first only the free blacks and a few white people opposed slavery. They formed abolition societies to protest against it. William Lloyd Garrison was one of the leaders in the fight against slavery. His newspaper, Liberator, won many white Americans to the abolitionist cause. These Americans helped black people mainly because they feared the power of southern slave owners. Slavery in the United States led to disagreements among the American people. The three sections of the United States were divided on the slavery issue. The South wanted slavery, whereas the North and West did not want it.

# LEARNING EXERCISES

## I. Remembering What We Have Read

Pick the best answer.

1. American Indians
   a. are related to people in India.
   b. speak the same language.
   c. have the same customs.
   d. were not all alike.
2. All the following tribes belonged to the Five Nations **except** the
   a. Seneca.
   b. Apache.
   c. Mohawk.
   d. Cayuga.
3. By 1860 the number of blacks in the United States who were free people was
   a. half of the black population.
   b. one out of every twenty-five blacks.
   c. one out of every ten.
   d. none.
4. Human rights include all of the following **except** the right to
   a. be treated with dignity.
   b. a speedy trial.
   c. own property.
   d. a jury trial.

## II. True or False

Is each of the following True or False?
1. The Constitution protects property rights.
2. American soldiers lived on reservations.
3. Hiawatha was a Mohawk Indian.
4. Slavery almost disappeared in Europe by the 1500s.
5. Indentured servants were slaves.

## III. Thinking About Things

Can you guess the answers to these questions? They are based on what you have been reading, but the answers are not in the book.
1. It has been said that slavery destroyed the soul of white Americans as well as black Americans. What might that mean?
2. Why is the United States today interested in human rights for people in all parts of the world?

# FREDERICK DOUGLASS

"At this moment you are probably the guilty holder of at least three of my own dear sisters, and my only brother—Sir, I desire to know how and where these dear sisters are. Have you sold them—are they living or dead? And my dear old grandmother whom you turned out like an old horse, to die in the woods—is she still alive?"

These words were written in 1848. They were part of a letter addressed to a slaveholder in Maryland. The letter was written by Frederick Douglass, an escaped black slave. His writings and speeches made him one of the great black leaders of all time.

Douglass was born a slave in Maryland in 1817. He was taken from his mother as a baby and raised by his grandmother. He managed to learn to read and write, though slaves were not allowed to do so. Before long Douglass was teaching other slaves to read and write. This led to his being punished severely. Once he was sent to a "slave breaker." This was a man hired to punish slaves and "break" their spirit. But Douglass refused to be "broken."

At the age of twenty-one he ran away to freedom.

Douglass lived first in New York, then in Massachusetts. He was always in danger of being caught by "slave catchers" and sent back to slavery. In 1841 Douglass attended an anti-slavery meeting. He was asked to tell of his life in slavery. Though this was a dangerous thing to do, he agreed to speak. Douglass was only twenty-four years old, but his speech was so forceful that he was cheered when he finished. The chairman of the meeting then asked the crowd, "Shall such a man ever be sent back to slavery?" The crowd roared, "No!"

For the next twenty years Frederick Douglass was an anti-slavery speaker. He traveled to many parts of the North and to Europe speaking against slavery. During the Civil War he helped enlist black soldiers for the Union Army. His own sons served as soldiers.

When the Civil War ended, Frederick Douglass was the most respected black leader in the United States. He founded a newspaper, held government posts, and spoke out for justice. He died in 1895, at the age of seventy-eight, still fighting for human rights. He spent his last day at a meeting being held to promote women's rights.

# How did the Civil War help end slavery?

CONFEDERATE STATES

BORDER STATES

UNION STATES

The United States is a union of states. These states have joined together freely over the years. But do the states have a right to leave the union which they joined? That was the issue that divided the United States in 1861. Southern leaders believed that states had the right to leave or secede from the Union. The northern and western states believed that no state had the right to secede. This difference was one of the things that brought on the Civil War.

The feelings of the different sections came to a head in the 1860 election. There were four candidates for president that year and the winner was Abraham Lincoln. He was a candidate of the newly formed Republican party.

Many southerners feared that Lincoln's election meant the end of states' rights. If the North and West joined forces, it could mean much less power for the South in Congress. Southern leaders felt this would mean the end of slavery. As a result, most of the slaveholding states decided to secede from the Union. They said they were within their rights in doing this.

The eleven southern states that seceded formed their own new nation. They called themselves the Confederate States of America. The Confederacy was to be a loose alliance of states. There was a central government, but it had almost no power.

President Lincoln and the Congress denied that states could leave the Union. Lincoln declared the southern actions were really a rebellion. He acted after southern troops fired upon a Union fort. Federal troops were sent to take back the power of the national government in the South. The result was the Civil War that lasted from 1861 to 1865.

At first President Lincoln did not seem interested in ending slavery. He declared his main purpose was to save the Union. In the early months of the war the Union troops suffered many defeats. In spite of this, the government refused to enlist black men as soldiers. The Union Army also did not try to free any slaves. However, more and more people in the North demanded action against these slave owners. Finally, President Lincoln issued the Emancipation Proclamation. It went into effect on January 1, 1863.

Emancipation means the freeing of people. But few slaves were actually freed by the Proclamation. It only freed slaves in areas of the South that had seceded. Slavery was not touched in border states like Maryland or Kentucky, which had not joined the Confederacy. President Lincoln hoped to keep these states from joining the Confederacy.

Many people felt the Emancipation Proclamation did very little. Most black leaders did not agree. They saw it as a first step in ending slavery. On December 31, 1862, thousands of people, blacks and whites, gathered in Boston at midnight. They waited for news of the Proclamation from Washington. When the news arrived, the crowd burst into cheers and sang the words:

> "Jehovah hath triumphed,
> His people are free."

*What do you think they meant in singing this song?*

After 1863 the Union Army allowed thousands of black men to enlist. Many also served in the Union Navy. The Civil War ended in 1865, with the Union winning. The Thirteenth Amendment to the Constitution was approved that year. It freed all slaves and ended slavery forever in the United States.

The victory that was won by the federal government in the Civil War also settled the question of whether a state could secede. The answer was "No."

# HARRIET TUBMAN

Harriet Tubman was born a slave and never learned to read and write. She was a small woman who suffered many illnesses all her life. But poor health and lack of schooling could not keep her down.

Harriet escaped from slavery when she was very young. She also helped her mother, father, and other members of her family to escape. Next, she became an undercover agent, or "conductor," for the Underground Railroad. This was a secret organization that helped slaves escape from the South. Harriet Tubman probably helped more than three hundred slaves find their way to freedom.

During the Civil War, Harriet served as a nurse, cook, and scout for the Union Army. As a scout, her main work was to spy upon southern troops. No one suspected the small, sickly-looking black woman was the famous Harriet Tubman.

After the war she filed a petition for a government pension. No action was taken for many years. Finally, in 1898, she filed another petition. It read:

"I was born and reared in Dorchester County, Md. . . . I married John Tubman who died in the State of Maryland in 1867. I married Nelson David, a soldier of the Civil War in March, 1869. . . . My claim against the U.S. is for three years' service as nurse and cook, and as commander of several men (eight or nine) as scouts. . . ."

The pension was granted the same year. Harriet Tubman died in 1913 at the age of ninety-two. This brave old lady was honored by her people as their "Moses."

*In what ways was Harriet Tubman like Moses?*

# Black soldiers in the Civil War

"Oh, boys, chains are breaking
Bondsmen fast awaking
Tyrant hearts are quaking
Southward we are making."

Imagine the surprise of the Confederate troops in South Carolina when they heard that song late in 1864. Imagine also their shock when they saw it was being sung by black Union soldiers.

The black Union troops, singing in battle, were the Colored Brigade. They were soldiers from the 54th and 55th Massachusetts Regiments. Many had once been slaves, but others were born free. At first all their officers were white men. Later some black soldiers became officers.

Frederick Douglass' sons were in one of the black regiments. The son of William Lloyd Garrison, the white abolitionist, was one of the white officers of the 55th Regiment. The black regiments from Massachusetts were the pride of the abolitionists. They proved the abolitionists had been right when they said black men would fight and die for freedom.

The Union Army had not been anxious to enlist blacks as soldiers. It was not until 1863 that President Lincoln finally gave his approval. Once the way was open, however, black men enlisted by the thousands. More than 200,000 blacks served in the Union Army. Thousands of others joined the Navy. About 100,000 of the black soldiers were former slaves from the Confederate states. Many others were from the border slave states that had not seceded. There were also about 40,000 free blacks from the North in the army. They left the safety of their homes to fight for their people.

More than 38,000 black soldiers died of wounds or disease during the Civil War. Twenty black soldiers and sailors won the Congressional Medal of Honor. Their conduct during the war proved the pledge they sang:

"No more for trader's gold
Shall those we love be sold
Nor crushed be manhood bold
In slavery's fold"

# SERGEANT CARNEY

William H. Carney was born a slave. He joined the Union Army and was a sergeant in the 54th Massachusetts Regiment. This was a black regiment led by white officers.

On July 18, 1863, the regiment tried to capture Fort Wagner in South Carolina. It was a fierce battle in which many of the black soldiers and their white leader, Colonel Shaw, died. During the fighting, Sergeant Carney took the flag of his regiment to lead the charge. In those days a sergeant carried the regimental flag near the colonel who was leading the troops into battle. When Sergeant Carney was close to the fort, he was wounded in the thigh. As he fell, he planted the flag and remained with it. Carney held the flag for over half an hour. Finally other soldiers came up to relieve the troops.

The regiment had failed to capture the fort and now fell back. Carney followed, creeping on one knee and holding up the flag. He had been wounded twice, once in the thigh and once in the head. His fellow soldiers cheered him and carried him to a field hospital. The official record reports he was covered with blood. But it states that "the flag never touched the ground."

In his heroic action that day, Sergeant Carney was an inspiration to the other soldiers. His bravery was rewarded with the Congressional Medal of Honor.

# Black Senators after the Civil War

In 1861 Jefferson Davis was a senator from Mississippi. Davis was a strong supporter of slavery. He resigned from the Senate when Mississippi seceded. Jefferson then became president of the Confederate States of America.

When the war ended, Davis and other Confederate leaders were not allowed to take office. In addition, Mississippi had to allow black men to vote and hold office.

HIRAM REVELS

In 1870 the Senate seat once held by Jefferson Davis was filled by Hiram Revels. Hiram Revels was born a free black in North Carolina. He was taken to Indiana where he grew up. After attending college, Revels became a minister of a black church. At the end of the Civil War he went south and settled in Mississippi.

Revels was chosen to be a senator in 1870 and served until 1871. It was the first time that a black person served in the Senate.

BLANCHE K. BRUCE

Four years later another black person was chosen as senator from Mississippi. His name was Blanche K. Bruce. Born a slave, Bruce escaped during the Civil War. He settled in Missouri where he set up a school for black people. At the same time, Bruce attended college to improve his education. After the war, he moved to Mississippi. Bruce soon became active in politics. He was a sheriff, and a superintendent of schools, before becoming a senator. Blanche K. Bruce served in the Senate from 1875 to 1881.

Hiram Revels and Blanche K. Bruce were our country's first black senators. After Senator Bruce left office in 1881, there were no other black senators until 1966. In that year, Edward W. Brooke of Massachusetts was elected to the United States Senate.

EDWARD W. BROOKE

# What has happened to black people since the Civil War?

Slavery was ended in the United States in 1865. Four million black people became free men and women. They soon found that the end of slavery did not bring full freedom. Many ex-slaves had no land, no jobs, or money. Most had received no education or training for skilled work. They had to start at the bottom and try to work their way up to a decent life.

*Why did ex-slaves have no land, money, education, or job training?*

The newly freed black people knew the importance of voting. Voting could help protect their freedom and give them a better chance. Now that they were free, they were able to vote. From 1867 to 1876 black people elected hundreds of black officials in the South. Many ex-slaves served as local officials, state legislators, and in Congress. Two black men were elected to the United States Senate. A black man became the acting governor of Louisiana. Fourteen blacks were

elected to the House of Representatives. Many laws were passed to help ex-slaves and poor whites in the South. These included setting up free public schools for all children.

The bright dream of freedom was nearly crushed after 1876. Black people found their right to vote taken away in many states. Blacks who tried to vote were often beaten, jailed, or killed. Racist organizations like the Ku Klux Klan used terror against black people. By 1900 there were very few black voters in the South.

Black people also faced other problems. These included prejudice and discrimination in jobs, education, and housing. Many states segregated black people in housing, schools, and trains. Black people protested against being treated as second-class citizens. They began forming organizations to fight for their rights.

In the early 1900s, some black leaders and concerned whites formed a new organization. It was called the National Association for the Advancement of Colored People (N.A.A.C.P.). The N.A.A.C.P. fought in the courts for the right of black people to vote and hold office. N.A.A.C.P. lawyers led the fight against segregated schools. They demanded all schools be integrated. The N.A.A.C.P. and the newly formed Urban League demanded jobs and decent housing for black people.

The N.A.A.C.P. won many court cases involving the unfair treatment of blacks. In 1954 the Supreme Court ruled that it was illegal to have separate schools for black people. The decision led to the great movement to integrate all American schools.

Black people have made many advances in the past fifty years. Great numbers of black people now vote. Blacks have become mayors, members of Congress, and senators, and hold other high office. There are growing numbers of black teachers, lawyers, engineers, and doctors. Black athletes can be seen in almost all the professional sports. In spite of these advances, much remains to be done. The N.A.A.C.P. and other organizations continue the fight for first-class citizenship for black people.

# W.E.B. DuBOIS

## and the N.A.A.C.P.

William E. B. DuBois was born in Great Barrington, Massachusetts, in 1868. He grew up in New England knowing little about the problems of other black people. All this changed when he went south to college. From that time he devoted his life to helping black people.

DuBois was a brilliant student. He later studied at Harvard College and earned a Doctor of Philosophy degree. His study of the African slave trade was written in 1896. It is still read today by students of history.

After more study and travel in Europe, the young Dr. DuBois returned to America. He taught at Atlanta University, a college for blacks in Georgia. Before long he was the center of stormy discussion. In 1903 he wrote an article urging black people to fight for their rights. This was a daring thing to say at the time, but DuBois did not stop there. Together with others, he organized the Niagara Movement. This group was pledged to fight for full civil rights for black people. The Niagara Movement was

active from 1905 to 1909.

In 1909 a group of whites joined with some blacks to set up a new organization. It was called the National Association for the Advancement of Colored People, or N.A.A.C.P. The N.A.A.C.P. was organized to help black people gain full rights of citizenship. In 1910 Dr. DuBois became one of the organization's directors. He was also in charge of its paper, called *Crisis.*

During the next fifty years, Dr. DuBois was a leader in the fight for justice for black people. He wrote, taught, and spoke in every part of the world. His message can be summed up in his own words:

"By every civilized and peaceful method we must strive for the rights which the world accords to men, clinging unwaveringly to those great words . . . 'We hold these truths to be self-evident: That all men are created equal' . . . ."

Dr. DuBois lived to the age of ninety-five and was active to the very end. He spent much of his time studying the African background of American blacks. His work opened the way for many of the studies of African life now going on. In his last years he moved to the new African nation of Ghana. He died there in 1963.

# MARTIN LUTHER KING

"Death doesn't matter to me now because I've been to the mountaintop. And I've looked over, and I've seen the promised land. . . . So, I'm happy. I'm not fearing any man. Mine eyes have seen the glory of the coming of the Lord."

Those stirring words were spoken by the great black leader, the Reverend Dr. Martin Luther King, Jr. One day later he was dead, the victim of an assassin's bullet.

Time and again, Dr. King put his life in danger to serve others. He was only a young minister of a black church when he first showed his courage and ability. In 1956 young Reverend King led a boycott of segregated city buses in Montgomery, Alabama. The boycott was a success and he became well-known to Americans.

In 1963 he helped organize a march by more than 250,000 Americans in Washington, D.C. All those people, whites as well as blacks, had joined to ask for equal justice for all Americans. One year later, in 1964, Dr. Martin Luther King, Jr., was awarded the Nobel Prize for peace. This is the highest award the world can give to any person.

Dr. King was known and respected throughout the world. He was honored by many important and powerful people. But his heart remained with those who were poor. In 1968 he came to Memphis, Tennessee, to help black garbage workers who were on strike. It was here that his life was threatened, and it was here that he died.

Perhaps the best way to tell the story of Dr. King is to read what he once said of himself. He felt that death was near, and in a sermon he urged those who might one day be at his funeral to "say that I tried to love and serve humanity."

# LEARNING EXERCISES

## I. Remembering What We Have Learned

Pick the best answer.

1. The abolitionists were opposed to
   a. factories.
   b. slavery.
   c. sectionalism.
   d. nationalism.
2. Hiram Revels and Blanche K. Bruce were
   a. Civil War generals.
   b. founders of the N.A.A.C.P.
   c. black senators.
   d. leaders of the Confederacy.
3. The person known as the "Moses" of black slaves was
   a. Frederick Douglass.
   b. Hiram Revels.
   c. Harriet Tubman.
   d. Abraham Lincoln.
4. One of the founders of the N.A.A.C.P. was
   a. Frederick Douglass.
   b. W.E.B. DuBois.
   c. Harriet Tubman.
   d. Hiram Revels.

## II. True or False

Is each of the following True or False?

1. Frederick Douglass escaped from slavery.
2. Abraham Lincoln was a candidate for president for the Republican party.
3. Black soldiers served in the Union Army.
4. The Emancipation Proclamation freed all the slaves.
5. The Niagara Movement sought to free black slaves.

## III. Thinking About Things

Can you guess the answers to these questions? They are based on what you have been reading, but the answers are not in the book.

1. Why are Americans still interested in the Civil War, which took place more than one hundred years ago?
2. In what ways can the N.A.A.C.P. help black people today?

## IV. Learning From Pictures

Each of the pictures tells us something about American history.
What does each picture mean to you?

## V. Learning From Headlines

What might be the story behind each of the following "headlines"?

"I'VE BEEN TO
THE MOUNTAINTOP"

A NEW "MOSES"
IN THE LAND

DAVIS SEAT
TO BLACK MAN

HIGH COURT RULES
AGAINST SCHOOL SEGREGATION

# What rights did women have 100 years ago?

In 1865, soon after the end of the Civil War, a woman wrote in her diary: "Commenced women's rights work in earnest." The woman was Susan B. Anthony. She had spent years fighting to end black slavery in the United States. Now she turned to the fight for women's rights.

Today we take it for granted that men and women have the same rights. Adults have the right to vote and hold office and to make and sign contracts. They also have the right to control any money they earn or inherit.

Many rights given to adults are not granted to minors. In some states a minor is any person under the age of eighteen. In other states it is any person under twenty-one. If you are a minor, you cannot vote, hold office, or make any legal contracts. Your parents or guardians must approve any contracts you make. They also control any money you make, or inherit, until you are of legal age.

One hundred years ago women were treated like minors. A forty-year-old woman had fewer rights than her fifteen-year-old son. Her son could expect to gain his rights when he came of age. Women never came of age in those days.

Most of the better jobs were closed to women. There were almost no women doctors or lawyers. Women could not sign contracts. They had no control over their money or property. In addition, women could not vote or hold office. Few women received any higher education. Almost none could go to college. Women were expected to do the housework and raise the children. They had no rights outside the home.

# How did American women gain their rights?

In 1848 a meeting was held in Seneca Falls, New York. The leaders of the meeting were Elizabeth Cady Stanton and Lucretia Mott. Both women had long been active in the fight to end slavery. Now they began organizing to also win greater freedom for women. The Seneca Falls meeting was one of the beginnings of the effort to gain full rights for American women.

Women used many methods to gain their rights. They drew up petitions and held meetings. Women also picketed and organized marches. It was a long, hard battle that took many years. Most men, even those who opposed black slavery, did not side with women. Public officials thought it foolish to give women the right to vote. President Grover Cleveland wrote in 1905:

"Sensible and responsible women do not want to vote. The importance of men and women were assigned long ago by a higher intelligence than ours."

*What do you think President Cleveland meant by this statement? Do you think there are people who would agree with it today?*

By the end of the 1800s, American women still had few rights. In the years that followed, they won more of their rights. Bit by bit, they gained the right to education and jobs. Many more

women also found jobs in offices and banks. However, most women did not gain equal pay with men. Equal pay for equal work remains an issue to this day.

The 19th Amendment to the Constitution was ratified in 1920. It gave women the right to vote. Today women are treated as adults. They can control their money and property the same as men. However, there is still much discrimination against women. In 1972 Congress approved an amendment to the Constitution. It would prohibit any discrimination against women in any aspect of American life. This Equal Rights Amendment, if it is ratified by three-fourths of the states (thirty-eight states), will become a part of the Constitution.

# Why did American workers form unions?

"It's the rich what gets the
    money.
It's the poor what gets the blame.
It's the same the wide world
    over.
It's a dirty, rotten shame."

These words, sung more than one hundred years ago, tell how many workers felt. It seemed to them that the harder they worked, the less they had to show for it. At the same time, the rich people seemed to be getting richer.

American workers did not have an easy time a hundred years ago. They worked from twelve to fourteen hours a day, six days a week. Many factories were dirty and unsafe. When workers were hurt on the job, it was considered to be their fault. They received no pay, or help, for any injuries they received while on the job.

Workers had no security on the job. They could be fired at any time for any reason. Wages were set by the employers, and a worker either accepted those wages or looked elsewhere for work. There was no unemployment insurance or old-age pension system. Those who had no jobs or who were too old to work had to live on their savings. When these were gone, they had to depend on charity.

Wages were low because there were often more workers than jobs. Women and children worked in many industries at very low wages. Workers lived in constant fear of losing their jobs. This would leave them without wages to support their families. Newly arrived immigrants were often used to drive wages down. These immigrants needed jobs. They were often willing to work for any wage. Many did not know how to protect themselves.

Suppose you were a worker at that time. The only way you could get a

American workers faced these problems one hundred years ago. They tried to help themselves by joining unions. A union is an organization formed by workers in the same industry. Its purpose is to bring better wages and working conditions to the workers in the industry. Members of the unions tried to win the right to collective bargaining. This means that the union and its officials will speak on behalf of the workers. Collective bargaining gives great strength to the individual worker. Unions often use strikes and picketing to help gain their demands. However, unions also bargain with the employers without having to engage in strikes.

raise was to ask your boss for more money. You had to do the same if you wanted safer and cleaner factories. But your boss might refuse. You might be fired for daring to ask for higher wages or better conditions. *What would you do to raise your wages and improve your working conditions?*

# SAMUEL GOMPERS
## and the A.F.L.

Samuel Gompers was born in England. He went to work when he was only thirteen years old. That same year the Gompers family moved to the United States. In the United States he worked at the skilled craft of cigar making.

Young Gompers had learned about unions in England. He joined the Cigarmakers' Union in the United States. In time he became the president of the union.

Samuel Gompers was a skilled worker and he favored other skilled workers. He believed skilled workers could have great power if they organized unions. Employers could easily hire new unskilled workers. But they could not do this to skilled workers. It was hard to find skilled workers to take the place of those who went on strike.

Gompers was mainly interested in forming craft unions of skilled workers. These unions could win higher wages and better working conditions. In time, their success would also improve life for unskilled workers. But Gompers felt that unions were to be mainly for skilled craft workers.

In 1886 Gompers and other craft union leaders formed the American Federation of Labor (A.F. of L.). This was a national union made up of many craft unions. They included cigar makers, plumbers, carpenters, bakers, and machinists. Gompers became the president of the A.F. of L. in 1886. He remained president until his death in 1924.

# How do unions help workers?

A union's main purpose is to give greater power to workers. One worker alone cannot do very much. But large groups of workers acting together have much more power. Unions have many ways of winning their demands. These include the use of collective bargaining, strikes, and picketing. Many unions have the slogan, "In union there is strength." *What do they mean by this?*

Collective bargaining means that the union acts on behalf of all the workers. Union officials meet with the employer and present the demands of the workers. The union officials have no reason to be afraid of the employer. The officials are paid by the workers, so they cannot be fired by the employer. Collective bargaining strengthens the worker, who has little power alone.

In a strike all the workers walk off the job. They remain out until an agreement is signed with the employer. The employer will lose money if that agreement is not reached quickly. Of course, workers also lose money while on strike.

The workers on strike try to keep others from taking their jobs. They do this by picketing, or walking in front of the struck business with signs. The signs tell people that the workers are on strike. They ask for help in that strike.

Strikes can hurt an employer, but they also mean a loss of pay for workers. Unions and employers often call in a third party to help settle the dispute. Using a third party is called mediation if they only want the opinion of that third party. It is called arbitration if they agree, in advance, to accept a third party's settlement. Mediation and arbitration have reduced the number of strikes that take place.

# A. PHILIP RANDOLPH

A. Philip Randolph was born in Florida in 1889. He was a self-educated person. By the time Randolph was twenty-eight he was a leader of black people. He started a newspaper, *The Messenger,* in 1917. His articles in the paper spoke out against the United States entering World War I. That same year, Randolph was arrested for his actions. This did not stop him from speaking out.

By the end of World War I, Randolph was convinced that black people needed unions. Unions could help them improve their wages and working conditions. In 1925 he organized the all-black Brotherhood of Pullman Car Porters. Randolph was active in union work for many years. He became a vice president of the A.F. of L., the national labor organization.

Randolph's chief work was fighting job discrimination. In 1941, just before the United States entered World War II, he organized a march on Washington. Its purpose was to end job discrimination for blacks. More than 100,000 people were to take part in the proposed march.

President Franklin D. Roosevelt asked Randolph to call off the march. In return, the president agreed to issue a special executive order. The order ended discrimination in all war industries. It also promised the end of segregation in the armed forces. Until that time black soldiers had been forced to serve in all-black units. The executive order issued in 1941 was the first step in changing many things. Today discrimination in industries is forbidden by federal law. Today, also, all armed forces units are fully integrated. A. Philip Randolph helped to make possible these important changes.

Another march on Washington was held on August 28, 1963. This time about 250,000 people—black and white—marched on Washington. They demanded more jobs, better housing, and equal education for all minority people. Once again, it was A. Philip Randolph, now seventy-four, who organized and led the march on Washington.

# LEARNING EXERCISES

## I. Learning From Pictures

Each of the pictures tells us something about life in the United States.

What does each picture mean to you?

1.

2.

3.

4.

## II. Thinking About Things

Can you guess the answers to these questions? The answers are not in the book.

1. Is there a women's rights movement today? What are its demands?

2. If you worked in a factory, would you be most interested in higher wages, better work conditions, or a steady job?

3. What are some examples of skilled jobs today? What are some unskilled jobs?

# What do graphs tell us about schools in the United States?

The American system of education has helped to make the nation strong. The time line below shows how the population of the United States has grown in one hundred ten years. It also shows the number of pupils in school during those years.

## TOTAL POPULATION OF THE UNITED STATES

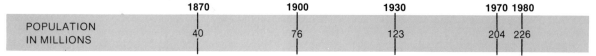

| | 1870 | 1900 | 1930 | 1970 | 1980 |
|---|---|---|---|---|---|
| POPULATION IN MILLIONS | 40 | 76 | 123 | 204 | 226 |

## PUPILS IN ALL PUBLIC AND PRIVATE ELEMENTARY AND HIGH SCHOOLS

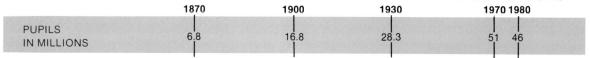

| | 1870 | 1900 | 1930 | 1970 | 1980 |
|---|---|---|---|---|---|
| PUPILS IN MILLIONS | 6.8 | 16.8 | 28.3 | 51 | 46 |

*What does the time line tell us about the growth of American schools in one hundred ten years?*

The numbers of pupils attending school is only one part of the story.

The bar graph below tells us another part. It shows the percentage of school-age pupils who were actually in school. The percentage number tells how many students out of one hundred were actually in school.

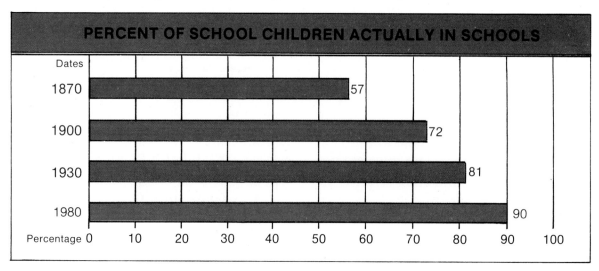

PERCENT OF SCHOOL CHILDREN ACTUALLY IN SCHOOLS

| Dates | Percentage |
|---|---|
| 1870 | 57 |
| 1900 | 72 |
| 1930 | 81 |
| 1980 | 90 |

Percentage 0 10 20 30 40 50 60 70 80 90 100

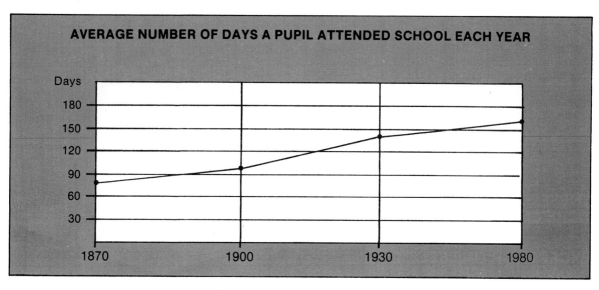

**AVERAGE NUMBER OF DAYS A PUPIL ATTENDED SCHOOL EACH YEAR**

Days: 180, 150, 120, 90, 60, 30

Years: 1870, 1900, 1930, 1980

*What does the graph above tell us about the growth of American education in one hundred ten years?*

The growing number of pupils in schools is only part of the story of American education. It is also important to know how much time pupils spend in school during the school year. Look at the line graph. *What does it tell us about the amount of time pupils spent in school during the school years from 1870 to 1970?*

The chart below tells us something about the number of young people who went to high school. It shows the number of pupils in high school in 1870, 1900, 1930, 1970, and 1980. It also shows the number of pupils graduating from high school in each of those years.

*What does the chart show us about the changes in high school education since 1870?*

| YEARS | PUPILS IN HIGH SCHOOL | PUPILS GRADUATING FROM HIGH SCHOOL |
|-------|----------------------|-----------------------------------|
| 1870 | 80,000 | 16,000 |
| 1900 | 100,000 | 74,000 |
| 1930 | 4,300,000 | 666,000 |
| 1970 | 12,250,000 | 1,864,000 |
| 1980 | 15,750,000 | 2,900,000 |

# How did free public education develop in the United States?

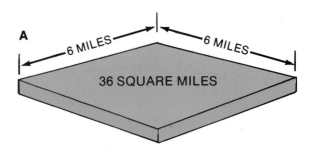

A TOWNSHIP
WAS DIVIDED
INTO 36 SECTIONS.
EACH ONE A SQUARE MILE.

THESE SQUARE MILE SECTIONS,
WERE SOLD AT PUBLIC AUCTIONS.

EXCEPT FOR ONE SECTION,
WHICH WAS KEPT AS A SITE
FOR A PUBLIC SCHOOL.

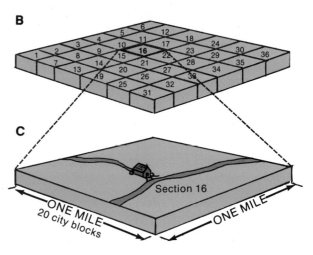

There were almost no free public schools in the United States before the Revolution. Parents had to send their children to private schools or hire private teachers. Most children in the United States received little or no education. Only the rich or the well-to-do could afford to provide education for their children.

The United States used its public lands to start a system of free schools. Congress, acting under the Articles of Confederation, passed a land ordinance or law in 1785. It provided for ways to sell lands owned by the national government.

First the public lands were surveyed into townships. Each township was six miles square in size. The townships were then divided into thirty-six parts or sections.

Each section was one square mile in size. These square mile sections were sold at public auction, except for one section. That one section was kept for use in setting up a public school.

These special sections of land were sold or used in other ways. The money gave free public education its start. In addition, villages and towns raised money by taxes to pay for the costs of the schools.

238

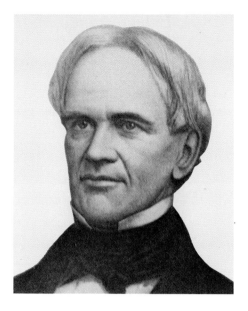

# HORACE MANN

Though poor, young Horace always loved books. He managed to go to college and decided to make education his life work. At the age of thirty-one he was elected to the Massachusetts legislature. Eight years later he helped to found the Massachusetts Board of Education. Its aim was to improve teaching and obtain good books. The Board also told parents about the need for good schools.

For twenty-four years Horace Mann traveled throughout Massachusetts speaking about schools. Parents and teachers came to the meetings. They heard what he had to say and gave their own ideas. The meetings helped to promote the idea of free public education.

Horace Mann also helped set up special colleges to train new teachers. Soon he was asked to visit other states and other countries. He brought back ideas from schools in Europe and helped to start a special magazine for teachers.

Horace Mann's work for free public education has helped in the fight for human rights. Education helps people understand what is meant by human rights and democracy. The public schools in our country are a living monument to the work of Horace Mann.

There were almost no public schools one hundred fifty years ago. Children of rich parents went to private schools or had private teachers. Most children were poor and did not go to school. They worked long hours on the family farm or in a nearby mill. They had little time to spend learning the three r's—"reading, 'riting, and 'rithmetic".

Some poor children went to church schools for a part of the day. Others went to one-room village schools. Many of these schools had broken seats and desks. They usually did not have chalkboards and few had maps or books. Village schoolteachers often had little learning and almost no understanding of children. Many teachers used a rod to punish children who did poorly or misbehaved. The result was that few children were ever really educated.

The man who helped to change this was born in Massachusetts in 1796. His name was Horace Mann. He is known as the father of American education for his work.

# LEARNING EXERCISES

## I. Learning From Graphs

Study this graph and answer the questions.

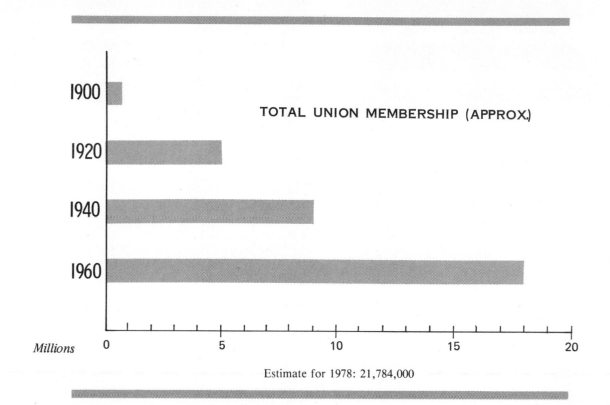

TOTAL UNION MEMBERSHIP (APPROX.)

*Millions*

Estimate for 1978: 21,784,000

1. When did the greatest percentage increase in union membership take place?
2. In the years between 1900 and 1940, did union membership increase about six times, ten times, or eight times?
3. World War I began in 1914; World War II began in 1939. What effect did these events seem to have on union membership?

# AMERICANS BUILD A MODERN NATION

# CONTENTS ☆☆☆☆☆☆☆☆☆☆☆☆☆☆☆☆

☆☆☆☆☆☆☆☆☆☆☆☆☆☆☆☆☆☆☆☆☆☆☆

# UNIT 6

# Where did Americans move after 1870?

Look at maps A and B on this page. They show where most Americans lived in 1860 and in 1920.

What differences do you see on these two maps? What do you think caused these differences?

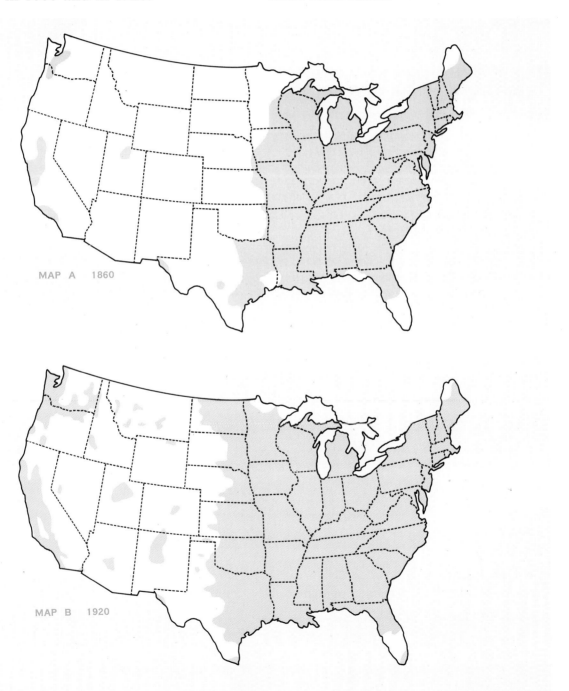

MAP A    1860

MAP B    1920

Look at map C. It shows the western and mountain states. Below this map is a graph showing the population of the western and mountain states over a forty-year period, from 1860 to 1900.

In which years did the greatest rate of increase take place in the West? The answer is: the years from 1870 to 1880. During these years the population of the area doubled. Most of this increase resulted from new settlers who moved west. Why were great numbers of Americans moving west after 1870?

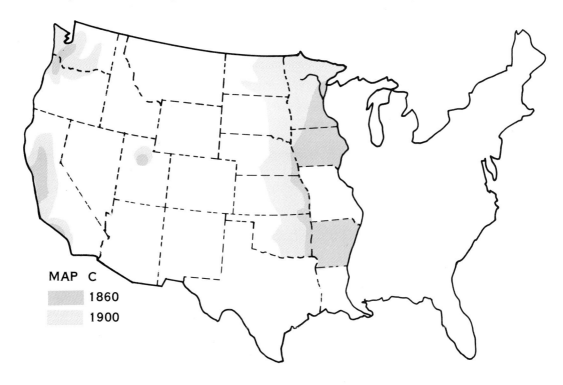

MAP C

1860

1900

POPULATION OF WESTERN AND MOUNTAIN STATES 1860 TO 1900

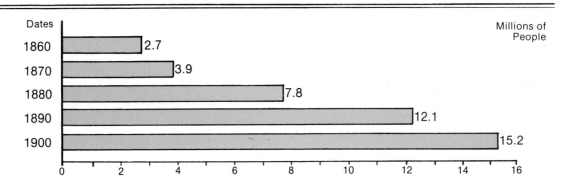

Dates | Millions of People

| 1860 | 2.7 |
| 1870 | 3.9 |
| 1880 | 7.8 |
| 1890 | 12.1 |
| 1900 | 15.2 |

0    2    4    6    8    10    12    14    16

# Why did Americans move west after 1870?

The Civil War ended in 1865. The next twenty years brought many changes to the United States. They brought a new way of life for many people.

The government made it easier for farmers to move west. In 1862 Congress passed the Homestead Act to help the farmers. This act offered one hundred sixty acres of land free to anyone who settled on it for five years. One hundred sixty acres is about the size of five city blocks by five city blocks. This was a good-sized homestead, or family farm. Many Americans left their smaller farms in the East and South. They moved to the free, new lands of the West.

Ways of living also changed in the South. Slavery was now ended and many white planters were ruined. Life was hard for all southerners. Many

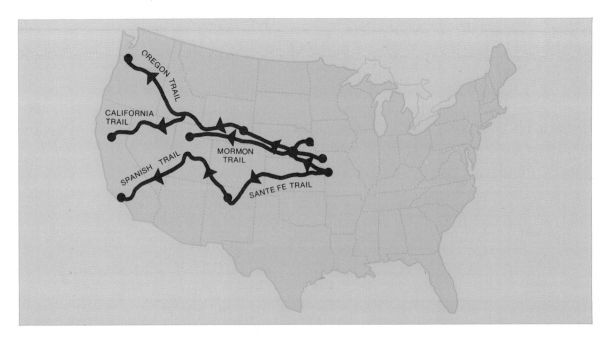

white southern farmers moved west to start a new life. Some newly-freed black people also moved to the North and the West.

Rich people were also interested in the West. The Civil War had brought new riches to some people. It had helped make many millionaires. Some of these people now put their money in timber and grazing land in the West.

Some people also put money in building railroad lines. However, the railroads could not make money unless more people moved west. People were needed to buy land, cut timber, herd the cattle, and build the railroads. Railroad companies joined with others to get people to move west.

Immigrants were attracted to the West after 1870. Some of these new Americans settled on homesteads and became farmers. Others, especially the Irish and Chinese, helped to build the new railroads. Immigrants also worked in the rich timberlands of the Pacific coast.

More people moved west when gold was discovered in Alaska in 1898. Many never reached Alaska, but settled in California, Oregon, and Washington.

Not all Americans went west for economic reasons. Some hoped to find adventure or to get away from dull jobs. Many fell in love with the beauty of the West. They stayed and urged their friends and families to come, too. Americans moved west after 1870 for many reasons. At times it is hard to tell which was most important to the settlers.

# What happened to the Indians when Americans moved west?

The first settlers in America had looked upon the American Indian as a savage. That idea was still held by most Americans in the 1800s. One writer once described Indians as "strangers in their own land." *What do you think was meant by this? How might Indians feel about being strangers in their own land?*

Indians and white Americans seemed unable to understand each other. Their languages and customs were very different. Indian family life, religion, dress, and foods were not only different, but hard for white people to understand. Many Americans could not accept Indians as equals. They saw them as inferior to white people. Many Americans also feared the Indians. To many western settlers the only good Indian was a dead Indian. *Why do you think they believed such a thing? What does this tell us about racism in the United States at that time?*

Many issues divided Indians and white Americans. Land ownership was one of these issues. The Indians held western lands that the white settlers wanted. As the white people moved westward, they often bought land from Indian chiefs. Many of the chiefs had no right to sell the lands of their people. The Indians looked upon land as the property of all the people. They saw themselves as caretakers, not owners. The soil, trees, and water belonged to the whole tribe now and in the future. The Indian chief Crazy Horse once explained, "One does not sell the earth upon which the people walk."

*What did he mean?*

There were some Indian lands that were intended only for one tribe or group of tribes. Indian custom did not permit white settlers to use this sacred land. But settlers moving westward were not interested in Indian customs. They moved onto lands without regard to the feelings of the Indians. The Indians were pushed farther and farther west. Soon there would be no free land left and no place for the Indian people to go.

In the meantime, buffalo hunting was carried on by white men. In a few years, about ten million buffalo were shot. They were killed mainly for their skins. These herds had been the chief source of food for many Indians living in the West. They also depended upon buffalo hides for clothing and shelter. Now the buffalo were nearly gone from the West and the Indians suffered.

There were about 200,000 Indians living in the West in 1870. These included the Apache, Comanche, and Sioux tribes. These brave, proud people knew they had to do something. Soon there would be no lands or buffalo left.

*What would you have done if you were an Indian living at that time? If you were a white American living at that time?*

# How were the Indians treated by the government?

The westward movement drove the Indians from their lands. White settlers set up farms on the lands once owned by Indian tribes. The settlers soon killed off most of the buffalo. The Indians now faced death by starvation and cold.

Some Indians fought back. They raided the settlements, destroyed property, and killed settlers. The army was called in to put down the Indians. More than 200 battles were fought in Indian Wars between 1869 and 1876. The Indians were led by such great chiefs as Sitting Bull, Running Bear, and Geronimo.

The American army troopers were often unable to defeat the Indians. The fast-riding Indians vanished before the slower American troops could swing into battle. One of the most famous army groups was the Seventh Cavalry Regiment. It was commanded by General George A. Custer, a hero of the Civil War. In 1876 Custer and a large number of his troopers were trapped and killed by Indians. The defeat made the United States determined to crush the Indians.

In the end the Indians were beaten. They were forced to move from their lands and were placed on reservations. These were special lands set aside for Indians. Most reservations were unfit for hunting, fishing, or farming. The proud Indian warriors were treated like beggars by the government.

*What do the following statements by Indians tell us about their feelings?*

"I don't want to settle. I love to roam the prairies. There I feel free and happy. . . ."

"They made us many promises, more than I can remember, but they never kept but one; they promised to take our land, and they took it."

Among the troops used in the Indian Wars were black soldiers. They made up about one-fifth of the American Army force in the West. The black soldiers were called buffalo soldiers by the Indians.

*Why do you suppose they were given that name?*

251

# GERONIMO

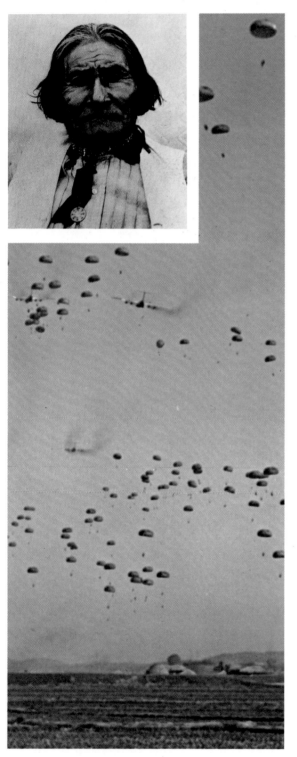

During World War II, American paratroopers shouted "Geronimo" when jumping into action. The battle cry was the name of a feared and famous Apache chief.

Geronimo was born in southwest Arizona. He must have been a very quiet baby, for he was given the name Goyathlay. In the language of the Apaches that name means "one who yawns." But the young man did not yawn very long. From early childhood he was trained as a warrior. By the time he was five he could run six miles through the desert without drinking water. As a youth, he became known for his strength and courage.

The Apaches were a warlike people. From their hideout in the Sierra Madre Mountains they attacked Mexican villages to the south. They took food, clothing, horses, and mules from these Mexican villages. Goyathlay, now a grown man, led many of the attacks. It was the Mexicans who gave him the name Geronimo. It means "Jerome" in the Spanish language. They learned to fear the very mention of his name.

In 1848 gold was discovered in California. Before long, the life of the Apaches changed. Many American settlers came through Apache country on their way to California. Some Americans stopped along the way and towns and settlements sprang up on Apache land. The settlers set traps to catch beaver, and they hunted deer and elk. The Apaches were angered by the settlers. They felt they would soon be losing their source of food. Disputes broke out between the Apaches and the American settlers. The result was fighting and attacks by the Apaches upon the settlements.

Geronimo led many of these attacks. His name struck terror among American settlers, as it had among the Mexicans. The United States Cavalry was sent to put down the Indian raids. This led to war between the Apaches and the United States Army. In 1876 the Apaches were forced to surrender. They had to agree to live on a reservation in Arizona.

Geronimo did not like the new arrangement. He felt the Americans were unjustly taking away land belonging to the Apaches. He, and a group of fifty warriors, fled over the border into Mexico. For the next ten years Geronimo fought against the United States Army. Geronimo and his followers lived in hideouts in the Sierra Madre Mountains. They attacked Mexican villages for food and horses. Then they attacked southwestern Arizona for rifles, ammunition, and clothing. During those years he was able to outrun and outfight the troops sent against him.

Finally, in 1886, Geronimo and his braves surrendered. The people of Arizona were still fearful of Geronimo. They would not allow him to stay on the Arizona reservation. He was sent to Florida, and later to Oklahoma. On March 5, 1905, Geronimo was invited to Washington. He was to take part in the inauguration of Theodore Roosevelt as president of the United States. As the seventy-six-year-old Indian chief rode by on his beautiful pony, the people shouted, "Geronimo! Geronimo!" They were paying their respect to a great chief. He had fought for his people in the only way he knew possible.

**Indians at the Inaugural parade of Theodore Roosevelt, 1905. Left to right: Little Plum, Buckskin Charlie, Geronimo, Hollow Horn Bear, American Horse, and Gray Wolf.**

# LEARNING EXERCISES

**I. Remembering What We Have Read**

Pick the best answer.

1. The Homestead Act offered free land to
   a. Indians.
   b. western settlers.
   c. industry.
   d. government agencies.

2. The American frontier moved from
   a. west to south.
   b. east to west.
   c. south to north.
   d. west to north.

**II. True or False**

Is each of the following True or False?

1. The Homestead Act helped farmers who wanted to move west.
2. The Civil War had helped make some people very rich.
3. Americans accepted Indians as equals.
4. The buffalo had been a chief source of food for many Indians in the West.
5. The Buffalo Soldiers were used for killing buffalo in the West.

**III. Thinking About Things**

Can you guess the answers to these questions? The answers are not in the book.

1. How might the United States have been different if there had been no Homestead Act?
2. What can the Indians in America teach us about caring for our land and its resources?

## IV. Learning From Pictures

What do these pictures tell us about the history of the United States?

1.

2.

3.

4.

## V. Learning From Graphs

Look at the graph below and answer these questions.

1. In the years between 1870 and 1880, did the population of the West triple, double, or only rise slightly?

2. Did the greatest increase in population in the West take place from 1860 to 1870, from 1880 to 1890, or from 1890 to 1900?

POPULATION OF WESTERN AND MOUNTAIN STATES 1860 TO 1900

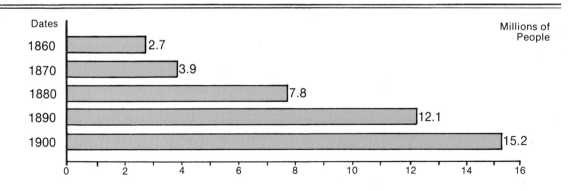

# Why did immigrants come to the United States after 1870?

An immigrant is someone who emigrates, or goes, from one country to another. It has been said that all Americans are immigrants or the descendants of immigrants. The only original Americans are the Indians. Even the Indians came from Asia many hundreds of years ago.

About twenty-eight million people came to the United States as immigrants between 1830 and 1910. This is about as many people as today live in New York, Massachusetts, and New Jersey.

Look at the chart below. *In which years did most of the immigrants come to the United States?*

Most immigrants to America were poor people. In many cases the man or woman who was the head of the family came first. They worked hard and saved money. Soon they were able to bring the rest of the family to a new home. Later, the family helped to bring relatives and friends. Whole villages

| IMMIGRATION TO THE UNITED STATES | 1831-1910 |
|---|---|
| 1831-1850 | 🧍🧍🧍 |
| 1851-1870 | 🧍🧍🧍🧍🧍 |
| 1871-1890 | 🧍🧍🧍🧍🧍🧍🧍🧍🧍 |
| 1891-1910 | 🧍🧍🧍🧍🧍🧍🧍🧍🧍🧍🧍🧍🧍🧍 |

🧍 – One Million Immigrants

moved from Europe to the United States. Moving to America became the dream of millions of poor people in all parts of the world.

Why did these millions of people come to the United States? Many who came were looking for economic opportunities. They hoped to find cheap farmland or high paying jobs in factories. Others came to find freedom. Many did not want to be called into the army in their homelands. Others fled cruel rulers.

Many immigrants wanted their children to have a chance for a better life. America had a good system of free education. There was a chance to train for high-paying jobs. This was impossible in many other parts of the world.

Immigrants came because they felt welcome. So long as immigrants were in good health, they were certain to be welcomed. Some people might make fun of their speech, clothing, and religion. But this usually did not last long. The new immigrants could become citizens in five years. As citizens they felt they were Americans the same as anyone born in the country.

Many immigrants passed through New York City. There they saw the Statue of Liberty. Written on the base of the statue were these words by the poet, Emma Lazarus:

"Give me your tired, your poor,
Your huddled masses yearning to
    breathe free,
The wretched refuse of your
    teeming shore.
Send these, the homeless,
    tempest-tossed, to me,
I lift my lamp beside the golden
    door."

*What was Emma Lazarus saying about how America felt about immigrants?*

The United states needed and welcomed immigrants. No wonder twelve and a half million immigrants poured into the United States in the years from 1891 to 1910!

# Why did immigration to the United States change after 1920?

The United States had needed immigrants during the 1800s. They were needed as farmers, workers, and household servants. Most of these early immigrants came from northern Europe. They were English, Irish, German, or Scandinavian people. Americans poked fun at the Germans, but they generally accepted them as neighbors. Irish Catholics ran into much more prejudice, but this was gradually overcome.

The early immigrants shared the customs and styles of dress of Americans. Many of them, especially the English and Irish, spoke the same language. Before long these early immigrants were accepted as Americans.

All this changed after 1890. The United States no longer needed more workers. Many American workers were now out of work. They feared immigrants would take over the jobs remaining. Most immigrants now came from southern Europe, Asia, and Mexico. They spoke strange languages and had different religions, customs, and styles of dress. Many Americans did not understand the new immigrants. This lack of understanding led to fear and prejudice. There was a demand for a limit to the number of immigrants allowed in the United States.

In 1921 Congress passed laws to limit immigration. They cut back sharply on immigrants from eastern and southern Europe. The laws favored immigrants from northern Europe. The result was a lowering in numbers of all immigration.

The immigration laws of the 1920s were changed in 1945. New laws allowing increased immigration have since been passed by Congress. The number of immigrants entering the United States, however, is still much lower than it was before 1920.

*What might be some advantages in increased immigration? What might be some disadvantages?*

| IMMIGRANTS ENTERING THE UNITED STATES | | | |
|---|---|---|---|
| | 1871-1880 | 1891-1900 | 1921-1930 |
| ENGLAND | 543,000 | 268,000 | 327,000 |
| IRELAND | 431,000 | 345,000 | 215,000 |
| GERMANY | 583,000 | 502,000 | 410,000 |
| POLAND AND RUSSIA | 47,000 | 594,000 | 311,000 |
| ITALY | 52,000 | 650,000 | 454,000 |

# LEARNING EXERCISES

## I. Remembering What We Have Read

Pick the best answer.

1. Immigrants came to the United States for
   a. cheap farmland.
   b. high paying jobs.
   c. freedom.
   d. all of the above reasons.

2. After 1890 most immigrants came from
   a. Ireland.
   b. northern Europe.
   c. southern Europe.
   d. Scandinavia.

3. New immigrants could become United States citizens in
   a. ten years.
   b. a few months.
   c. one year.
   d. five years.

4. Before 1890, most immigrants to the United States came from
   a. England.
   b. Ireland.
   c. Germany.
   d. all of the above.

## II. Fact or Opinion

Is each of the following a Fact or an Opinion?

1. Many immigrants ran into prejudice in the United States.

2. Most immigrants to America were poor people.

3. Immigrants wanted to live on farms, not in big cities.

4. There are more advantages to immigration than disadvantages.

5. Immigration was limited by law after 1920.

## III. Thinking About Things

Can you guess the answers to these questions? The answers are not in the book.

1. Some immigrants to the United States soon returned to the Old World. What might have been some reasons for going back?

2. It has been said that immigrants and their children have divided loyalties. They are Americans, but they also feel loyalty to the old country. Do you think this is a real problem?

## IV. Learning From Pictures

What do these pictures tell us about the history of the United States?

1.

2.

3.

4.

## V. Learning From Graphs

Look at the graph below and answer these questions.

1. In which periods did fewer than ten million immigrants come to the United States in a twenty-year period?

2. In what period did fewer than four million immigrants come to the United States?
3. How many immigrants came to the United States in 1851–1870; 1891–1910?

| IMMIGRATION TO THE UNITED STATES 1831–1910 | |
|---|---|
| **1831–1850** | 🧍🧍🧍         🧍 — One Million Immigrants |
| **1851–1870** | 🧍🧍🧍🧍🧍 |
| **1871–1890** | 🧍🧍🧍🧍🧍🧍🧍🧍 |
| **1891–1910** | 🧍🧍🧍🧍🧍🧍🧍🧍🧍🧍🧍 |

# How did transportation change after 1870?

1832

1870

MODERN

1911

1920

1980

1903

1929

1940

MODERN

The pictures show some of the changes in transportation after 1870. These changes were so great that we call them a revolution. The revolution in transportation is still going on today. Supersonic jet planes can travel faster than the speed of sound. This is more than 738 miles an hour. Spacecraft have reached speeds of 17,000 miles an hour!

Great changes in transportation

have taken place on sea and land. By 1870 steamboats were on the Mississippi River. Larger steamships began crossing the oceans to Europe and Asia. These steamships soon replaced the wind-driven sailing ships. After 1900 motor ships were developed that ran on diesel engines. Today ships can cross the Atlantic Ocean in less than a week.

In the 1800s the steam-driven locomotive replaced the horse-drawn wagon on land. The first railroads had been built in the early 1840s. Most railroad trains ran for only short distances. By 1869, however, the east and west coasts were linked by the first transcontinental railroad line. The chart below shows the rapid growth of American railroads in the next sixty years.

1840

### MILES OF RAILROAD TRACK

Thousands of Miles

| | 1870 | 1890 | 1910 | 1930 |
|---|---|---|---|---|
| | 53,000 | 156,000 | 240,000 | 260,000 |

250
150
50

1892

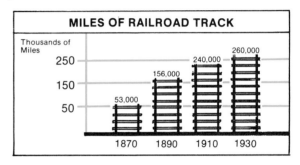
1869

MODERN

# The WRIGHT BROTHERS

Wilbur and Orville Wright grew up in Dayton, Ohio. The two brothers always enjoyed working together and showed great skill as mechanics. They were encouraged in all their projects by their mother. She had a special ability for mechanical work.

One day the boys decided to build a sled. They asked their mother to help them. Mrs. Wright used pencil, ruler, and paper to draw a plan. The sled she designed was low, narrow, and long. She told the boys that the sled's shape would cut down wind resistance. This ought to make the sled go faster than other sleds. Sure enough, the sled they built was the fastest in the neighborhood. The brothers learned about wind resistance from this experience. They also learned the importance of planning a project in advance. It was a lesson they always remembered.

When the boys were older, they became interested in flying. They made drawings of kites, and built and flew them in contests. As a result they learned more about wind and wind resistance. Soon they were making kites and selling them for twenty cents apiece. They did a brisk business selling kites.

Later the young men went into the bicycle business. Once again they showed their skill. Orville shortened the metal upright holding the handle bars. He also dropped the handle bars down. Now he could bend forward instead of having to sit upright on the seat. This cut down the wind resistance of his body. It made it possible for him to go faster without tiring. Orville's new model bicycle brought them good profits. But the Wright brothers were less interested in money than in testing new ideas.

Their interest soon turned again to flying. Wilbur had read a book by a German scientist who had built a glider. A glider, like a kite, depended on the wind to carry it. The big difference was that the glider had carried a man aboard. Once in the air, the man glided about for almost a full minute. Wilbur and Orville grew excited as they discussed the problems of gliders. They were sure of their knowledge of wind resistance and design. This could enable them to build a better glider.

The brothers first built many large

box kites and studied how they flew. Finally, they built a glider and prepared to test it. They wrote to the U.S. Weather Bureau which suggested the village of Kitty Hawk, North Carolina. Kitty Hawk was surrounded by empty, sandy beaches and had a steady wind blowing in from the ocean. It seemed the perfect place to test flying machines.

In 1900 Wilbur flew the first glider built by the brothers. It flew one hundred feet and landed safely. Two years later he flew an improved model for a distance of over five hundred feet. It was the longest distance ever flown by a piloted glider. Now the brothers were ready to test a new type of flying machine. Unlike the glider it would not depend only on the winds. The machine, called an airplane, would also use the power of a gasoline-driven engine for flight.

On December 17, 1903, the Wright brothers were back at Kitty Hawk. They tossed a coin to see who would take the risk of the dangerous test. Orville won and he piloted the airplane on its first flight.

Only five people witnessed the flight that day. They saw a machine built like a huge box kite with wings. Orville first warmed up the engine and then started the propeller. Next, he had to lie down on the lower wing since there was no seat for the pilot. He used both his hands and feet to operate the controls of the airplane.

On the first flight the machine rose ten feet in the air. It was in the air for twelve seconds and traveled over one hundred feet. When it landed, the brothers and the others danced for joy. It was the first flight ever made by an airplane.

The same day Wilbur flew the airplane almost two hundred feet. Orville then tried again and came down after fifteen seconds. On the next try, Wilbur was in the air for fifty-nine seconds. He rose to a height of twenty feet and flew a distance of eight hundred feet. The witnesses at Kitty Hawk could hardly believe their eyes. At long last people were flying.

**Orville Wright**

**Wilbur Wright**

# ROBERT GODDARD

## and American Rocketry

Today the world takes giant rockets for granted. Hundreds of spaceships have been launched by rockets. Many rockets weigh tens of thousands of pounds. Imagine the tremendous power that is needed to lift such rockets off the earth!

Fifty years ago rockets were only a dream in the minds of a few people. One of those people was Robert Goddard. He became interested in rockets in 1917 during World War I when he worked for the Army. As a scientist he was interested in jet propulsion and other means of flight. Rockets were being used to send signals. Goddard believed they might also be used for flight.

After World War I, Goddard worked as a college teacher. He continued his studies of rockets and conducted many experiments. Most of

these early efforts ended in failure. Then he hit on the idea of new fuels for making rockets "blast off." Up to then a black powder had been used to provide power for the takeoff. Goddard now decided to use liquid fuels in place of the powder. It would be a mixture of gasoline and liquid oxygen. He believed this new mixture would give far greater power to rockets. It would blast them high into the sky.

On March 16, 1926, Goddard and his assistants put the liquid fuels to the test. The launch site was a farm near the college. The launcher was built and a ten-foot rocket placed within its thin brackets. Next, the fuel valves were

opened allowing the fuel to escape slowly. A blowtorch was then applied to the fuel mixture! There was a loud roar and the fuel burned for about three seconds. The rocket rose into the air. It traveled 184 feet and reached a speed of sixty miles an hour. Then the rocket curved and fell to the earth. That test does not seem like much today. But it was the first successful firing of a rocket using liquid fuel. The experiment was as important as the first airplane flight by the Wright brothers in 1903.

Robert Goddard continued his experiments, though there was no great interest in rockets. Most people did not believe a rocket could travel very long distances at high speeds. Goddard argued that future rockets would reach speeds of thousands of miles an hour. They would fly into space past the pull of the earth. Such rockets, he claimed, could someday reach the moon!

Fifty years ago such talk seemed impossible to believe. Goddard worked on, alone, with very little help, until his death in 1945. One of his best efforts came in 1935 when one of his rockets reached a height of 7,500 feet. It flew at an average speed of about 550 miles an hour.

Germany's use of rocket bombs toward the end of World War II reawakened interest in rockets. Then,

in 1957, the Soviet Union used a giant rocket to put the unmanned satellite, Sputnik I, into space. Before long, the United States was also developing space rockets. In 1969 the United States used a 3,000 ton rocket to send men to the moon. Modern science makes such projects possible. But it was Robert Goddard who showed it could be done!

# How did communication change after 1870?

Listening to the telegraph

The early 1800s were a time of very slow communication. It had taken weeks for the news of the ending of the War of 1812 to reach the United States from Europe. In the meantime, the battle of New Orleans was fought. It was a battle that need never have been fought.

Communication did not improve much until the 1840s. Most Americans depended upon written messages sent by mail or delivered by messenger. The first great change in communication came in 1844. In that year Samuel F. B. Morse built a telegraph line from Washington, D.C. to Baltimore. The telegraph could send messages over great distances in a matter of seconds.

In 1866 Cyrus W. Field linked Europe and the United States by telegraphic cable. The cable stretched for more than 3,000 miles across the floor of the Atlantic Ocean. Most

people felt that little more could be done to speed communication or to improve it. They were soon proved wrong.

In 1876 came the telephone. The wireless, radio, and television were all invented in the next fifty years. People no longer had to wait hours for newspapers to bring them the latest news. They could now get up-to-the-minute news on radio or television.

The changes in communication have been truly revolutionary. Today more than 82 billion pieces of mail are delivered each year in the United States. This is about 400 pieces of mail

a year per person. About 140 million telegraph messages are sent each year. However, it is the telephone that handles most of America's messages. There are more than 115 million telephones in the United States. More than 460 million calls are made every day.

*How many phone calls do you make in the average day?*

There are now more than 225 million radios in use in American homes. More than nine out of every ten American homes also have a television set.

*How do radio and television affect your life? How would your life be changed if you had no radio or television?*

The revolution in communication has not done away with interest in newspapers. In 1920 when radio first started to expand, nearly 28 million newspapers were sold each day. Today, nearly every American home has a radio or television set. But more than 62 million newspapers are sold each day.

*Which newspaper does your family read? Which parts of the newspaper do you like best?*

# ALEXANDER GRAHAM BELL

The telegraph brought about a revolution in communication. But the telegraph also had its problems. The message had to be sent in a code of short and long sounds called dots and dashes. These sounds were sent over an electric wire. The trained operator tapped out the message. It was received by another operator who decoded the dots and dashes into words. The message was then delivered to the person to whom it had been sent. All this took time and was costly. Inventors began looking for a faster and cheaper form of communication.

A new and faster form of communication was found by Alexander Graham Bell. Like others, he had hoped to invent a machine that allowed people to talk to each other directly. His great invention was the telephone.

Alexander Graham Bell was born in Scotland. Like his father, he was a teacher of the deaf. In 1870 the Bell family moved to Canada. The next year Alexander went to Boston where he opened a school for the deaf. In his spare time he conducted experiments in sending the human voice over wires. Bell formed a partnership with a mechanic, Thomas A. Watson. Together, they tried to develop a telephone.

One day, Bell was working with a new type of speaker. It had wires attached to a metal cup filled with acid. Wires from the cup ran to a

receiver in another room where Watson was sitting. Suddenly Bell spilled some acid on his clothing. He called into his speaker, "Mr. Watson, come here. I want you." Watson in the other room heard every word as it came over the electric wire. This was the first time a human voice had been sent over an electric wire. The telephone had been invented.

Bell decided to show the new invention, in 1876, at a fair in Philadelphia. He hoped it might interest people in investing money to start a telephone company. Meanwhile, Bell continued to teach his deaf pupils. Mabel Hubbard was one of the pupils in the school. She could neither talk nor hear, but could communicate in sign language. She knew about the invention and was very excited. Mabel was sure it would be a great success.

For some reason, Bell suddenly changed his mind about showing the telephone at the fair. Mabel Hubbard learned of this decision and disagreed with it. She "spoke" to Bell and convinced him he must demonstrate the telephone at the fair. This was one time when a teacher listened to his pupil. It proved to be the right decision for Bell.

One of the visitors to the fair was the emperor of Brazil. He knew about Bell

and had visited his school in Boston. Now he asked to see, and hear, the new "talking machine." When he watched the demonstration he cried out, "It talks!" He was wrong, of course, but it did not matter. His words spread quickly and the telephone became the hit of the fair. Crowds came to see it.

The telephone soon became a great success. Alexander Graham Bell became a millionaire and received many honors. And what happened to Mabel Hubbard, the young lady who convinced Bell to show the telephone at the fair? She became Mrs. Alexander Graham Bell.

# What were the effects of changes in transportation?

Railroads had speeded the settlement of the Far West. This brought the far-flung nation closer together. Railroads also changed people's ideas about transportation and travel. The railroad whistle seemed a call to a great future. People living in small towns felt the railroad tied them to the whole country. It was truly a revolution in their lives.

Americans were barely used to the railroad when the automobile was invented. There did not seem much future for the first automobiles. They broke down easily and often had to be towed by horses. Youngsters, accustomed to the swift rush of locomotives, called out to automobile drivers to "get a horse."

By 1901 there were fewer than 15,000 automobiles in the United States. But, by 1910, the automobile industry had solved many of its problems. The manufacturing of automobiles grew rapidly, as did the road building programs in many states. Today there are more than 145 million automobiles, buses, and trucks in the United States.

Transportation revolutions on sea and land were soon matched by a revolution in the skies. The use of airplanes expanded after the 1930s. The fleet of 102 commercial airliners in 1930 has risen to over 3,600 airliners today. Nearly all of today's airliners are jet propelled.

Young Americans once dreamed of navigating ships. Later they dreamed of becoming locomotive engineers. Today many dream of becoming pilots or astronauts. Their changing dreams tell the story of the changes in transportation in the past one hundred years.

Changes in transportation have brought many benefits to the American people. They have also brought many new problems. *Can you give some of the benefits and some of the problems of the transportation revolution?*

# LEARNING EXERCISES

## I. Remembering What We Have Read

Pick the best answer.

1. The most recent transportation invention is the
   a. diesel engine.
   b. steamship.
   c. supersonic jet plane.
   d. locomotive.
2. An unmanned satellite is used in
   a. railroad building.
   b. space.
   c. modern ships at sea.
   d. airplanes.
3. Rockets became a success after Robert Goddard started using
   a. powder fuels.
   b. gasoline engines.
   c. liquid fuels.
   d. dynamite.
4. All the following names are connected with improvements in communication **except**
   a. Cyrus W. Field.
   b. Alexander Graham Bell.
   c. Orville Wright.
   d. Samuel F. Morse.

## II. Learning From Pictures

Each of the following pictures tells us something about changes in transportation and communication. What does each picture mean to you?

1.

2.

3.

## III. Yesterday and Today in Pictures

Look at the four pictures of methods of transportation shown below. Each picture has a letter above it. In what order would you put the letter to show which method of transportation was used first, second, third, and most recently?

A.

B.

C.

D.

## IV. Thinking About Things

Can you guess the answers to these questions? The answers are not in the book.

1. Would the United States be better off if it had fewer television sets? Give reasons for your answer.

2. Will railroads make a comeback in the future? Give reasons for your answer.

# How did American industry change after 1870?

We have read about revolutions in transportation and communication after 1870. There were also revolutions in agriculture and industry at the same time. All of these brought changes to the American people.

The first Industrial Revolution began in the 1840s. Many small factories were built. These factories used steam-powered machines to produce small amounts of goods. This changed after 1870 when the United States entered upon its second Industrial Revolution. The chart shows how this second Industrial Revolution affected American industry.

Many new factories were built during the second Industrial Revolution. The new factories were often very large and employed thousands of workers. These factories used complicated, expensive machines run by electricity. They were able to produce vast amounts of goods at low cost. Electric power and the mass production of goods were two of the changes brought to American industry after 1870.

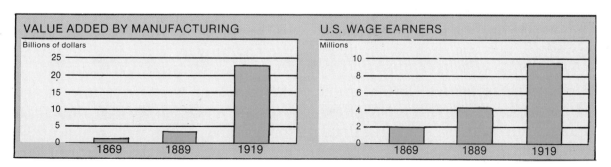

VALUE ADDED BY MANUFACTURING
Billions of dollars
25
20
15
10
5
0
1869  1889  1919

U.S. WAGE EARNERS
Millions
10
8
6
4
2
0
1869  1889  1919

# What changes were brought by the Industrial Revolution?

The second Industrial Revolution brought many changes to the United States. American business had grown slowly and steadily during the 1800s. It grew much more rapidly after 1870.

American industrial companies grew much bigger and richer after 1870. The first billion-dollar company was the United States Steel Corporation. It was formed in 1901. It was soon followed by other billion-dollar companies. Today there are hundreds of American companies that are each worth more than a billion dollars. They have helped to make the United States the land of big business. This is one of the changes brought by the Industrial Revolution.

Production of goods was greatly increased by American industries. Much of the production went into what is called consumer goods. Consumer goods include automobiles, radios, television sets, furniture, dishwashers, and clothing. These are goods we use every day. The mass production of consumer goods helped give Americans the highest standard of living in the world.

The Industrial Revolution led to the rise and growth of the factory system. The new factories needed tens of thousands of workers. Many of the workers came from the farms and from foreign lands. Cities sprang up near the factories and changed American life.

Before 1870 most Americans had been farmers. Only about one American in four, or twenty-five percent, lived in cities, or urban areas. The rest lived on farms or in small towns and villages called rural areas.

The chart shows how cities, or urban areas, grew after 1870. The Industrial Revolution changed the United States from an agricultural nation to an industrial nation. It also changed the United States from a rural-based nation to an urban-based nation.

**AMERICANS LIVING IN CITIES AND FARM AREAS**
DATA FOR 30 YEAR INTERVALS

| DATE | CITIES | FARM AREAS |
|------|--------|------------|
| 1880 | 28% | 72% |
| 1910 | 45% | 55% |
| 1940 | 56% | 44% |
| 1970 | 75% | 25% |

# HENRY FORD and his "FLIVVER"

Henry Ford was born and grew up near Detroit, Michigan. He had little schooling, but he was a good mechanic. As a young man he worked as a farm machinery repairman. Ford also worked as an engineer for an electric company in Detroit. But his main interest was in automobiles. He built his first car in 1896.

Automobiles cost a lot of money at that time. Each car was different and had its own parts. It took a day and a half to put the parts together to produce a single car. The cost was very high. Only the rich could afford to own one of these automobiles.

Henry Ford found a way to bring down the price of cars. His idea was to make all his cars alike. This could be done by making all the parts alike, or standardized. It was now possible to

interchange parts in every car of the same model. Thus, a fender for one of the cars would fit on any other car of the same model. Spare parts could be made cheaply.

Ford next set up an assembly line for production. The car being assembled moved down a belt past a line of workers. Each worker put on a different part of the car. When the car reached the end of the line, it was fully assembled.

Ford's methods of production led to the first low-cost cars in the world. His Model T, or flivver as it was called, sold for as little as $300. Millions of Americans rushed to buy it.

Henry Ford's great contribution to American industry was more than the cheap Model T car. His idea of assembly line production created a revolution in manufacturing. It helped make the United States the greatest industrial nation in the world.

# How did American farming change after 1870?

The United States started as a nation of small farmers. The farm families did most of the work. They planted and harvested crops using simple hand tools and farm animals.

Most American farms before 1870 were family farms. The farmers produced mainly for themselves and their families. They sold their surplus, or extra products, but did not depend upon cash crops. Cash crops are raised to be sold rather than to be used by the family. Cotton and tobacco are examples of cash crops.

American farming began to change in the 1840s. The steel plow of the 1830s made working in the thick soil of the Midwest possible. At about the same time, Cyrus McCormick invented the automatic reaper. It speeded the work of cutting grain. Other machines, such as the thresher and harvester, followed. These machines were run by steam engines rather than animals. They could do the work of dozens of farmers.

During the 1830s a new machine was invented. It could cut, thresh, and clean and bag the grain all at once. The combine, as it was called, marked the start of a revolution in agriculture.

In 1800 the average farmer could barely attend to ten acres of land. By 1900 the average farmer could attend to more than 130 acres! This made it possible for thousands of people to leave the farms. They moved to the cities where many of them became factory workers. This movement from the farms did not cut down on farm production. Now one person could do the work once done by 300 farmers fifty years earlier.

| YEARS | TRACTORS | HORSES AND MULES |
|-------|----------|------------------|
| 1870 | — — | 8,000,000 |
| 1890 | — — | 20,000,000 |
| 1920 | 250,000 | 22,500,000 |
| 1950 | 3,400,000 | 4,300,00 |

Chemical fertilizers helped to enrich the soil. The newly invented tractor replaced animals in moving heavy farm machinery. The chart shows how tractors affected the use of animals on the farms.

The railways made it possible for farmers to speed their products to market. At the same time, new scientific farming methods helped produce larger crops. New and better ways of plowing were developed.

New machinery and improved farming methods brought bigger harvests. This was done with fewer farm workers than before. After 1870 the production of corn rose more than 400 percent and wheat 300 percent. At the same time the number of farms and farmers dropped.

After 1870 farmers produced more cash crops. The average size of farms increased as machines and farm labor were used in cash crop farming. The charts tell the story of the changes on American farms.

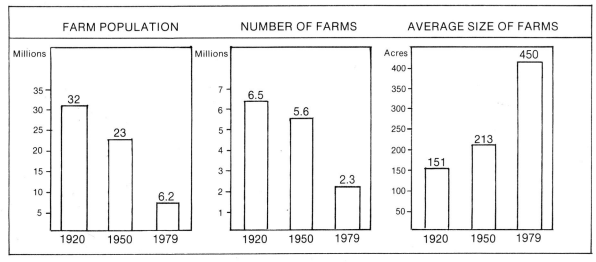

# LEARNING EXERCISES

## I. Remembering What We Have Read

Pick the best answer.

1. The percentage population of urban areas of the United States today is
   a. less than it was in 1880.
   b. only slightly higher than it was in 1880.
   c. the same as it was in 1880.
   d. very mugh higher than it was in 1880.
2. Mass production is connected with
   a. modern machines.
   b. the Industrial Revolution.
   c. changes in American industry.
   d. all of the above.
3. Ford's production methods were based upon
   a. assembly line production.
   b. interchangeable parts.
   c. standardized parts.
   d. all of the above.
4. The second Industrial Revolution involved all the following **except**
   a. electric power.
   b. large factories.
   c. steam power.
   d. mass production of goods.

## II. Learning From Pictures
Each of the following pictures tells something about the Industrial Revolution. Write a sentence about each one.

1.

2.

3.

## III. Fact or Opinion

Is each of the following a Fact or an Opinion?

1. The Industrial Revolution led to the expansion of factories.
2. Tobacco is a cash crop.
3. Modern farming methods led to the ruin of the family farms.
4. The average size of farms increased after 1870.
5. Too much of American production has gone into consumer goods.

## IV. Who Are They?

On a separate sheet of paper write 2 or 3 sentences about each of the following people.

HENRY FORD

CYRUS McCORMICK

## V. Learning To Use Graphs

Three bar graphs are used in this reading selection. On a separate sheet of paper change each of the bar graphs to a line graph.

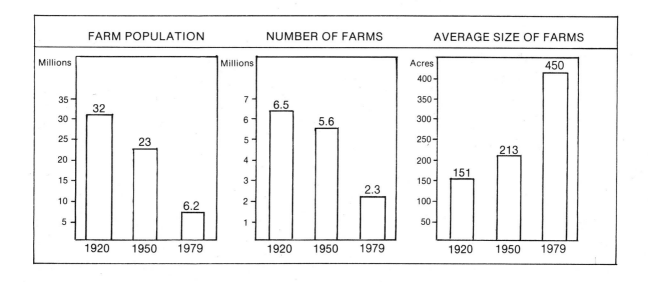

| FARM POPULATION | NUMBER OF FARMS | AVERAGE SIZE OF FARMS |
|---|---|---|
| Millions | Millions | Acres |
| 1920: 32, 1950: 23, 1979: 6.2 | 1920: 6.5, 1950: 5.6, 1979: 2.3 | 1920: 151, 1950: 213, 1979: 450 |

# How did American foreign policy change after 1870?

| CONSTITUTION | |
| --- | --- |
| **PRESIDENT** | **CONGRESS** |
| Chooses Secretary of State - Appoints Ambassadors Makes Treaties | Approves President Appointments Ratifies Treaties Provides Funds |

The Constitution gives the president control of foreign policy. It is the job of the president to deal with other countries. But, Congress also has the power to keep check on the president. For example, the Senate must approve the people the president appoints as ambassadors. The Senate also has to approve the secretary of state. This is the official who directs foreign policy for the president. In addition, the Senate must approve all treaties made with foreign countries. Congress must vote the money the president needs to carry out the foreign policy.

American foreign policy has always had three main aims. They are:

1. To protect American lives and property in foreign lands.

2. To encourage trade between the United States and foreign countries.

3. To settle disputes between the United States and foreign countries.

During its first hundred years, the United States had an isolationist foreign policy. This meant that it tried not to get involved in Europe's affairs. President Washington was partly responsible for this. When he took office in 1789, most of Europe was at war. Washington was afraid the United States would get entangled, or mixed up, in these wars. In 1797 before he left office, Washington warned about "entangling alliances." This warning marked the start of American isolationism.

The foreign policy of isolationism seemed to make sense. The United

States was separated from Europe by 3,000 miles of ocean. It took weeks for a ship or a message to cross the ocean. In the 1800s Americans were busy settling the West and fighting the Civil War. They had no time to worry about Europe or Asia.

American foreign policy changed after 1870. The revolutions in transportation and communication brought Europe and the United States closer. The Industrial Revolution led to greater American interest in trade. Americans needed raw goods for their factories. They also wanted markets where they could sell the products they made. Some Americans favored imperialist policies like those of European nations. This meant taking control, or making colonies, of foreign lands. These lands would provide the raw goods American factories needed. They would also serve as markets where finished products could be sold. Colonies would also bring a sense of importance to the United States. All of this helped lead the United States into the Spanish-American War in 1898.

Americans did not give up the idea of isolationism after 1870. They remained isolationist in regard to European affairs. But the United States was also interested in colonies and imperialism in Asia. It was not until the 1940s that the United States finally gave up isolationism. Today, the United States has no colonies. It has given up the old-fashioned idea of imperialism. American foreign policy is now based on internationalism. It seeks cooperation with all the nations of the world.

# How did World War I affect American foreign policy?

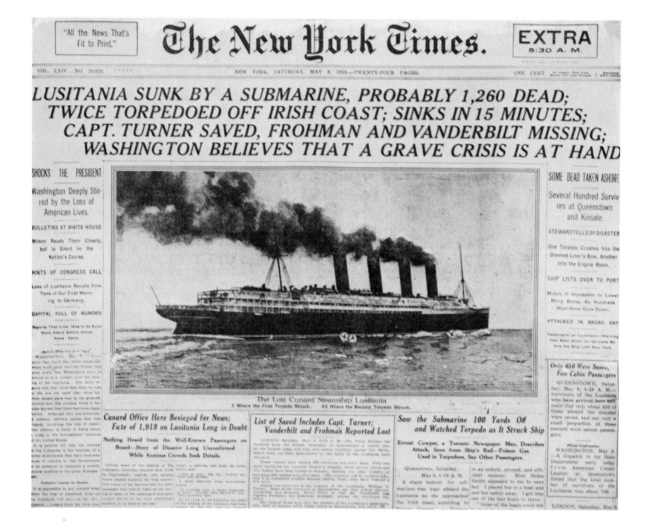

"All the News That's Fit to Print."

# The New York Times.

EXTRA 5:30 A.M.

VOL. LXIV...NO. 20,923.       NEW YORK, SATURDAY, MAY 8, 1915—TWENTY-FOUR PAGES.       ONE CENT

## LUSITANIA SUNK BY A SUBMARINE, PROBABLY 1,260 DEAD; TWICE TORPEDOED OFF IRISH COAST; SINKS IN 15 MINUTES; CAPT. TURNER SAVED, FROHMAN AND VANDERBILT MISSING; WASHINGTON BELIEVES THAT A GRAVE CRISIS IS AT HAND

**SHOCKS THE PRESIDENT**

Washington Deeply Stirred by the Loss of American Lives.

**BULLETINS AT WHITE HOUSE**

Wilson Reads Them Closely, but Is Silent on the Nation's Course.

**HINTS OF CONGRESS CALL**

Loss of Lusitania Recalls From Tone of Our First Warning to Germany.

**CAPITAL FULL OF RUMORS**

*The Lost Cunard Steamship Lusitania*

**SOME DEAD TAKEN ASHORE**

Several Hundred Survivors at Queenstown and Kinsale.

**STEWARD TELLS OF DISASTER**

One Torpedo Crashes Into the Doomed Liner's Bow, Another Into the Engine Room.

**SHIP LISTS OVER TO PORT**

**ATTACKED IN BROAD DAY**

**Cunard Office Here Besieged for News; Fate of 1,918 on Lusitania Long in Doubt**

**List of Saved Includes Capt. Turner; Vanderbilt and Frohman Reported Lost**

**Saw the Submarine 100 Yards Off and Watched Torpedo as It Struck Ship**

**Only 650 Were Saved, Few Cabin Passengers**

---

American isolationism fell apart during World War I. That war broke out in 1914 in Europe. England, France, and Russia, known as the Allies, were on one side. Germany and Austria, called the Central Powers, were on the other side. Italy was neutral at first, but later it joined the Allies.

At the start of the war, the United States said it was neutral. However, most Americans wanted the Allies to win. German submarine attacks on American ships angered the American people. In 1917 the United States entered the war on the side of the Allies. This was the first time American troops fought in a European war. The United States seemed to be moving away from isolationism. Woodrow Wilson was then President of the United States.

World War I ended in 1918 with a victory for the Allies. The United States now joined the Allies in drawing up a peace treaty. That treaty set up a world organization called the League of Nations. Its chief task was to settle disputes before they led to wars.

The United States seemed about to give up its isolationist foreign policy. President Wilson had thought up the idea of a League of Nations. If the United States joined the League, it would mean a great change in foreign policy. This did not happen, however. The Senate did not approve the peace treaty. The United States did not join the League of Nations.

World War I had only partly brought the United States out of its

isolationism. During the 1920s many Americans seemed more anxious than ever to keep out of the affairs of Europe or Asia.

*How might this have been a result of World War I?*

# How did World War II affect American foreign policy?

The time line shows some events that took place between 1918 and 1945. This was a time of great change in the world. It was also a time of change in the foreign policy of the United States.

American foreign policy remained isolationist, in many ways, after World War I. For example, the United States never joined the League of Nations.

However, the United States did join other nations in disarmament meetings. These meetings tried to reduce the size of the navies of the great powers. The United States, Britain, France, and Japan agreed to reduce the size of their navies. It was hoped this would save money and lessen the chances for war.

Meanwhile, a warlike dictator

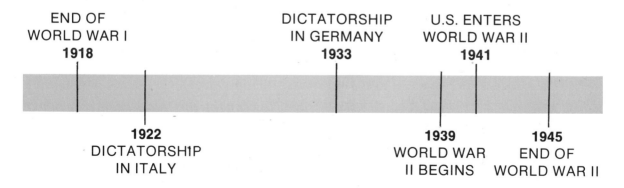

END OF
WORLD WAR I
**1918**

DICTATORSHIP
IN GERMANY
**1933**

U.S. ENTERS
WORLD WAR II
**1941**

**1922**
DICTATORSHIP
IN ITALY

**1939**
WORLD WAR
II BEGINS

**1945**
END OF
WORLD WAR II

Hitler

Mussolini

Tojo

named Mussolini rose to power in Italy in 1922. Ten years later a group of military leaders took control of Japan. In 1933 a dictator named Adolf Hitler led his Nazi party to power in Germany. All these dictators wanted power even if it meant war. The Japanese seized most of northern China in 1931. Italian troops invaded Ethiopia, in Africa, in 1935. The Germans, led by Hitler, began to rearm and prepare for war.

The dictator nations of Italy, Japan, and Germany became known as the Axis powers. They agreed to help one another in case of war. World War II began in 1939, when Germany invaded Poland. Britain and France joined in the fight against Germany, but Poland was soon defeated. Then the Germans, helped by the Italians, defeated France. There was fear that Germany could invade and defeat the British unless Britain was helped.

# How was the United States involved in World War II?

The United States was not involved in World War II when it began in 1939. However, the United States sent ships and guns to help Britain. President Franklin D. Roosevelt took this action in spite of the fear of being involved in the war. He warned that a British defeat might mean an end to democracy in the world.

In 1939 Germany and the Soviet Union had signed a friendship treaty. But in 1941 Germany expanded the war by invading the Soviet Union. The Soviet Union and Britain now became allies in the war against the Axis powers.

In December 1941, Japanese airplanes bombed the American fleet at Pearl Harbor, Hawaii. The United States was soon at war with Japan, Germany, and Italy. During the next

four years American troops fought in Africa, Europe, and Asia.

World War II ended American isolationism. The United States joined with its allies to plan a new world organization. It would take the place of the old League of Nations. The name of the new organization was the United Nations. It was formed while the United States, Britain, and the Soviet Union were fighting the Axis powers in World War II.

World War II ended with the defeat of the Axis nations in 1945. That same year, the United Nations held its first meeting. The United States became the first member to join the United Nations. Internationalism rather than isolationism was now America's foreign policy. The United States was ready to be a world leader.

# Pearl Harbor

"Air raid, Pearl Harbor. This is no drill." This message was sent by Army radio operators early in the morning of December 7, 1941. It was the first word of the Japanese attack on the American naval base at Pearl Harbor, Hawaii.

The Japanese attack came as a complete surprise. The United States and Japan were not at war at the time. However, the United States was helping Britain and Russia, who were at war with Germany. Japan and Germany were allies and they expected the United States to enter the war against them. Japan's military leaders hoped the surprise attack would give them a head start in the war against the United States.

The attack went on for two hours. More than 400 Japanese bombers were launched from aircraft carriers. They struck the American navy base and nearby airfield. More than 3,600 Americans were killed or wounded in the attack. Nineteen ships, including five giant battleships, were sunk or badly damaged. At least 150 American airplanes were destroyed. The Japanese surprise attack almost wiped out the entire American Far East Fleet and Air Force. Luckily, the American aircraft carriers were not in Pearl Harbor at the time.

Americans were angered by the Pearl Harbor attack. It had taken place even as Japanese officials were talking peace with the American government. President Roosevelt called December 7, the day of the attack, "a day that will live in infamy." Congress was called the next day to a special meeting and the United States declared war on Japan. Three days later, Germany and Italy, Japan's allies, declared war on the United States.

During World War II, the words "Remember Pearl Harbor" became a unifying cry for all Americans. After the war, the sunken ship *Arizona* was a memorial to those who died at Pearl Harbor. It rests in shallow waters of the harbor. Part of the ship can be seen by the thousands of visitors who come to honor the dead.

# The first atomic bomb is dropped

In April 1945, President Franklin D. Roosevelt died. Vice-President, Harry S. Truman, became president. The next month, Germany surrendered, and the war in Europe ended. But the war against Japan continued.

American soldiers and marines had driven the Japanese from many Pacific islands. Most of the Japanese fleet had been sunk or damaged. American bombers had destroyed many Japanese cities and factories. In spite of this, Japan would not surrender. President Truman had to decide what to do next. He could order American troops to invade the mainland of Japan. This might cost the lives of many American soldiers and Japanese civilians. The president could also order the use of a new type of bomb against Japan. American scientists had just developed and tested an atomic bomb. One atomic bomb had the force of thousands of ordinary bombs. The new weapon might force Japan to surrender without the loss of many lives.

President Truman finally decided to use the atomic bomb. On August 6, 1945, a single atomic bomb was dropped on the Japanese city of Hiroshima. The city was almost completely wiped out. More than 160,000 Japanese were killed or injured by this one bomb. Three days later a second atomic bomb was dropped on the city of Nagasaki. Once again thousands of people were killed or injured. Within a week Japan surrendered and World War II was over.

After the war, many people felt it had been wrong to use the atomic bombs. President Truman said he had asked that the bomb be used only on a military target. However, the terrible power of the bomb killed many people who were not soldiers or sailors. The bomb also caused destruction of parts of the city that were not military targets. Many people also believed that Japan might have surrendered without an invasion or the use of atomic bombs. The question of whether it was right to use the atomic bomb on Japan is still argued. *What do you think?*

# LEARNING EXERCISES

## I. Remembering What We Have Read

Pick the best answer.

1. All United States treaties must be approved by
   a. a vote of the American people.
   b. the Senate.
   c. the Supreme Court.
   d. both houses of Congress.
2. The dictator nations, called the Axis powers, included
   a. Germany, Italy, and France.
   b. Germany, Italy, and Russia.
   c. Germany, Italy, and Japan.
   d. Germany, Japan, and Russia.
3. American foreign policy is controlled by the
   a. Cabinet.
   b. Congress.
   c. president.
   d. ambassadors.
4. The League of Nations was set up
   a. before 1914.
   b. after 1918.
   c. during World War I.
   d. during World War II.

## II. True or False

Are the following True or False?

1. The United States followed an isolationist foreign policy for its first hundred years.
2. George Washington warned about becoming involved in European wars.
3. American foreign policy is now based on internationalism.
4. Russia was one of the Central Powers in World War I.
5. World War II began when Poland invaded Germany.

## III. Thinking About Things

Can you guess the answers to these questions? The answers are not in the book.

1. Why do some people feel it is impossible for the United States to be isolationist in the modern world?
2. Do you think nations will ever be able to disarm?

# Why did the United States join the United Nations?

The United States did not join the League of Nations after World War I. American isolationist feelings led to this refusal to join the League. The American action greatly weakened the League. It was never strong enough to prevent the coming of World War II in 1939.

The United States was neutral when World War II began. However, almost all Americans supported Britain and France against the German and Italian dictatorships. When France was defeated, President Roosevelt acted to give direct aid to Britain. Ships, guns, and ammunition were sent to help Britain, which was in danger of a German invasion. This was a big step away from isolationism. It was the start of a very new foreign policy for the United States.

President Roosevelt declared the United States would be an "arsenal of democracy" though it was not at war. *What is an arsenal? What do you think he meant by that statement?*

In August 1941, the United States changed much of its foreign policy. It took a big step away from isolationism and imperialism. The United States, though not in the war, joined Britain in a plan for the future. President Roosevelt and Prime Minister Winston Churchill issued the Atlantic Charter. The Charter said they would seek no new territories at the end of the war. It also promised the return of self-government to nations that had been conquered by the Axis powers.

The Charter also declared that Britain and the United States would work for a system of world peace and security. What this meant was soon made clear. In December 1941, the United States was in the war. Together with its allies, Britain and Russia, it acted to form a new world organization. The United Nations, as it was called, was established in 1945. The United States joined it because Americans no longer believed in isolationism. They felt that only world cooperation could prevent future wars or the threat of war.

# How does the
# United Nations operate?

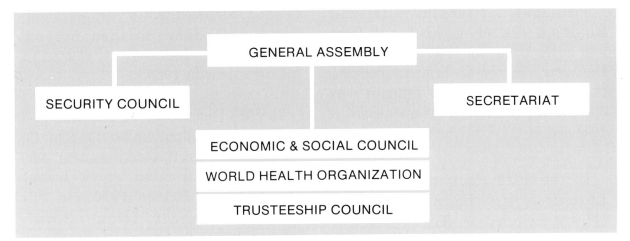

GENERAL ASSEMBLY

SECURITY COUNCIL

SECRETARIAT

ECONOMIC & SOCIAL COUNCIL

WORLD HEALTH ORGANIZATION

TRUSTEESHIP COUNCIL

The chart shows how the United Nations, or UN, is organized. The General Assembly is made up of all the members of the United Nations. Each member nation has one vote in the Assembly. The General Assembly is the place where issues are discussed. However, the Assembly cannot order that any action be taken by the United Nations.

The Security Council is made up of fifteen members. Five of the members are permanent members. This means that they are always members of the Council. The permanent members are known as the Big Five. They are the United States, England, France, the Soviet Union, and China. The other ten members of the Council are elected for two-year terms.

Only the Security Council can order the UN to take action. To do this, nine members of the Security Council must vote for the action. These nine must include all of the Big Five. If one of the Big Five permanent members votes against the action, it is vetoed, or turned down.

The UN has other agencies besides the Assembly and the Security Council. The World Health Organization works to improve health in all parts of the world. The Economic and Social Council tries to improve education, science, work conditions, and human rights. The Trusteeship Council looks after colonies until they are ready to become new, independent nations.

The day-to-day work of running the United Nations is handled by the Secretariat. This is a staff of workers from all over the world. It is headed by the secretary-general, who is elected by the UN members. The United Nations has its headquarters in New York City. Most of its meetings are held there.

# United States Presidents since 1945

President Franklin Delano Roosevelt was serving his fourth term when he died in 1945. The Vice-President, Harry S. Truman became the new president. Mr. Truman was elected as president in his own right in 1948.

In the 1952 election, Dwight D. Eisenhower was chosen as president. He was reelected to office in 1956.

John F. Kennedy was elected president in 1960, but was assassinated in 1963. Mr. Kennedy's vice-president, Lyndon B. Johnson then became president. Mr. Johnson was elected in his own right in 1964.

In 1968 Richard M. Nixon, who had been vice-president under Dwight D. Eisenhower, was elected president. Mr. Nixon was reelected in 1972, but resigned the office in 1974. He was succeeded by the vice-president, Gerald Ford. In 1976 Mr. Ford was defeated for the presidency by Jimmy Carter. Mr. Carter lost the election of 1980 to Ronald Reagan.

Enrichment

# Gerald R. Ford and Nelson D. Rockefeller take office without being elected

The United States Constitution is the highest law of the land. It must be obeyed by every person and by every state. From time to time the Constitution is changed or amended. The 25th Amendment was passed in 1967. It set up a new way to replace a president or vice-president who left office by death, resigning, or removal.

Vice-President Agnew resigned in 1973. President Nixon followed the rule set forth by the 25th Amendment. He asked Congress to approve Gerald R. Ford as vice-president. This was done. One year later, Mr. Nixon resigned as president. Vice-President Ford now became the new president.

He asked Congress to approve Nelson D. Rockefeller as vice-president. This was done.

From then on, until January 1977, President Ford and Vice-President Rockefeller would serve in office. They were the first president and vice-president to take office without being elected by all the people.

296

# United States foreign policy since 1945

The United States and the Soviet Union had been allies during World War II. When the war ended in 1945, that alliance fell apart.

American foreign policy after 1945 was aimed at containing the Soviet Union. Economic and military aid was given to many nations to help them resist communism. The United States also signed treaties of alliance with many nations.

In 1950 fighting broke out in Asia between North Korea and South Korea. The Soviet Union supported the pro-Communist North Koreans with military supplies. Communist Chinese troops also came to the aid of North Korea. The United States and the United Nations supported the South Korean government. Thousands of American troops fought in Korea until the war ended in 1953. A truce finally ended the war. It left North and South Korean boundaries almost as they had been in 1950.

In the 1960s fighting broke out between North and South Vietnam. American soldiers helped the South Vietnam government against the pro-Communist North Vietnam troops. More than 46,000 American soldiers died in Vietnam. All American forces were removed from Vietnam in 1973. After they left, the North Vietnamese took control of all Vietnam.

By the mid-1970s American foreign policy aimed to improve relations with the Soviet Union. The United States also established normal relations with the new Communist government in China. The People's Republic of China had taken control of the Chinese mainland in 1949. At first the United States refused to recognize the new government. Finally, in 1976, it recognized the Chinese Communist government. By that time the Chinese Communist leaders were engaged in disputes with the Soviet Union.

In 1979 the Soviet Union sent troops into the neighboring nation of Afghanistan. The United States protested strongly. It led the United Nations in condemning the Soviet Union. Relations between the United States and the Soviet Union worsened.

# The election
## of 1980

The United States today has two main political parties. They are the Democratic party and the Republican party. Each party tries to elect its members to office in the cities, states, and the nation. Each party especially tries to win the elections for the Congress and the president.

In 1976 Jimmy Carter, a Democrat, was elected President. He narrowly defeated President Gerald R. Ford, the Republican candidate. The Democratic party also won control over the Congress of the United States.

President Carter faced many problems in his four year term in office. In 1979 the Shah of Iran was overthrown. Later in the year the leaders of the revolt in Iran seized more than sixty Americans. Some were later released but fifty-three Americans were held as hostages. By the end of 1980 they were still being held in Iran. Many Americans were angered by this action. Some blamed President Carter for failing to free the hostages though it was not clear what he could do about it.

The president was also blamed for the inflation that led to rising prices. Efforts by the government to control inflation failed. Many people felt that a change was needed. In 1980 the Republicans nominated Ronald Reagan for the presidency. The Democrats again selected Mr. Carter. The election in November 1980 resulted in a strong Republican victory. Mr. Reagan was elected president and took office in January 1981. The Republicans also gained control of the Senate and increased its members in the House of Representatives.

At last in January 1981, the hostages were released. This event took place on the same day as the inauguration of Ronald Reagan. The hostages had been held captives for 444 days.

## LEARNING EXERCISES

**I. Remembering What We Have Read**

Pick the best answer.

1. The Big Five of the United Nations does not include
   a. China.
   b. France.
   c. Japan.
   d. the Soviet Union.
2. In World War II the arsenal of democracy was
   a. Britain.
   b. the United States.
   c. the United Nations.
   d. none of the above.

3. The Security Council of the United Nations has
   a. nine members.
   b. one member for each nation in the United Nations.
   c. five members.
   d. fifteen members.
4. Three vice-presidents who succeeded to the presidency included all the following **except**
   a. Gerald Ford.
   b. Lyndon B. Johnson.
   c. Dwight D. Eisenhower.
   d. Harry S. Truman.

**II. Learning From Headlines**

What might be the story behind each of the following headlines?

### PRESIDENT PLEDGES AID TO BRITAIN

### UN ELECTS NEW SECRETARY–GENERAL

### PRESIDENT RESIGNS: VICE-PRESIDENT SWORN IN

**III. Thinking About Things**

How does the United States try to help other nations and people of the world?

# How has science made
# the United States a great nation?

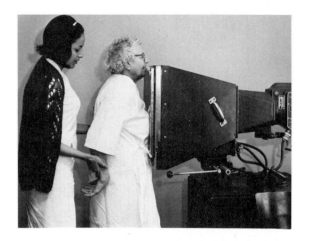

Nations were once considered great because of their power to make wars. Today the greatness of nations can be measured in other ways. Science, industry, and art are better signs of greatness than big armies or war victories.

Science has improved the health of the American people. One hundred years ago the average American could expect to live only thirty-five years. Today, the average American can expect to live for more than seventy years.

One hundred years ago almost one-third of all children died before they were one year old. In 1900 more than sixteen percent of all children died before the age of one. Today only 2 percent die. Childhood diseases such as measles, diphtheria, and polio, or infantile paralysis, have been conquered by science. Medical science has also helped older children and adults. Today more than 330,000

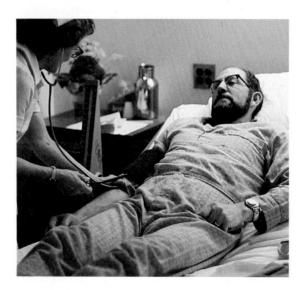

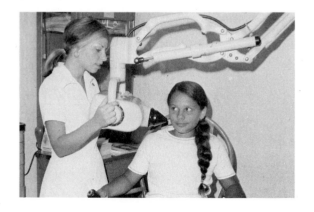

doctors, 600,000 nurses, and 100,000 dentists help to keep Americans healthy. They are helped by thousands of scientists who work in laboratories. Every year these scientists find new cures for diseases.

Science also makes our lives richer and fuller in other ways. Inventors have used the discoveries of scientists to create new products. Scientists who studied sound and light made possible the invention of the telephone, radio, and TV. Scientific study led to the invention of steam power, electric power, and atomic energy. Scientists helped make fast, safe jet air travel possible. They are now studying ways to cut down on airplane noise and pollution.

Science has brought revolutions to American industry, communication, transportation, and agriculture. It has brought greater health, and longer life, to Americans. Science has made the United States a great nation.

# CHARLES P. STEINMETZ

## The Wizard of Schenectady

On June 2, 1889, a boatload of immigrants arrived in New York harbor. Immigration officials questioned the people before permitting them to go ashore. They especially questioned a bearded, lame man less than five feet tall. His name was Karl P. Steinmetz. He was twenty-three years old and spoke no English. There was some doubt that he should be allowed to enter the country. He probably had no job skills and might not be able to support himself.

Just when it seemed that Karl Steinmetz would be kept from going ashore, an American came aboard. The American, Oscar Asmussen, took Steinmetz by the arm. He greeted Steinmetz like an old friend. Then he said to the officials, "This man is a German scientist. I will be responsible for him in America." The officials signed the papers and Steinmetz entered the country. The United States was his home for the rest of his life. His ideas helped make America great.

Steinmetz was born with many physical handicaps. However, his mental ability was very great. When he was a child, he was an outstanding student in mathematics and in science. As a university student, he often knew more than his teachers. In spite of his ability, he had to leave Germany because of things he said against the German government. Steinmetz settled in Switzerland, where he met Oscar Asmussen. Asmussen loaned him money to come to the United States and helped him settle here.

In America, Steinmetz changed his first name to Charles. He soon found work as an electrical engineer. Three years later, he joined the General Electric Company in Schenectady, New York. Steinmetz remained with General Electric until his death in 1923, at the age of fifty-seven.

Before long Steinmetz was known as the wizard of Schenectady. His laboratory poured out all kinds of electrical information and inventions. One invention was a way to send electricity over long distances. It could then be used in factories many miles away.

Steinmetz was more than a great scientist. He was also a very friendly, easygoing person. The children of Schenectady often came to special "magic" shows that he put on. He also had his own private zoo of snakes, alligators, and crows. Within his handicapped body was a heart filled with love for animals and people.

303

# Men on the moon

**Armstrong's First Step on Moon**

"That's one small step for man, one giant leap for mankind." With these words, Neil A. Armstrong, an American astronaut, stepped from a space-landing craft to the surface of the moon. The date was July 20, 1969. Armstrong was the first man ever to walk on the moon.

*What do you think he meant by "a small step for man and a giant leap for mankind."?*

Millions of people watched Neil Armstrong take his historic step. They were able to watch because it was televised from the landing craft. It had taken the spaceship about four days to reach the moon, but it took less than two seconds for the television picture to go from the moon to the earth. This made it possible for the entire world to have a ringside seat at the first moon walk.

Armstrong was soon joined on the surface of the moon by another astronaut, Edwin E. Aldrin. They had both guided the landing craft from the spaceship to the moon's surface. A third astronaut, Michael Collins, remained in the spaceship and circled the moon. Together, Armstrong and Aldrin planted the American flag on the moon. Then they walked on the moon for about two and a half hours. They set up scientific instruments that would send back information to scientists on earth. The astronauts also collected about fifty pounds of sample rocks and soil from the moon. These would later be studied by scientists on earth. Much would be learned about the history of the moon from these samples of moon rocks and soil.

of hard work and study by American scientists. Other nations were also interested in space flight. For a while it seemed the Soviet Union might be the first to land men on the moon. In the end, it was the United States that was first.

Finally, the two astronauts got into their landing craft and lifted off the lunar surface. They rejoined the spaceship in which Michael Collins had been circling the moon. Four days later, the three astronauts returned safely to earth.

Getting the astronauts to the moon was one of the great victories of American science. It took many years

MOON ROCKS

# How has industry made the United States a great nation?

Huge sums of money, or capital, are needed to run the mines and factories. Much of this money is raised by selling shares of ownership in the industries. Anyone can buy these shares, or stocks. When you buy some stock in a business, it means you own a part of it—usually a very small part. If you want to own a larger part of the business you have to invest more of your money in it.

*Do you, or does anyone in your family, own stock in a business? Why was it bought?*

Raw materials, good transportation, skilled workers, and business people made the United States a great industrial nation. Together, they have led to record-breaking industrial production.

American industry has built millions of homes, schools, and buildings. It has produced the food, the clothing, and the shelter we need for our daily lives. American industry has created jobs for workers and profits for those who invest their money in business. It has given the American people the highest standard of living in the world. American industry also helps to keep our country strong.

It has been said that Americans take for granted many things that other people only dream about. *What does this mean? Can you give an example?*

| THIS CHART SHOWS HOW PRODUCTION ROSE IN SEVEN IMPORTANT INDUSTRIES. | | | |
|---|---|---|---|
| | **1895** | **1955** | **1979** |
| COAL (Million Tons) | 135 | 500 | 776 |
| STEEL (Million Tons) | 13 | 126 | 136 |
| OIL (Million Barrels) | 53 | 2,500 | 3,108 |
| AUTOMOBILES (Millions) | — | 8 | 11⅓ |
| RADIOS (Millions) | — | 14½ | 40 |
| TELEVISION (Millions) | — | 7½ | 16½ |
| LEATHER SHOES (Million Pairs) | — | 293 | 357 |

# What raw materials does the United States possess?

The chart below shows the leading nations of the world in eight main industries. *What does the chart tell us about the United States?*

Do you know why the United States is a great industrial nation? The answer is a combination of things. The United States has plentiful raw materials, good transportation, and skilled workers. It also has business people willing to invest their money, or capital.

The United States is rich in such raw materials as iron ore, coal, oil, and copper. The map shows where these raw materials are located in the United States.

Raw materials will not guarantee a nation's industrial growth. The materials must be brought together in mills and factories. For example, iron ore and coal are needed to make steel.

## LEADING PRODUCERS AMONG NATIONS IN 1979

|  | 1ST | 2ND | 3RD | 4TH |
|---|---|---|---|---|
| COAL | SOVIET RUSSIA | U.S. | POLAND | UNITED KINGDOM |
| IRON ORE | SOVIET RUSSIA | U.S. | AUSTRALIA | CANADA |
| LEAD ORE | U.S. | AUSTRALIA | CANADA | MEXICO |
| ZINC ORE | CANADA | AUSTRALIA | U.S. | JAPAN |
| OIL | SOVIET RUSSIA | SAUDI ARABIA | U.S. | IRAQ |
| NATURAL GAS | U.S. | SOVIET RUSSIA | CANADA | ROMANIA |
| COPPER | U.S. | CHILE | ZAMBIA | CANADA |
| CARS AND TRUCKS | U.S. | JAPAN | WEST GERMANY | FRANCE |

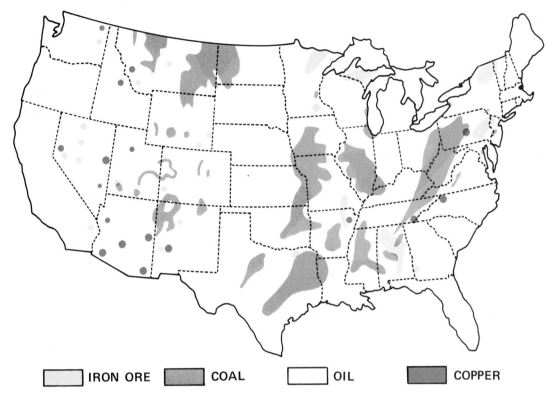

| IRON ORE | COAL | OIL | COPPER |

American coal deposits are in the East and the iron ore is in the Midwest. The American transportation system of barges, ships, and railroads brings the iron and coal to the steel mills. There skilled workmen use the iron and coal to make steel.

America's factories need skilled workers to run the machines. They also need trained managers to direct the work. The United States has a good supply of skilled workers and managers. This helps to make the United States an industrial nation.

# ANDREW CARNEGIE

Andrew Carnegie was born in Scotland in 1835. His parents were hard-working cloth weavers. In 1848 he and his family moved to the United States. They had to borrow money to pay the fare, but they hoped to find jobs soon. A relative had promised to help them when they came to America.

Young Andrew was only thirteen when he left Scotland. His family had been very poor. They often had little to eat. He made up his mind he would change all that in America. He would work hard and become a success.

Andrew's first job was in a cotton factory. It paid only $1.20 a week. He later worked for a railroad as a telegraph operator. His good work won the attention of the managers and he was promoted. Meanwhile, Andrew was saving his money and investing it in new companies. His investments brought huge profits. Before long, he was a wealthy man.

In 1864 Carnegie, then only about thirty, went into business for himself. He manufactured rails, axles, and iron bridges. This business brought him greater wealth than before. But this was not enough for him. He also believed that steel was better than iron. Steel is strong, flexible, and does not crack in cold weather. Carnegie felt it was the product of the future. He decided to enter the steel business with his profits.

Carnegie visited London in 1872 to study the latest steel making methods. When he returned, he formed the Carnegie Steel Corporation. It became the largest producer of steel in the world. In 1901 he sold his company to the newly formed United States Steel Corporation. He was paid 400 million dollars in cash for his company. There were no federal taxes at the time. That meant Carnegie kept every dollar he was paid. He became one of the richest men in the world.

During the last eighteen years of his life, Carnegie gave away many of his millions. His idea was that people who made money ought to use it to help others. "To die rich is to die

disgraced," he would say. This belief led him to give millions to build almost 3,000 public libraries in the United States. He gave millions more to help support education in American schools. It was his way of thanking the nation which made him a millionaire industrialist.

# GEORGE WESTINGHOUSE

George Westinghouse was one of the greatest American inventors and industrialists. He was born in 1846, and served as a Union soldier in the Civil War. After the war, he worked in his father's agricultural tool shop. He often tinkered with engines. When Westinghouse was twenty, he had patented several inventions for an improved steam engine. In 1869 he patented his greatest invention. It was the first air-brake for trains. His brake system used air pressure to stop railroad cars swiftly and smoothly. It is still in use today.

Westinghouse next turned to the use of electricity to bring greater safety to the railroads. One of his inventions was an electric signal system. It helped railroad engineers adjust their speed and warned them of dangers ahead. Westinghouse also developed some other important industrial devices. One

of these made it possible to send natural gas over long distances through pipe lines.

Westinghouse became a very rich man, but he did not stop working. He grew interested in electricity again and this led to new inventions. These included a trolley car motor, electrical brakes for subway cars, and shock absorbers. He also invented special steam turbines for producing electricity for ships.

At the time of his death in 1914, he held patents on more than 400 inventions. He was one of the founders of the Westinghouse Electric Company. It was one of the giants of American industry. George Westinghouse's work was an important part of the great Industrial Revolution after 1870.

## LEARNING EXERCISES

### I. Remembering What We Have Read

1. Andrew Carnegie was
   a. an inventor.
   b. a scientist.
   c. an industrialist.
   d. all of the above.

2. The person best known as an electrical scientist was
   a. Neil Armstrong.
   b. Hetty Green.
   c. Andrew Carnegie.
   d. Charles Steinmetz.

### II. Thinking About Products

Three important raw products of the United States are shown in the pictures below. Each picture has a letter.
Answer these questions. The answers are not in the book.

1. Which product is used to make steel?
2. Which product is used to make pipes and tubing?
3. Which product is used to make gasoline?

A. Copper

B. Iron

C. Oil

### III. Learning From Headlines

What is the story behind each of the following headlines?

**WIZARD OF
SCHENECTADY HONORED**

**CURE FOR DEADLY
CHILDHOOD DESEASES**

**GIANT LEAP
FOR MANKIND**

# How have artists made the United States a great nation?

In 1820, an Englishman asked, "Who reads an American book?" He was poking fun at Americans by saying they had no important authors. Americans were supposed to be too busy building their farms and cities to write books.

That Englishman was very wrong. There were Americans writing books in 1820. Before long, Englishmen were reading and enjoying those books. One American writer of the 1820s was James Fenimore Cooper. His book *The Last of the Mohicans* is still widely read today. Many other Americans were also just starting to write books and poems. Among the most popular was Washington Irving. He wrote about Rip Van Winkle and Ichabod Crane.

By 1900 America had hundreds of well-known writers. One of the best loved was Samuel Clemens, or Mark Twain. He wrote *Tom Sawyer* and *The Adventures of Huckleberry Finn.* These are two books young people still read and enjoy. The stories have also been shown on television.

The man who poked fun at the American writers in 1820 would not do so today. The United States is not only rich in giant industries, but also rich in great artists. American books, paintings, and music are known and respected all over the world.

The music known as jazz and blues was created by black Americans. Today it is heard throughout the world. American songwriters, such as Stephen Foster, Scott Joplin, and Richard Rodgers, are also well known. The American people have also shown their love for classical music. Many American cities have their own orchestras giving concerts of classical music. The Metropolitan Opera House is in New York. It is one of the world's outstanding and beautiful opera houses.

There are art galleries and museums in all parts of the United States. They exhibit the works of American artists as well as foreign artists.

What do these writers, artists, and musicians tell us about the United States? They tell us that there is more to this country than rich farmlands, giant industries, and superhighways. They tell us that Americans have the ability to see and love the world about them. In bringing this message, the artists have helped make the United States a great and cultured nation.

# MARK TWAIN

Samuel Langhorne Clemens was born in 1835 in Hannibal, Missouri. His boyhood was a happy one. With his friends he went barefoot and roamed the woods. They fished and swam in the nearby Mississippi River.

Sam Clemens and his friends often played at being pirates. They explored the nearby caves and searched for buried treasure. But every river boy's dream in the 1840s was to become a river-boat pilot. Sam Clemens was one of the few whose dream came true. He actually did become a river-boat pilot when he was twenty-one.

When the Civil War cut off river traffic, Sam Clemens left for Nevada. There he took a job with a newspaper. Though he had little schooling, he showed skill as a writer. Before long his articles, written under the name of Mark Twain, were well known. He moved to San Francisco and became a full-time writer.

Samuel Clemens, now known as Mark Twain, wrote about his memories of boyhood. And, of course, he wrote about the river. In fact, the words "Mark Twain" came from the river. It was the signal that was called by crewmen to the pilot. It told the pilot the water was deep enough for safe passage. This and other facts about river-boat life were told in one of his books called *Life on the Mississippi.*

Today Mark Twain is best known for his stories about Tom Sawyer and Huckleberry Finn. No doubt, Tom Sawyer is the kind of boy Sam Clemens was. The happy, lovable, dirty Huckleberry Finn may have been Samuel Clemens' boyhood friend, Tom Blankenship. *The Adventures of Huckleberry Finn* is considered one of the greatest American books ever written.

In spite of his success, Mark Twain was often in debt. For several years he traveled to many parts of the world giving lectures. He was a popular speaker and made enough money to pay off his debts. His sense of humor won him friends everywhere. He became so well known that letters addressed to "Mark Twain, America" were delivered to him by the post office.

# ROBERT FROST

On January 21, 1961, John F. Kennedy was to be sworn in as President of the United States. Thousands of people came to Washington, D.C. They wanted to see the ceremony in spite of the bitter cold. Millions of others watched on television. One of the honored guests was Robert Frost, the country's oldest poet. The eighty-seven-year-old Frost had been invited to recite his patriotic poem, "The Gift Outright."

Frost had a surprise for the new President. He had written a new poem for this special occasion. He did not know the words from memory and had written them on a piece of paper. When it was his turn to speak, he began to read. The bitter cold and strong wind made it hard for him to continue. The glare of the sun kept him from seeing what he had written. His voice hesitated and his hands trembled. The spectators and television viewers felt anxious for this nervous old man. Suddenly, Frost gave up trying to read his new poem. He stuffed the paper back into his pocket, lifted his head, and recited from memory his old poem "The Gift Outright."

> "The land was ours before we
>   were the land's.
> She was our land more than a
>   hundred years.
> Before we were her people.
> She was ours in Massachusetts,
>   in Virginia,
> But we were England's still
>   colonials. . ."

These words were the beginning of the poem. They thrilled those who watched in person or on television. People felt pride in their country and in the courage of this gentle, old poet. But many who saw and heard him that day knew little about Robert Frost.

Like many other poets, success did not come easy to Frost. He lost his father at the age of ten and had to support himself through high school. He worked on a nearby farm and in a shoemaker's shop. Whenever he could, he loved to walk through the New England countryside. The young man would observe the trees, flowers, and the beautiful scenery. Many of his poems told about the New England countryside. In later life he was known as the Poet of New England.

Frost grew up, married, bought a farm, and taught school. He continued to write poetry, but was discouraged. Nobody cared for his poems or wanted to publish them. At the age of thirty-eight, Frost and his family moved to England. There he became friends with many of the British poets. A British publisher printed a book of his poems about New England. It was a great success and he became known in Britain as an outstanding American poet.

After three years in England, he returned to the United States. By this time he was famous in his own country. He gave lectures, read his poems, and taught at different colleges. Frost traveled to many parts of the world. He was received everywhere with honors, and invited to read his poems to large audiences.

Although most of Frost's poetry was serious, he also had a sense of humor. This was shown in his poem "The Hardship of Accounting."

> "Never ask of money spent
> Where the spender thinks it went
> Nobody was ever meant
> To remember or invent
> What he did with every cent."

Everyone, young or old, who has ever wondered how he spent his money can understand what Robert Frost was saying.

# LANGSTON HUGHES

"The night is beautiful
So the faces of my people
The stars are beautiful
So the eyes of my people
Beautiful, also, is the sun
Beautiful, also, are the souls of
  my people"
(from the poem "My People" by
  Langston Hughes)

Some poets look at nature. They write about the flowers, birds, or the stars in the sky. Other poets look at the people about them, and the lives they lead. These poets try to tell about the lives of the people. Langston Hughes was such a poet—a poet who wrote about people.

As a black man, he recorded his feelings and the feelings of black people. He wrote about the problem of living in a world where white people and black people do not always understand each other. Langston Hughes filled his pages with the story of black people. He told their story to all Americans, and to people in many parts of the world. He came to be considered the voice of the black people of America.

Langston Hughes was born in Missouri in 1902. He died in New York City in 1967. As a baby, he was raised by a grandmother in Kansas. She told young Langston many stories

Moscow. He was also a teacher at Atlanta University.

Langston Hughes started to write poetry when he was very young. From the start, his poetry dealt with the lives of black people. He wrote about their sorrows and problems, but also described their humor and love of life. In addition to poems, he wrote novels, histories, biographies, plays, and songs. In later years, he wrote many books for young readers. These books were about black heroes, musicians, jazz music, and Africa.

Langston Hughes wanted to tell of the sense of pride among black people. They had risen above slavery and hard times. All of this had given them the strength to go on and try to improve their lives. Langston Hughes thought of this when he wrote "My soul has grown deep like the rivers."

about freedom and slavery. The stories were filled with the names of black leaders such as Frederick Douglass and Harriet Tubman. He never forgot those stories.

Young Langston began attending school in Kansas. He was a good student and loved to read books. He later moved to Cleveland where he finished high school. He then attended college, but looked for his education in many places besides college. He lived in New York's Harlem area, in Mexico, Spain, Africa, and Moscow. To support himself, he took many jobs. These included dishwasher, cabin boy on a freighter, and movie maker in

# GEORGIA O'KEEFFE

Georgia O'Keeffe was born in Wisconsin in 1887. As a young person she showed great artistic talent. But there seemed to be little future in the United States for artists. There was even less future for women artists. In spite of this, Georgia O'Keeffe studied and taught art in Chicago, Texas, and New York.

Few of the art galleries were willing to show paintings by a woman artist. However, Georgia's charcoal drawings caught the attention of Alfred Stieglitz. He was a photographer and art gallery owner. Stieglitz exhibited the work of Georgia O'Keeffe in 1918. This helped to advance her career. Eight years later Stieglitz and Georgia O'Keeffe were married.

After 1920 Georgia O'Keeffe's work drew attention in all parts of the world. She was famous for her landscapes, desert scenes, and flower studies. Her art has been described as modern and American.

Today Georgia O'Keeffe is recognized as one of the great American artists. Her work is exhibited in the great museums and galleries of the world.

# JOHN PHILIP SOUSA
## "The March King"

On May 24, 1865, young John Philip Sousa saw and heard something that turned him ever afterward toward marching music. That day the eleven-year-old boy and his father watched the Grand Review of the Union Army in Washington, D.C. The parade was in honor of the army that had just won the Civil War. Young John never forgot the excitement and the thrill of thousands of marching men. He always remembered the many marching bands of the victorious regiments.

Two years later Sousa studied in the United States Marine Band. He was only thirteen years old when he became a Marine bandsman. Sousa remained with the Marine Band for eight years. He left it in 1875, but returned as director of the Marine Band in 1880.

Sousa made the Marine Band an outstanding musical group. He wrote his first marches for their concerts. The march "Semper Fidelis" (Ever Faithful) took the slogan of the Marine Corps and made it into a stirring march. He followed this by "The Washington Post March" in honor of a Washington, D.C. newspaper. It became a popular march and dance number. In 1892 Sousa left the Marine Corps and formed his own band. He called it the New Marine Band and made it world famous. Sousa wrote many new marches including "El Capitan" and "Stars and Stripes Forever."

When Sousa died in 1932, many new styles of music were being played in the United States. In spite of these changes, his marching music never lost its popularity. To this day John Philip Sousa remains the March King and all the world is familiar with the music he wrote.

# HELEN HAYES

## "First Lady of the Theater"

In 1955 the Fulton Theater in New York was renamed the Helen Hayes Theater. Having a theater named for you is a great honor for an actor or actress. No one doubts that Helen Hayes deserved that honor.

Helen Hayes Brown was born in Washington, D.C. in 1900. In later years she dropped her last name and used the stage name of Helen Hayes. She was only five years old when she went on stage, playing the part of a boy. At the age of eight she came to New York with her mother. Mrs. Brown was determined to make young Helen a star, and she succeeded.

At fourteen, Helen Hayes played opposite John Drew. He was one of the great actors of the time. When Helen was eighteen, she was called the greatest young actress of her age. From then on, success followed after success. Her best-known role was that of Queen Victoria of England. She played the queen as both a young girl and an old woman. The play ran on Broadway for three years and brought her worldwide fame.

Helen Hayes went on to perform in movies, radio, and TV. She was a "hit" in all of these. But she was more than a great actress. Busy as she was, she found time to help other actors and actresses. She also worked to get the government to help actors, dancers, and painters. Her whole life was devoted to bringing better art and better theater to the American people. No wonder she had become known to Americans as the first lady of the theater.

# LEARNING EXERCISES

## I. Remembering What We Have Read

Pick the best answer.

1. James Fenimore Cooper was a famed
   a. scientist.
   b. writer.
   c. inventor.
   d. musician.
2. The person whose name is best known to theatergoers is
   a. James Fenimore Cooper.
   b. Samuel Clemens.
   c. Georgia O'Keeffe.
   d. Helen Hayes.
3. Two famed American poets were
   a. Georgia O'Keeffe and Robert Frost.
   b. Washington Irving and Samuel Clemens.
   c. Robert Frost and Langston Hughes.
   d. Washington Irving and Langston Hughes.
4. The character Huckleberry Finn was created by
   a. Robert Frost.
   b. Samuel Clemens.
   c. James Fenimore Cooper.
   d. Washington Irving.

## II. Thinking About Things

What is your opinion in these matters?

1. Is the space program worth the billions of dollars it costs the American people?
2. Would you rather be a scientist, a writer, an actor or actress, or an industrialist? What are your reasons?
3. If you could invent one thing, what would it be?

# LEARNING EXERCISES

## III. Reviewing People and Events

How well do you remember the people and events appearing in this unit?

Below are the names of five people listed in Column A. Next to these names are five events listed in Column B.

On a separate sheet of paper, match the events in Column B with the names that are in Column A.

COLUMN A
People
1. Orville Wright

2. Alexander Graham Bell

3. Harry S. Truman

4. Mark Twain

COLUMN B
Events
a. First practical telephone is shown in public.
b. *Tom Sawyer* is a best-selling book.
c. An airplane makes its first flight.
d. President orders use of the atom bomb.

## IV. Reviewing the Meaning of Graphs

How well do you remember the story that graphs can tell? Below are two graphs used in this unit. What story does each of these graphs tell you?

### LEADING PRODUCERS AMONG NATIONS IN 1979

|  | 1ST | 2ND | 3RD | 4TH |
|---|---|---|---|---|
| COAL | SOVIET RUSSIA | U.S. | POLAND | UNITED KINGDOM |
| IRON ORE | SOVIET RUSSIA | U.S. | AUSTRALIA | CANADA |
| LEAD ORE | U.S. | AUSTRALIA | CANADA | MEXICO |
| ZINC ORE | CANADA | AUSTRALIA | U.S. | JAPAN |
| OIL | SOVIET RUSSIA | SAUDI ARABIA | U.S. | IRAQ |
| NATURAL GAS | U.S. | SOVIET RUSSIA | CANADA | ROMANIA |
| COPPER | U.S. | CHILE | ZAMBIA | CANADA |
| CARS AND TRUCKS | U.S. | JAPAN | WEST GERMANY | FRANCE |

### THIS CHART SHOWS HOW PRODUCTION ROSE IN SEVEN IMPORTANT INDUSTRIES.

|  | 1895 | 1955 | 1979 |
|---|---|---|---|
| COAL (Million Tons) | 135 | 500 | 776 |
| STEEL (Million Tons) | 13 | 126 | 136 |
| OIL (Million Barrels) | 53 | 2,500 | 3,108 |
| AUTOMOBILES (Millions) | — | 8 | 11½ |
| RADIOS (Millions) | — | 14½ | 40 |
| TELEVISION (Millions) | — | 7½ | 16½ |
| LEATHER SHOES (Million Pairs) | — | 293 | 357 |

326

# AMERICANS LOOK TO THE FUTURE

# CONTENTS ☆ ☆ ☆ ☆ ☆ ☆ ☆ ☆ ☆ ☆ ☆ ☆ ☆ ☆ ☆ ☆

☆ ☆ ☆ ☆ ☆ ☆ ☆ ☆ ☆ ☆ ☆ ☆ ☆ ☆ ☆ ☆ ☆ ☆ ☆

**UNIT 7**

☆ ☆ ☆ ☆ ☆ ☆ ☆ ☆ ☆ ☆ ☆ ☆ ☆ ☆ ☆ ☆

☆ ☆ ☆ ☆ ☆ ☆ ☆ ☆ ☆ ☆ ☆ ☆ ☆ ☆ ☆ ☆ ☆ ☆ ☆ ☆ ☆

# What is the United States doing for world peace?

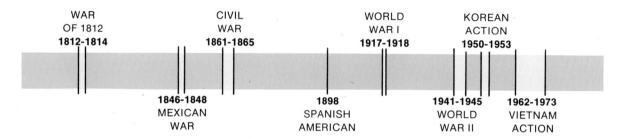

WAR OF 1812
1812-1814

CIVIL WAR
1861-1865

WORLD WAR I
1917-1918

KOREAN ACTION
1950-1953

1846-1848 MEXICAN WAR

1898 SPANISH AMERICAN

1941-1945 WORLD WAR II

1962-1973 VIETNAM ACTION

The time line tells a sad story. It is the story of the major wars fought by the United States.

Since the end of World War II in 1945 there have been several small wars. At times the world was close to some big wars. The United States and the Soviet Union were allies in World War II, but came close to war soon afterward. The United States felt the Soviet Union wanted to force communism on other countries. The Soviet Union felt the United States wanted to destroy communism. Each side stored atomic bombs and missiles to scare the other side. But the Soviet Union and the United States were also anxious to avoid an open war.

In our modern world there will probably be no real winners in an atomic war. Atomic fallout of deadly rays could kill off the winners as well as the losers. Even neutral nations, hundreds of miles from the bombings, might be destroyed by atomic fallout. The United States and other nations know this. One way to prevent future wars is to settle disputes between different nations. It is especially important for the United States and the Soviet Union to live in peace.

In 1972 the United States and the Soviet Union signed an important agreement. It was the first step seeking to limit their atomic weapons. This could lead to further agreement in the future. But the Soviet move into Afghanistan in 1979 hurt Soviet-American relations. New disputes are likely to arise.

The United States is now trying to improve relations with the People's

Republic of China. In 1949 the Communist forces of China won control of that country. During the next twenty-five years there was often danger of war between China and the United States. Chinese troops and American soldiers actually fought each other during the conflict in Korea.

In 1964 China produced its first atomic bomb. At the same time, the Chinese began to have serious disputes with the Soviet Union. The United States felt that both these actions might be a threat to world peace. Action had to be taken to avoid any chance of war. As a result, the United States reexamined its relations with the People's Republic of China.

The United States had refused to recognize the People's Republic of China since 1949. This led to bad relations between the two countries. It had also kept the People's Republic of China out of the United Nations. In 1972 the United States took steps to improve relations with China. The People's Republic of China was admitted to the United Nations with the support of the United States. Next, President Nixon visited China. Both actions helped to bring the two nations closer and to lessen the dangers of war. In 1978 the United States recognized the People's Republic of China. It was hoped that normal relations between the two nations would improve the chances for world peace.

# Why is housing a problem in the United States?

The United States has faced a serious housing problem for the past thirty-five years. The lack of good housing has grown worse each year. This is especially true in the inner city areas of New York, Chicago, and other large cities.

One of the reasons for the housing problem has been the growth in population in the United States. In 1940 there were 130 million people in the United States. That number rose to 180 million by 1960. Today there are about 225 million people living in the United States. Population growth has helped make the housing situation worse.

Many problems have also arisen because of the rising cost of homes. Inflation and the cost of labor and materials have made it difficult for many people to buy their own homes. At the same time, there has been a rise in the cost of borrowing money. People who want to borrow money to buy a home must pay higher rates of interest to the banks.

Lack of good housing remains a serious problem in the United States. Efforts to clear up this problem have not been successful up to the present time. It remains to be seen if the United States will be more successful in the future.

# Why is transportation a problem in the United States?

The United States is an urban industrial nation. Transportation is important to its daily life. This includes local transportation as well as long-distance forms of transportation.

There are two main forms of transportation in use. Individual transportation means moving a single person or small groups of people from one place to another. The automobile is the main form of individual transportation used in the United States. Today it is the most commonly used method of transportation for most American people.

Mass transportation means moving great numbers of people. Buses and railroads are forms of mass transportation. During the past twenty-five years mass transportation has lost out to the use of automobiles by many people.

The problem of transportation has worsened in recent years. Part of this is because of the breakdown of the mass transportation systems that once existed. Many railroad lines no longer carry passenger cars or offer commuter services. The high cost of fuel and the many fuel shortages have worsened transportation problems. The United States is now trying to develop greater use of buses and railroads by the people. This can only be done if costs are kept reasonable. But people must also want to use mass transportation in place of the automobile wherever possible. The future will decide if this happens.

# What are some problems of American working people?

American working people have the highest living standard in the world. In spite of this, American workers face many problems. These include wages, work conditions, job security, and old age security.

The wages of American workers have risen steadily during the past forty years. Your grandparents probably worked for as little as twenty dollars a week. Today the average American worker earns nearly eight times more. But many workers still feel they are not earning a living wage. This is because of the rising cost of food, rent, and clothing. Workers feel they must get higher wages to support their families.

Work conditions today are much improved over those of earlier times. People used to work under dangerous conditions in firetraps and dreary "sweatshops." Many bad conditions have now been corrected, but some still remain. The safety and health of workers often depend on the work conditions in the shop or factory.

Job security has become an important demand of American workers. They want to feel that there will always be work for them if they want it. Many workers fear that new machines will take the place of workers. It has been said that about 400,000 jobs disappear each year because of new machines. Of course, many of those who lose their jobs will find other jobs. Some will work at jobs created by the new machines. However, this could take time. Workers fear they will be left without jobs or wages for weeks or months.

Old age security is one of the great concerns of working people. This is especially true if workers must support a family on low-paying jobs. Often they do not earn enough to save for their old age, when they can no longer work. Moreover, the costs of illness can use up an elderly person's savings. Most workers are proud and do not want to depend on charity in their old age. They want a way to be found to provide security for older people who have retired.

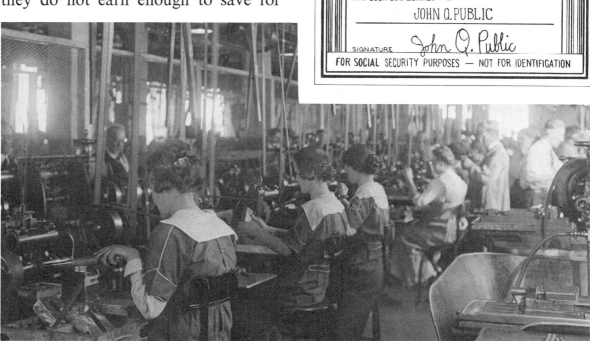

SOCIAL SECURITY

ACCOUNT NUMBER

000-00-0000

HAS BEEN ESTABLISHED FOR

JOHN Q. PUBLIC

SIGNATURE John Q. Public

FOR SOCIAL SECURITY PURPOSES — NOT FOR IDENTIFICATION

# How are the government, business, and unions helping working people?

The government, private business, and labor unions all help American workers. They do not always agree with one another. However, they all have something to contribute.

All three groups have helped wages to rise steadily. In addition, business people have developed many new products and industries. This has helped to provide jobs and wages for American workers. In many cases businesses have raised wages in order to attract workers to the industries. At other times, wages have risen because of action taken by the government and by labor unions.

The United States government has helped workers by passing a national minimum wage law. The minimum wage is the least amount that can be paid to workers in many industries. The first wages and hours law was passed in 1938. It set the minimum wage at forty cents an hour for a forty-hour week. Some people feared this would ruin the country, but they were wrong. Since then the wages and hours law has been changed many times. By 1981 the minimum wage was $3.35 an hour. Minimum wages have helped to raise all wage levels.

Labor unions helped to get the

wages and hours laws passed. But the minimum wage is only the least amount that can be paid. Workers may need much more than that to support their families. For this reason, labor unions have tried to win higher wages for workers. However, the problem of higher wages is part of the problem of inflation. Inflation leads workers to demand higher wages, but higher wages can also be one of the causes of inflation.

Working conditions are as important to many workers as wages. There has been general agreement about the need to improve working conditions. Many business people understand that good working conditions bring higher production. At the same time, local and state government officials help to improve work conditions. They do this by checking on work conditions in shops and factories. Unions also check to make sure that safety rules are enforced. They also see that work areas are clean, well lighted, and either properly cooled or heated at all times.

# How have American workers gained greater security?

Job security remains a problem for many workers. There are many times when a business is forced to close down. This means many workers lose their jobs. At other times, the use of machines means fewer workers are needed. This usually means that the last people to take jobs in the factory are now the first to be fired. Such a system gives job security only to some of the workers. It often means that minorities and women are the first to lose their jobs.

Many labor unions have been trying to win greater job security for all people. They want the government to guarantee that every worker who is willing to work will have a guaranteed income. When a person is out of work, the government will try to help that person find a job. If there are no jobs, the government will pay such people wages as if they were working. This would provide security for those workers who are without jobs through no fault of their own.

The idea of a guaranteed income is still new to most people. It is not yet popular with many Americans. They fear a guaranteed income would be expensive. It might lead to some people not wanting to work.

There is some security for workers in a federal insurance-type plan. This plan is called Social Security. Since

1935 it has provided for payments for the unemployed, the disabled, and the elderly in the United States.

Unemployment insurance is not a form of charity. It is a worker benefit and it is paid for by a tax on wages. This tax is paid by the employer, or boss, just as if it were wages to the worker. The payments are made to the federal government, which gives money to the states for unemployment insurance. Workers who lose their jobs apply for unemployment insurance from the state unemployment insurance offices.

The insurance system for the disabled and elderly is also based on the tax on wages. Workers and their employers pay for this tax. When workers are hurt or disabled so that they can no longer work, they can receive payments from Social Security.

There is also a plan to give security to older workers. They can now retire at age sixty-two. These workers receive benefits from Social Security for the rest of their lives. The amount they receive will depend on how much they have paid to the retirement fund by their Social Security tax payments.

In 1965 the Social Security system added medical insurance for older people. This system of care is known as Medicare. It helps provide security for

older people against the high cost of doctors and medicines.

# LEARNING EXERCISES

## I. Remembering What We Have Read

Pick the best answer.

1. The problems of housing have been made worse by
   a. high labor costs.
   b. inflation.
   c. high rates of interest.
   d. all of the above.
2. American workers today have all the following **except**
   a. minimum wage laws.
   b. social security.
   c. old age pensions.
   d. guaranteed income.
3. Medicare is concerned with
   a. job security for older people.
   b. insurance for the disabled.
   c. security against medical costs for older people.
   d. unemployment insurance for older workers.
4. "Fallout" is a term connected with
   a. pollution control.
   b. schools.
   c. medical care.
   d. atomic explosions.

## II. Thinking About Things

Can you guess the answers to these questions? The answers are not in the book.

1. Do you think it will ever be possible to wipe out race prejudice?
2. It has been said that there is less chance of atomic war because all the big powers have the atomic bomb. Do you agree?

## III. Learning From Pictures

Each of the pictures tells us something about life in the United States. What does each picture mean to you?

1.

2.

## IV. Learning From Headlines

What might be the story behind each of the headlines below?

**SHORTAGE OF ELECTRICITY FEARED**

**MORE COPS NEEDED FOR INNER CITY**

**PRESIDENT ASKS PEOPLE TO DRIVE LESS**

**PRESIDENT VISITS AT GREAT WALL**

# Why are race relations a problem in the United States?

There are more than 225 million people living in the United States. They come from many different lands and belong to many different races. When we speak of races, we usually mean light-skinned people, black-skinned people, and people with yellow skins or brown skins. All these people have different skin colors, but they are not really different as people. Race and skin color have nothing to do with brains or ability. There are wise men and fools in all races.

The great majority of Americans are light-skinned, or white people. Nearly nine of every ten Americans are light skinned. The next largest group is the Negroes or blacks. One of every ten Americans is black. Fewer than two Americans of every one hundred is an Indian, Asian-American, or Latin American. These may seem to be small numbers of people. However they add up to over 22 million blacks, one million Mexican-Americans, one million Puerto Ricans, and about 600,000 Indians. There are also a total of nearly one million Japanese-Americans, Chinese-Americans, and Filipino-Americans.

All of these nonwhite people are minority groups in the United States. The majority group is made up of white people. Most of the minority

groups suffer from some form of race discrimination. This means they often have difficulty in finding good jobs, decent housing, and a good education. As a result, they are more likely to be poor than people who belong to the majority group.

Race discrimination is the result of prejudice. Some Americans believe they are better than the racial minorities. This idea developed more than one hundred years ago when black people were slaves in the United States. Racial prejudice did not die out when slavery ended. It is still a great problem in the United States to this day.

Prejudice and discrimination cause anger and bad feeling. Race prejudice is one of the most serious problems facing the United States. In a sense, it

has divided the country into two groups. Race prejudice does great harm to nonwhites—the black people, Indians, Asian-Americans, and Latin Americans. At the same time it also harms the white people who make up the great majority of Americans. Prejudice causes many American people to fear their neighbors and to doubt themselves. The United States is based on the idea that appears in the Pledge of Allegiance—"one nation, under God, indivisible, with liberty and justice for all." That idea cannot live side by side with race prejudice.

# How are Americans trying to improve race relations?

Most Americans understand that race prejudice is a serious problem. However, improving race relations is not easy. It took many years for Americans to admit that there was a problem. Now they are trying to decide which are the best means for dealing with it.

One hundred years ago most white Americans accepted race prejudice. It was a part of their daily lives. They thought of it as a natural thing that was neither good nor bad. White Americans believed they were better than Indians, blacks, or Asian-Americans. Such racist thinking went side by side with distrust of Catholics, Jews, and nearly all foreigners. Racist ideas were to be found in the newspapers, theaters, schools, and in the home. The idea of people being truly equal was not accepted in spite of the fine words in the Declaration of Independence.

Much of this has now changed. Today the American people are very much aware of racial problems. They know that Indians have been badly mistreated in the past and that some are still being mistreated. Most Americans also know that minority groups suffer from prejudice and discrimination. There is still much racism and prejudice in the United States, but much has been done to end them.

Americans are now more aware of the need for action to improve race relations. Many laws have been passed to stop discrimination in housing and employment. Such laws make it possible for minority groups to get better jobs and live in better homes. Slums are being replaced by large, modern apartment houses. Poor people can rent apartments in these newly built houses for very little money.

Trade unions have sometimes been a problem for blacks and other minorities. The unions have helped win job security and higher wages for many workers. This has often helped black people, but it has also hurt some of them. The unions have sometimes kept black people from joining as members. At times, the union rules meant that black people who were the last to be hired would be the first to be fired. Much of this has changed during the last few years. Today many unions are helping to provide jobs for blacks and the other minority groups. The union rules are being changed in many places. Many now provide greater job security for blacks and other minorities.

Education is also helping to improve race relations. More opportunities are being provided for racial minorities to attend good schools. Special programs have been developed to help them go on to college. Steps are also being taken to teach all pupils the dangers of racism. The textbooks used today give more information about blacks, Indians, Asian-Americans, and Latin Americans. In this way, these people learn about themselves and take pride in their history. At the same time, many white pupils can learn the contributions of other racial groups.

Racism remains a dangerous and evil part of American life today. It is not easily removed from our thoughts and actions. American people are learning to act against such things as prejudice and discrimination. But all of us still have to guard against the racism that is part of our world. We may not always be able to remove it completely from our thoughts. However, our awareness of racism will help reduce the damage it does.

# Why is ecology important to Americans?

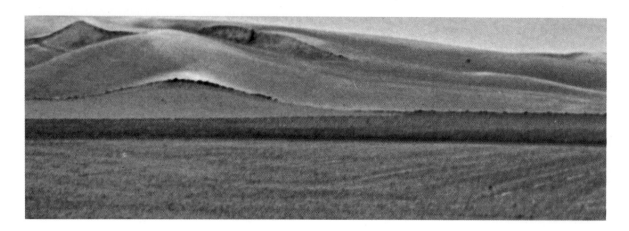

Ecology is an important science. It studies how plants, birds, animals, fish, and the environment affect each other. Each of these things depends upon the others. If they are not in balance, life on earth can be in danger. How can this happen? Let's take a simple example:

Animals depend on plants for food. Plants depend on water and air in the environment for their growth. If water and air become polluted, plants will die. This can mean that animals will not get the food they need. Animal life might then suffer or die out for lack of food. Somehow, there must be a proper balance between what plants and animals need and the environment supplying those needs. This balance of nature can be thrown off balance. It can happen if too many animals are killed, if too many forests are destroyed, or if the water and air we use are polluted.

Americans have not paid much attention to ecology in the past. They allowed their forests to be cut down

carelessly. This left many animals without shelter or food. Rivers and lakes were polluted by factory chemicals and sewage wastes. This resulted in the killing off of fish and other forms of marine, or water life.

Sometimes science has helped to upset the balance of nature. Many poisonous sprays were developed by scientists. These sprays killed insects and pests on crops. The crops were kept free of these insects, but the result was not always all good. Insects and worms that ate the crops became poisoned. They, in turn, poisoned the birds and animals that ate them. Sometimes the sprays remained in the crops. They poisoned the animals and people eating them. In addition, some of the poison spray was washed by rainwater into nearby streams. The poison polluted the waters and killed the fish in them.

Today Americans are aware of the importance of ecology. Unless we keep the balance of nature, we may be endangering life on earth.

# Why is conservation important to the United States?

The United States is rich in human resources and natural resources. Its human resources are the people of this country. Their energy and intelligence are important to the United States. Our natural resources include iron, coal, oil, forests, soil, water, and air. Americans use these resources every day. Without them the United States would be a very poor country.

Resources can be damaged or used up. That is why the conservation of resources is so important. Conservation means the protection

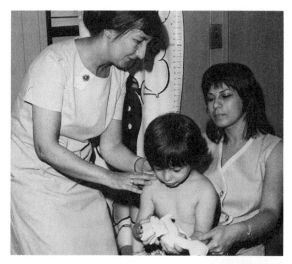

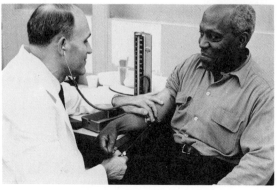

and wise use of all resources. It helps make sure there will still be enough resources for future use.

The conservation of human resources means care for the health and safety of people. It also means providing a good education for young Americans. Young people will someday take the place of their elders as leaders. They must be healthy and well-educated if the United States is to remain a good place to live. Everyone agrees about the need to conserve human resources. Of course, not everyone is ready to pay the costs involved. Health programs, schools, and libraries can be expensive. This has sometimes kept Americans from doing more for the conservation of human resources. But, in general, the United States has done much in this area of conservation.

The natural resources of the United States were once believed to be limitless. Americans thought their

forests, minerals, soil, and waters would last forever. Today we know better. The natural resources of any country are limited. If they are used carelessly, they may disappear at some future date. That is why the conservation of natural resources is almost a matter of life and death for the United States.

There are two types of natural resources. The first one is called a renewable resource. This means it can be used many times if it is used properly. Forests are one example of a renewable resource. A forest can be re-grown after its trees have been cut. Air, water, and soil are other examples of renewable resources. They can be used over and over again if they are not spoiled or polluted.

The second type of natural resources are called nonrenewable. They are usually obtained by mining or drilling under the surface of the earth. These are resources that are used up and can never be replaced. Coal and oil are nonrenewable resources. It takes millions of years for nature to deposit coal and oil in the earth. Once they are taken from the earth, they can never be replaced. They are gone forever. Someday a country may find that it no longer has any of these resources.

*What other resources can you name that are nonrenewable?*

Conservation is important if the United States is to remain rich and strong. Ways must be found to take better care of human resources. Renewable resources must be used in ways that make sure they will not be spoiled or polluted. Nonrenewable resources must not be wasted. Instead, substitutes should be found and used whenever possible.

*Can you think of any substitute materials we are now using?*

# How are Americans conserving their renewable resources?

The United States is trying to conserve its human resources. It is spending billions of dollars to remove slums and build new, low-cost housing. More billions are being spent to improve education for young people. Large sums of money have also been used to improve health care, especially for the poor and the elderly. These programs all show concern for the human resources of the country. Much has been done, but much more remains to be done.

The United States is also acting to conserve its soil resources. To do this, the government works with farmers to help conserve the soil. Crop rotation is one method used. It helps prevent the soil being exhausted, or used up, by certain crops. Tobacco and cotton, for example, use up many chemicals in the soil. After a while the soil can become useless. Farmers can save their soil resources by rotating, or changing, their crops every so often. They can plant peanuts, soybeans, and certain other crops. These help to replace the soil chemicals that were used up.

Farmers also can keep their soil from being blown away by wind or

washed away by rain. They can do this by planting trees and shrubs. The roots will hold down the soil. Contour plowing, rather than plowing in straight lines, also helps to hold the soil. The government helps by educating farmers about the need to conserve the soil. It also has a system of payments for farmers who practice conservation. In this way, the soil upon which crops are grown is made truly renewable. Lands once called dust bowls now produce crops.

Water is another renewable resource that must be conserved. It is very important to save water because it is needed by our fast growing population. More and more water is needed for the farms, industries, and cities of America. Water from rainfall is often allowed to run off into the earth, and the seas, as waste. To prevent this, many dams are being built to conserve water. The water stored in dams can be used to irrigate the drier farmlands. It can also supply factories and homes.

Some water is being wasted through pollution of streams, rivers, and lakes. The government is now taking steps to prevent pollution. The dumping of raw sewage or chemicals in waters is being stopped. It is hoped these actions, by the local and national governments, will clean up many of the water sources we need and use.

*How can you help conserve water?*

# How are Americans conserving their nonrenewable resources?

The conserving of the nonrenewable resources is difficult. Everyone agrees it must be done, but there is disagreement about how to proceed. It cannot be done in a way that might hurt industry and throw people out of work. This might happen if Americans mine less iron ore and copper or drill for less oil. Such actions would slow down industries that depend upon these resources.

No serious-minded person wants to keep American industry from producing vital goods. At the same time, ways must be found to conserve nonrenewable resources. One way is to find better ways of taking these resources from the earth. Years ago, half the oil in a well might never be taken out. This was because of the pumping methods used at that time. Pumping methods used today are much better. Much more oil is taken from wells and there is much less waste.

The mining of mineral resources has also been much improved. In the past, the methods of mining were very bad. Much of the coal, iron, and other minerals being mined were left in the earth. Today better mining methods are cutting down on this waste.

Another way of conserving nonrenewable resources is by recycling. Many used metals can be crushed into scrap. The scrap is then melted down and used to make another, new metal product. When that has been used, it will also be melted down as scrap and recycled into another type of use. No product need be thrown away as waste after a single use. It can be recycled for continued use in the future.

## How are Americans affected by the energy crisis?

The United States is an urban, industrial nation. This means that it depends upon many important sources of energy. Energy is needed to run the many factories, motor vehicles, and airplanes. Energy is also needed to heat homes and to provide electricity. Today's main sources of energy are coal, oil, natural gas, and electricity. Fifty years ago coal was the most important source of energy. It was gradually replaced by gas and oil.

Coal and oil are used to run the generators that produce electricity. Oil also provides the gasoline used as fuel for automobiles and trucks. The United States used to produce all the oil, gasoline, and natural gas it needed. Today the United States has to import about forty percent of the oil it uses.

The rising cost of oil has hurt many American industries. It has also meant an increase in the cost of gasoline and home heating oil. In addition, the United States is forced to depend upon foreign nations for its oil.

The oil shortage has caused an energy crisis in the United States. The crisis also exists in other parts of the world. The United States is trying to meet the problem by conserving its use of oil. It is also trying to find new sources of energy. One new source of energy is atomic power. However, this has proceeded slowly in recent years.

Many Americans are afraid it is not a completely safe way to produce energy. Instead, there is an effort to make use of the large amounts of coal in the country. There is also interest in solar energy, wind power, and synthetic fuels. In spite of these efforts the energy crisis remains a very serious problem.

# How are Americans fighting pollution?

Many Americans believe that pollution is a serious problem. They agree that steps must be taken to bring it under control. But how is this to be done? Can we shut down the factories, mills, and mines that produce goods? Can we force one hundred million Americans to stop using their cars? These do not seem like very practical ideas. Somehow, the United States must solve the problem of pollution. At the same time, it must try to keep the many things that the people want and enjoy.

One way to reduce air pollution is to pass special laws. Factories now have to use special equipment in their machines and smokestacks. This helps control the amount of smoke and gas going into the air.

The local and national governments are also trying to end pollution caused by automobiles. Manufacturers of new automobiles are making many changes in auto engines. These changes will cut down the smoke and fumes from automobile exhaust.

Oil companies are now producing new types of gasoline. These will cut down on chemical waste by automobile engines. In the meantime, researchers are looking into types of engines that will not use gasoline. Electrical engines may someday take the place of gasoline engines.

hundreds of tons of garbage and metal waste clog our streets. Old newspapers, paper cartons, tin and aluminum cans, and broken-down automobiles and refrigerators are part of this garbage waste. Most of these items can be recycled. The metal objects can be crushed, melted down, and made into usable metal materials. Old paper can be turned into pulp and made into usable paper goods. Recycling can help conserve nonrenewable resources. It can also reduce pollution in our cities.

*What can you do to help cut down pollution?*

Many cities and states have also taken action to prevent water pollution. Laws have been passed against the dumping of chemical wastes in lakes and rivers. In addition, raw sewage and garbage are being treated chemically before being dumped at sea. This special chemical treatment helps to make certain that the ocean waters will not be polluted.

Americans can stop wasting resources and also help end certain types of pollution. For instance, many

# LEARNING EXERCISES

## I. Remembering What We Have Read

Pick the best answer.

1. Ecology is a word that fits together with
   a. race.
   b. prejudice.
   c. environment.
   d. religion.
2. Human resources deals with
   a. forests.
   b. people.
   c. waterways.
   d. all of the above.

3. Recycling is useful in
   a. ending race prejudice.
   b. transportation.
   c. finding jobs for older people.
   d. conserving resources.
4. The greatest number of Americans are
   a. black-skinned.
   b. Oriental or Latin Americans.
   c. not light-skinned.
   d. light-skinned.

## II. Thinking About Things

Can you guess the answers to these questions? The answers are not in the book.
1. What can each of us do to help end race prejudice in the United States?
2. Suppose we had to cut back on the amount of electricity we use because of the energy crisis. Which electric items would you be willing to do without?
3. Do you think you will smoke cigarettes when you are older in spite of health warnings? Explain your answer.

# GLOSSARY

## A

**abolition societies** [AB uh LISH un suh SY uh teez] groups of black and white people against slavery. Page 213

**A.D.** [AY DEE] after the birth of Christ. Page 51

**adelantados** [ah day lahn TAH dos] Spanish explorers or scouts. Page 65

**alliance** [uh LI uns] agreement or friendship between nations. Page 297

**Allies** [AL ize] World War I alliance of England, France, Russia, and the United States. Page 286

**almanac** [ALL me nak] a book and calendar with helpful information. Page 158

**amendments** [uh MEND munts] changes made in a law, bill, and the Constitution. Page 136

**American Revolution** [uh MER i kun REV uh LOO shun] the 1775-1783 war that freed American colonies from British rule. Page 114

**ancestors** [AN ses turz] relatives from whom we are descended; great-grandparents. Page 4

**ancient** [AYN shent] very old; of times long past. Page 10

**Ancient Times** [AYN shent TYMZ] period ending about 500 A.D. Page 50

**anthem** [AN thum] a song of praise or patriotism. Page 170

**anti-Federalists** [AN tye-FED er ul ists] political party led by Thomas Jefferson against strong government. Page 150

**anti-slavery** [AN tye-SLA ver ee] opposed to or against slavery. Page 182

**arbitration** [AR buh TRA shun] union and employer agreement to accept a third party's (outside person's) settlement of labor disputes. Page 233

**armada** [ar MA da] a fleet of warships. Page 96

**arsenal** [AR sen ul] a stockpile of weapons. Page 294

**Articles of Confederation** [AR ti kuls uv kun FED uh RA shun] first body of laws of the United States. Page 134

**assembly line** [uh SEM blee LYNE] piecing together alike products on a moving belt. At the end, the product is complete. Page 279

**astronaut** [ASS truh nawt] pilot or crew member of a spacecraft. Page 304

**Atlantic Charter** [at LAN tik CHAR ter] World War II agreement between United States and Great Britain to seek no new territories and to return self-government to conquered countries. Page 294

**atomic bomb** [uh TOM ik BOM] a bomb made powerful by splitting atoms. Page 292

**atomic energy** [uh TOM ik EN er jee] energy made by controlling nuclear fission. Page 12

**atomic fallout** [uh TOM ik FAWL owt] deadly rays from the explosion of an atom bomb. Page 300

**automatic reaper** [AW tuh MAT ik REE per] a machine that speeded the work of cutting grains. Page 280

**Axis powers** [AK sis POW rz] dictator nations of Italy, Japan, and Germany during World War II. Page 289

**Aztec Indians** [AZ tek IN dee unz] powerful people of Mexico that fell to the Spanish. Page 65

## B

**balance of nature** [BAL ens uv NA cher] differences between what living things need and the ability of the environment to supply those needs. Page 346

**baron** [BAIR un] ruler of a manor in the Middle Ages. Page 55

**barter** [BAR ter] trading goods or services without using money. Page 55

**Battle of Bunker Hill** [BAT l uv BUNK er HIL] an early battle of the American Revolution. Page 110

**B.C.** [BEE SEE] before the birth of Christ. Page 51

**Big Five** [BIG FIVE] five permanent members of the United Nations Security Council (U.S., England, France, Soviet Union, and China). Page 295

**bigots** [BIG uts] people who form beliefs without judging fairly. Page 90

**bilad al sudan** [bee LOD al su DON] ancient black kingdoms of West Africa. Page 8

**Bill of Rights** [BIL uv RITES] first ten amendments to the Constitution. Page 150

**blockade** [blah KADE] military blocking to control who or what goes into or out of a place. Page 169

**borough** [BUR oh] one of five districts of New York City. Page 25

**Boston Massacre** [BAW stun or BAH stun MASS uh ker] a 1770 clash between colonists and British soldiers. Page 102

**Boston Tea Party** [BAW stun or BAH stun TEE PAR tee] colonist protest against British tea tax. Page 106

**boycott** [BOY kot] to unite in refusing to buy, sell, or use a product or service. Page 225

**"bread colonies"** [BRED KOL uh neez] American middle Atlantic colonies that grew grains as cash crops. Page 83

## C

**capital** [KAP uh tul] total wealth owned or used by a firm or person. Page 306

**caretakers** [KAIR take erz] those who watch over something but do not own it. Page 249

**cash crops** [KASH KROPS] crops grown to be sold. Page 280

**Central Powers** [SEN trul POW rz] World War II alliance between Germany, Austria, and Italy. Page 286

**Central Time Zone** [SEN trul TYME ZONE] standard time in central United States. Page 38

**checks and balances** [CHEKS and BAL un sez] system to control and keep equal power between branches of government. Page 144

**chief justice** [CHEEF JUS tis] head of the U.S. Supreme Court. Page 148

**Christianity** [kris chee AN uh tee] religion based on the teachings of Christ. Page 56

**Cibola** [SEE bo luh] cities of gold in Indian stories. Page 73

**city-state** [CIT ee-STAYT] a city that rules itself as a country. Page 54

**civil rights** [SIV ul RITES] rights of citizens. Page 140

**climate map** [KLY mit MAP] map showing the kind of weather a place has. Page 35

**collective bargaining** [kuh LEK tiv BAR gun eeng] right of a union to speak for workers about work conditions and wages. Page 231

**colonial powers** [kuh LO nee ul POW rz] countries who control or have power over colonies. Page 96

**colonies** [KOL uh neez] settlements in lands distant from countries that govern them. Page 5

**combine** [KOM bine] a machine that cuts, threshes, cleans, and bags grain. Page 280

**communication** [kuh MYU nuh KA shun] system of exchanging news or information. Page 172

**communism** [KOM yuh niz um] political form in which a single party controls and manages the country, as in the Soviet Union. Page 297

**commuter** [kuh MYU ter] person who daily travels short distances, usually to and from work. Page 333

**compass** [KUM pus] instrument for showing directions with a needle pointing North. Page 42

**compromise** [KOM pruh mize] settlement of a dispute in which each side gives up a part of what they want. Page 197

**Congressional Medal of Honor** [KON gresh un l MED ul uv ON er] the highest military award for bravery. Page 219

**conquistador** [kon KEES tah dor] a Spanish soldier and explorer. Page 65

**conservation** [KON ser VA shun] the protection and wise use of all resources. Page 348

**consumer goods** [kun SU mer GUDZ] products we buy and use every day. Page 276

**continent** [KON tuh nent] one of seven large land masses on earth. Page 5

**contour plowing** [KON tur PLOW eeng] plowing a field along curves in the land to hold soil in place. Page 351

**contribute** [kun TRIB yute] to offer or give. Page 336

**craft unions** [KRAFT YU nyenz] groups of skilled workers. Page 232

**crop rotation** [KROP ro TA shun] changing what crop is planted in a field to conserve the soil. Page 350

**cross-country** [KRAWS-KUN tree] across an entire country. Page 7

**crusades** [kroo SADZ] Christian religious wars against Moslems during the Middle Ages. Page 56

**cultured** [KUL cherd] to have and to make use of books, poetry, music, art, and drama. Page 315

**customs** [KUS tumz] long-used habits or ways of living. Page 4

## D

**decathlon** [di KATH lon] athletic contest of ten events. Page 26

**Declaration of Independence** [DEK luh RAY shun uv IN di PEN dens] colonists' statement written by Thomas Jefferson saying they were free and no longer ruled by England. Page 133

**decoded** [dee KO ded] changed from code into plain language. Page 270

**degrees** [dih GREEZ] numbered sections or units used to measure the earth, temperature, and angles. Page 44

**democractic government** [dem uh KRAT ik GUV ern munt] a system of ruling that is run by the people or their representatives. Page 115

**descendants** [deh SEN dants] people born of a certain family. Page 9

**descent** [di SENT] family line; ancestors. Page 8

**deserters** [dee ZER terz] members of an army who run away from duty. Page 169

**dictators** [DIK tay turz] people who rule a country with total power. Page 6

**diesel engines** [DE zul EN jenz] motors that run on oil. Page 263

**diplomat** [DIP leh mat] person who handles relations between their nation and other nations. Page 162

**disarmament** [dis AR ma munt] limiting or eliminating weapons and military forces. Page 288

**discriminate** [dis KRIM uh nayt] to show a difference in the way one treats another person or group. Page 24

**discrimination** [dis KRIM uh nay shun] a system of unfair treatment by a person or group against another person or group. Page 212

**division of power** [de VIZH en uv POWr] separation of control or rule into different parts taken by different people. Page 140

**dust bowls** [DUST BOWLZ] lands used up by farming without conservation methods. Page 351

## E

**Eastern Time Zone** [EEST ern TYME ZONE] standard time in the eastern United States. Page 38

**ecology** [e KOL uh jee] study of how plants, birds, animals, fish, and the environment affect each other. Page 346

**economic** [E kuh NOM ik *or* EK uh NOM ik] having to do with money or trade. Page 247

**economic opportunity** [E kuh NOM ik *or* EK uh NOM ik OP er TOO ni tee] new ways for people to make money or to provide for themselves. Page 257

**Economic and Social Council** [E kuh NOM ik *or* EK uh NOM ik and SO shul KOUN sul] United Nations agency to improve education, science, work conditions, and human rights. Page 295

**Electoral College** [ih LEK ter ul KOL ej] group of people chosen to elect the U.S. president and vice-president. Page 156

**emigrates** [EM uh grates] leaves one country to settle in another country. Page 256

**emperors** [EM per erz] those who rule empires. Page 54

**energy** [EN er jee] power that is used to run our industrial urban nation. Page 353

**environment** [en VI ren munt] the world around us that affects our life and health. Page 346

**Equal Rights Amendment** [E kwul RITES uh MEND munt] proposed amendment to the U.S. Constitution to stop discrimination against women. Page 229

**equator** [ee KWAY ter] imaginary east-west line dividing the earth in half. Page 43

**exhaust** [ig ZOST] smoke and fumes from the used gasoline of automobile and other engines. Page 354

## F

**Fall of Rome** [FAWL uv ROME] end of the Roman Empire (about 500 A.D.). Page 54

**federal governments** [FED er ul GUV ern munts] systems of ruling countries. Page 134

**Federalists** [FED er ul ists] early American political party favoring a written constitution. Page 150

**First Continental Congress** [FERST KON tuh NEN tl KONG ris] a 1774 group to unite the colonists in dealing with the British. Page 107

**Five Nations** [FIVE NA shunz] the Mohawk, Cayuga, Oneida, Seneca, and Onondaga tribes united by Hiawatha. Page 209

**flagship** [FLAG ship] ship that carries the officer in command; displays a flag indicating the officer's rank. Page 170

**49ers** [FOR tee NY nerz] people who went to California to find gold. Page 196

**French and Indian Wars** [FRENCH and IN dee un WORZ] war in 1754-1763 between French and English in North America. Page 98

## G

**General Assembly** [JEN ur ul uh SEM blee] United Nations (U.N.) body made up of the members of the U.N. Page 295

**generators** [JEN e ray terz] machines that produce electricity. Page 353

**geographers** [jee OG ruh ferz] experts in the study of the earth's surface. Page 60

**glider** [GLY der] light aircraft with no motor that depends on wind currents to keep it in the air. Page 264

**Great Compromise** [GRATE KOM pruh mize] decision that provided for two houses of Congress in the U.S. government. Page 138

**grid** [GRID] lines of latitude and longitude on a map or globe. Page 44

## H

**hemisphere** [HEM uh sfeer] half of a globe or the earth's surface. Page 32

**heritage** [HAIR i tij] what is handed down from one generation to the next. Page 9

**Hessians** [HESH enz] German troops that helped the British fight against the colonists in the American Revolution. Page 117

**Homestead Act** [HOME sted AKT] 1862 law offering free land for farmers who settled western territories. Page 246

**House of Representatives** [HOWS uv REP ri ZEN tuh tivs] lower house of the U.S. Congress whose membership is based on each state's population. Page 138

**human resources** [HYU mun REE sor sez] people of the nation. Page 348

# I

**immigrants** [IM uh grunts] people who come to a new country to live. Page 4

**impeach** [im PEECH] trial of a public official for suspected wrongdoing during office. Page 145

**imperialist** [im PEER ee ul ist] extending the power and rule of one country to other countries. Page 285

**import tariffs** [IM port TAIR ifs] duties or taxes on products coming into a country. Page 181

**impressment** [im PRESS munt] people seized and forced to serve in an army or navy. Page 169

**inaugurated** [in AW gye ray ted] taking office with ceremony. Page 184

**Inca Indians** [ING ka IN dee unz] an ancient and powerful people of Peru. Page 65

**indentured servants** [in DENT cherd SER vents] people who came to a new country paying for their travel by working without wages. Page 211

**independence** [in di PEN dens] freedom from control by others. Page 114

**independent** [in di PEN dunt] free from control of others. Page 8

**individual transportation** [in de VIJ you ul TRAN sper TA shun] moving a single person or small group from one place to another. Page 333

**industrial production** [in DUS tree ul pruh DUK shun] the making of products by industry. Page 306

**industrial revolution** [in DUS tree ul REV uh LOO shun] time when American manufacturing grew greatly by using electricity and methods of mass production. Page 275

**inflation** [in FLAY shun] a sudden rise in prices that results from too much paper money or credit. Page 298

**inland** [IN lund] away from a coast or border. Page 85

**inlets** [IN lets] narrow strips of water running from a larger body of water into the land. Page 181

**inner city** [IN er SIT ee] the central, often poor, areas of larger cities. Page 332

**integrated** [IN tuh gra ted] races of people who live and work together; children of different races in school. Page 223

**interchange** [in ter CHANJ] to change or substitute for another. Page 279

**intermediate directions** [in ter MEE dee it dye REK shunz] compass directions between the main directions: northwest, southwest, southeast, northeast. Page 42

**internationalism** [in ter NASH uh nel izm] a foreign policy that seeks cooperation among all nations. Page 285

**irrigation** [eer uh GAY shun] supplying land with water. Page 70

**Islam** [ISS lam *or* iss LAM] religion based on the teachings of Mohammed. Page 57

**isolationist** [eye suh LAY shun ist] a country that believes it should keep apart from other nations. Page 284

**isthmus** [ISS mus] a narrow strip of land connecting two larger bodies of land. Page 49

**jet propulsion** [JET pruh PUHL shun] to power a rocket by a jet engine. Page 266

**job security** [JOB si KYUR i tee] demand of workers that there will always be work if they want it. Page 334

**journal** [JER nl] a daily record of events. Page 164

**justice** [JUS tis] fairness; fair treatment. Page 25

# K

**key** [KEE] an explanation of symbols on a map. Page 33

# L

**laboratories** [LAB ruh tor eez] places for scientific work. Page 21

**land ordinance** [LAND OR dn ens] 1785 law that provides ways to sell government land and to keep sections for public schools. Page 238

**landforms** [LAND formz] the different kinds of land masses on the earth's surface. Page 34

**latitude** [LAT i tood *or* LAT i tyud] distance north and south of the equator, measured in degrees. Page 43

**League of Iroquois** [LEEG uv EER uh kwoy] the Mohawk, Cayuga, Oneida, Seneca, Onondaga, and Tuscarora tribes united by Hiawatha. Page 209

**League of Nations** [LEEG uv NA shunz] world organization after World War I to settle international disputes. Page 287

**legislature** [LEJ i SLAY chur] group of elected people who make laws for a state or nation. Page 239

**living wage** [LIV eng WAJE] money for work that is enough to pay for a person's needs. Page 334

**local governments** [LO cul GUV ern munts] systems of ruling for a certain place. Page 134

**locomotive** [LO kuh MO tiv] a steam-driven engine. Page 263

**longitude** [LON jeh tood *or* LON jeh tyud] distance east or west on earth's surface, measured in degrees. Page 43

**loose alliance** [LOOS uh LI uns] a central government with little or no power. Page 216

**lunar surface** [LOO ner SER fis] outside or crust of the moon. Page 305

## M

**mainland** [MANE lund] the main part of a continent or country. Page 85

**majority** [ma JOR i tee] the larger number; more than half. Page 145

**manors** [MAN urz] large estates in Europe during the Middle Ages. Page 55

**mass production** [MASS pruh DUK shun] a factory method of making the same product over and over again for profit. Page 275

**mass transportation** [MASS TRAN sper TA shun] moving large numbers of people from one place to another. Page 333

**Mayflower Compact** [MAY flowr KOM pakt] Pilgrim settler's agreement for self-rule in America. Page 86

**mediation** [MEE dee A shun] use of a third party (outside persons) to settle disputes between unions and employers. Page 233

**Medicare** [MED e kair] medical insurance money from taxes for older people. Page 339

**mercenaries** [MER suh NAIR eez] soldiers who are paid to serve in a foreign army. Page 117

**merchant ships** [MER chunt SHIPS] ships that carry goods to be bought and sold. Page 120

**Middle Ages** [MID l A jez] time between about 500 A.D. and 1500 A.D. in Europe. Page 50

**Middle East** [MID l EEST] region including Sudan, Egypt, and Turkey in the west to Iran in the east, and countries in southwest Asia. Page 7

**migrant** [MY grunt] someone who moves from place to place. Page 16

**minimum wage law** [MIN uh mum WAJE LAW] U.S. law stating the least amount that can be paid to workers in many industries. Page 336

**minors** [MY nerz] persons under the state legal age of adulthood, usually 18 or 21 years of age. Page 228

**minutemen** [MIN it men] American colonists who fought the British during the Revolution. Page 110

**missionaries** [MISH un air eez] people sent on religious missions. Page 86

**Modern Times** [MOD ern TYMZ] time from 1500 A.D. to the present. Page 50

**Mountain Time Zone** [MOUN tn TYME ZONE] Standard time in Rocky Mountain regions of the U.S. Page 38

## N

**N.A.A.C.P.** [EN DUB l AY SEE PEE] National Association for the Advancement of Colored People —an organization to help blacks gain civil rights. Page 24

**nationalism** [NASH uh nuh lizm] feelings or actions of loyalty to one's country. Page 175

**natural barriers** [NACH ur ul BAIR ee erz] mountains and rivers forming divisions between countries or continents. Page 46

**natural resources** [NACH ur ul REE sor sez] useful elements and materials produced by nature. Page 348

**navigators** [NAV uh gay turz] people who sail or steer a ship. Page 60

**neutral** [NOO trul or NYOO trul] taking no side of a quarrel or dispute. Page 168

**neutral nations** [NOO trul or NYOO trul NA shenz] nations not officially allied with a major world power. Page 330

**Niagara Movement** [ny AG ruh MOOV munt] 1905-1909 group begun by William E. B. Dubois that fought for black civil rights. Page 224

**Nisei** [NEE say] second generation U.S. citizens of Japanese descent. Page 22

**Nobel Prize** [no BEL PRIZE] any of six internationally honored prizes established by Alfred B. Nobel (Sweden). Page 12

**nonrenewable resources** [non ri NOO ubl REE sor sez] resources that, once used up, can never be replaced. Page 349

**Norse** [NORS] people living in northern Europe during the Middle Ages. Page 59

## O

**orbit** [OR bit] oval path of a planet (earth) or other heavenly body in space. Page 37

## P

**Pacific** [puh SIF ik] ocean west of North and South America. Page 69

**Pacific Time Zone** [puh SIF ik TYME ZONE] standard time in westernmost parts of the United States. Page 38

**paratroopers** [PAIR uh TROO perz] soldiers who parachute into battle from an airplane. Page 252

**Parliament** [PAR luh munt] lawmaking body in Great Britain. Page 102

**patented** [PAT n ted] a new invention with government papers giving inventor sole rights to make and sell it. Page 312

**patriotic** [pay tree OT ik] having or showing loyalty and devotion toward one's country. Page 318

**patriotism** [PA tree uh TIZ em] loyal support of one's country. Page 175

**pension** [PEN shun] an allowance paid regularly for service. Page 218

**pentathlon** [pen TATH len]   an athletic contest of five different events. Page 26

**petition** [puh TISH un]   formal request to an authority. Page 113

**picket** [PIK it]   an event, usually a march with printed signs, to protest something or to keep others from entering a workplace on strike. Pages 229 and 231

**Pilgrims** [PIL grimz]   English settlers of Plymouth colony. Page 86

**plains** [PLAYNZ]   low, flat lands. Page 34

**plantations** [plan TAY shunz]   large farms, especially in tropical or semitropical regions. Page 65

**plateau** [pluh TOE]   high, flat land. Page 34

**political map** [puh LIT i kl  MAP]   map showing nations of the world or states of a country. Page 35

**politics** [POL uh tiks]   the science and art of government. Page 25

**pollution** [puh LOO shun]   making air and water unclean by factory wastes, poison sprays, automobile smoke, and fumes. Pages 301 and 354

**prejudice** [PREJ uh dis]   opinion formed without judging fairly. Page 223

**Prime Meridian** [PRIME  meh RID ee un]   an imaginary north-south line dividing the earth in half. Page 43

**property rights** [PROP er tee  RITES]   rights protected by the Constitution to own goods or land. Page 204

**pueblos** [poo EHB lohs]   mud-covered homes of Zuñi Indians. Page 73.

**Puritans** [PYUR uh tns]   members of the Church of England who settled Plymouth colony for religious freedom. Page 89

## Q

**Quakers** [KWA kerz]   a group of religious settlers that founded Pennsylvania. Page 89

## R

**racism** [RA siz m]   the belief that one race is better than another race. Page 345

**rates of interest** [RATES  uv  IN ter ist]   the cost of borrowing money. Page 332

**ratified** [RAT i fide]   approved or confirmed; accepted. Page 150

**raw goods** [RAW  GUDZ]   materials in a natural condition; not manufactured. Page 285

**rearm** [ree ARM]   rebuilding stores of weapons and armies. Page 289

**recycling** [ree SY kleeng]   re-using products or materials instead of throwing them away after one use. Page 352

**reelection** [ree i LEK shun]   election again. Page 182

**region** [REE jun]   a large part of the earth's surface. Page 10

**relief map** [ruh LEEF  MAP]   a map showing the landforms of an area. Page 35

**religious prejudice** [ri LIJ us  PREJ uh dis]   unfair feelings or judgement based on religious beliefs. Page 60

**renewable resources** [ree NYU ubl  REE sor sez]   a resource that, when used properly, can be used many times. Page 349

**representatives** [REP ri ZEN tuh tivz]   those who act in place of, who speak and act for. Page 127

**republic** [ri PUB lik]   a country whose citizens elect the representatives to run government. Pages 140 and 190

**reservations** [REZ er VA shunz]   special, often poor lands set aside by U.S. government for Indians forced off their lands. Page 207

**retired** [re TIRED]   stopped working every day for wages. Page 335

**revolution** [REV uh LOO shun]   the movement of the earth around the sun (*See also* American Revolution). Page 37

**road map** [RODE  MAP]   a map showing highways and distances between places. Page 35

**rockets** [ROK its]   a jet powered machine used to move fireworks, missiles, and space vehicles. Page 266

**rotate** [RO tayt]   to move around a center or axis; to turn in a circle. Page 36

**rotation** [ro TAY shun]   the turning of the earth on its axis; turning in a circle. Page 37

**rural** [ROOR ul]   in the country; away from the city. Page 7

**rural areas** [ROOR ul  AIR ee uhz]   in the country or farm lands. Page 277

## S

**sacred** [SA krid]   of spiritual or religious value. Page 249

**satellite** [SAT l ite]   an object launched by rocket into orbit around the earth or other celestial body. Page 267

**scale of distance** [SKALE  uv  DIS tens]   a key showing how many actual miles are equal to one inch on the map. Page 33

**secede** [si SEED]   to leave or withdraw from the union or association. Page 216

**Secretariat** [SEK re TAIR ee uht]   United Nations headquarters staffed by workers from all over the world. Page 295

**secretary-general** [SEK re TAIR ee-JEN er uhl] leader of the United Nation's (U.N.) Secretariat who is elected by the U.N. members. Page 295

**secretary of state** [SEK re TAIR ee uv STAYT] federal official who directs foreign policy for the president. Page 284

**section** [SEK shun] a part of a nation with concerns that may be different from other parts. Page 180

**Security Council** [si KYUR i tee KOUN sul] United Nations agency made up of five permanent members and ten elected members. Page 295

**segregation** [SEG ruh GAY shun] separation of racial groups from one another. Page 24

**self-government** [SELF-GUV ern munt] government by those of one's own country rather than by a foreign power. Page 294

**self-rule** [self-ROOL] self-government. Page 86

**Senate** [SEN it] upper house of the U.S. Congress. Page 138

**separation of power** [sep uh RA shun uv POW r] dividing the rule of a nation between different branches of the government. Page 147

**serfs** [SERFS] slaves who were not sold off the lands, but passed with the land to new landowners. Page 55

**Seven Cities of Cibola** [SEV en CIT eez uv SEE bo lah] imaginary golden cities. Page 75

**shares of ownership** [SHAIRZ uv O ner ship] small parts of a factory or other business that may be owned by a buyer. Page 306

**Six Nations** [SIKS NA shunz] the League of the Iroquois. Page 209

**smuggled** [SMUG uld] brought into or taken out of a country secretly and against the law. Page 106

**Social Security** [SO shul si KYUR i tee] federal plan that provides payments to unemployed, disabled, and elderly. Page 338

**solar energy** [SO ler EN er jee] energy from the sun that may be used for heat and electricity. Page 353

**Sons of Liberty** [SUNZ uv LIB er tee] American colonists that protested against British laws. Page 102

**sphere** [SFEER] a ball or globe. Page 32

**Stamp Act** [STAMP AKT] British tax on American colonial newspapers and legal papers. Page 102

**standard of living** [STAN derd uv LIV eeng] manner or amount of goods and materials used in daily life. Page 307

**standardize** [STAN der dize] to make all parts alike. Page 278

**state church** [STAYT CHERCH] a religion favored or adopted by a state or federal government. Page 163

**state governments** [STAYT GUV ern munts] systems of ruling for a state. Page 134

**states' rights** [STAYTS RITES] powers that belong to the states rather than the federal government. Page 185

**statesmen** [STAYTS men] persons skilled in managing public or national affairs. Page 162

**strait** [STRAYT] a narrow channel of water connecting two larger bodies of water. Page 69

**strikes** [STRYKES] work stopped by unions and workers to improve pay or work conditions. Page 16

**supersonic** [SOO per SAHN ik] able to travel faster than the speed of sound. Page 262

**surplus** [SER plus] amount over what is needed. Page 280

**symbols** [SIM bulz] something that stands for or represents something else. Page 33

**synthetic fuels** [sin THET ic FYU elz] anything burned to make power and made by human industry rather than taken from the earth. Page 353

# T

**tariffs** [TAIR ifs] taxes on goods coming into or leaving a country. Page 185

**taxation without representation** [tak SA shun with OUT REP ri zen TA shun] paying extra money (taxes) for goods with no voice or vote about whether those taxes are good or fair. Page 102

**telegraph** [TEL uh graf] a device that sends or receives messages by electric pulses. Page 268

**telegraphic cable** [TEL uh GRAF ik CAB l] electric wires used to carry telegraph messages. Page 268

**telephone** [TEL uh fone] a system for sending and receiving speech by electricity. Page 270

**Three-Fifths Compromise** [THREE-FIFTHS KOM pruh mize] 1787 ruling in Constitution that southern states count each five slaves as three citizens. Page 139

**time line** [TYME LYNE] a chart, divided like a ruler, showing when events took place. Page 50

**time zones** [TYME ZONEZ] twenty-four regions of the earth within which the same standard time is used. Page 36

**transcontinental** [TRANS kon ti NEN tl] crossing from one side of the country to the other. Page 263

**treason** [TREE zn] to betray one's country; to help enemies of one's country. Page 112

**treaties** [TREE teez] official agreements made between nations. Page 284

**Trusteeship Council** [truh STEE ship KOUN sul] United Nations agency that looks after colonies until they become independent nations. Page 295

## U

**unconstitutional** [uhn kon stuh TU shun ul] against or contrary to the U.S. Constitution and therefore not proper. Page 147

**Underground Railroad** [uhn der GROUND RAYL rode] a secret organization that helped slaves escape from the South. Page 218

**unemployment insurance** [uhn em PLOY ment in SHUR ens] money for workers who lose their jobs. Page 339

**unions** [YU nyenz] workers in the same industry organized to improve working conditions and pay. Page 231

**United Nations** [yu NY ted NA shunz] world organization working for world peace and security. Page 290

**United States Supreme Court** [yu NY tid STAYTS suh PREEM CORT] branch of the U.S. government that decides the meaning or properness of laws. Page 148

**urban areas** [UR bun AIR ee uhs] cities and suburban lands around cities. Page 277

## V

**veto** [VEE toe] right of a government leader to reject bills passed by the lawmaking body. Page 145

**Vikings** [VI keengz] Norse sailors and warriors. Page 59

## W

**west coast** [WEST KOSTE] U.S. western shorelands. Page 7

**wind resistance** [WIND ri ZIS tuns] any force that tends to stop or hinder the motion of wind. Page 264

**World Health Organization** [WERLD HELTH OR guh ni ZA shun] United Nations agency to improve world health. Page 295

## Z

**Zuñi Indians** [ZOO nee IN de unz] Native Americans living in Arizona and New Mexico. Page 73

# SUBJECT INDEX

# NAME INDEX

## A

Adams, John (patriot and president, 1797-1801), 105, 107, 148, 163, 169, 182

Adams, John Quincy (patriot and president, 1825-1829), 182

Adams, Samuel (patriot), 103, 104, 106, 107, 110, 111, 182

Agnew, Spiro T. (vice-president, 1969-1973), 296

Aldrin, Edwin E. (astronaut), 305

Allen, Ethan (Revolutionary War soldier), 110

Armstrong, Neil A. (astronaut), 304-305

Attucks, Crispus (killed in Boston Massacre), 103, 104, 121

## B

Balboa, Vasco Nuñez de (Spanish explorer), 66-67, 75

Barjonah, Isaish (patriot), 121

Beanes, Dr. William (American prisoner in War of 1812), 170

Bell, Alexander Graham (inventor, telephone), 270-271

Berson, Solomon (medical researcher), 21

Blackwell, Elizabeth (first U.S. woman doctor), 186

Bonaparte, Napoleon (ruler of France), 161, 168

Brooke, Edward W. (U.S. senator), 221

Bruce, Blanche K. (black U.S. senator, post-Civil War), 221

Burr, Aaron (vice-president, 1801-1805; dueled with Hamilton), 157

## C

Cabot, John (Italian explorer for England), 82, 184-185

Cabral, Pedro (Portuguese explorer), 62

Carnegie, Andrew (industrialist and philanthropist), 310-311, 313

Carney, William H. (black Civil War soldier), 220

Carter, Jimmy (president, 1977-1981), 296, 298

Cartier, Jacques (French explorer), 76

Chavez, Cesar (Chicano union leader), 16

Chisholm, Shirley (first U.S. black congresswoman), 25

Churchill, Winston (British prime minister), 294

Clark, William (American explorer), 164-165

Clemens, Samuel Langhorne, *See* Twain, Mark

Clemente, Roberto (baseball star), 19

Cleveland, Grover (president, 1885-1889), 229

Collins, Michael (astronaut), 305

Columbus, Christopher (Italian explorer), 59, 63, 64, 65, 75, 84

Cooper, Anna Julia Haywood (black educator), 18

Cooper, James Fenimore (American author), 314

Cornish, Samuel E. (black newspaper publisher), 183

Coronado, Francisco Vasquez de (Spanish explorer), 73

Cortes, Hernando (Spanish conquistador), 65, 70-71, 75

Crosby, Governor (of New York colony), 91

Craft, Samuel (patriot), 121

Crazy Horse (Indian chief), 249

Custer, George A. (general in Civil and Indian wars), 250

## D

Da Gama, Vasco (Portuguese explorer), 62, 68

Davis, Jefferson (president of the Confederate States of America), 221

Dawes, William (patriot), 110, 111

Dayton, Jonathan (delegate to Constitutional Convention), 137

De Champlain, Samuel (French explorer), 76

De Kalb, Baron (German soldier in American Revolution), 117, 123

Dix, Dorothea (educator and social reformer), 186

Douglass, Frederick (anti-slavery speaker), 215, 219, 321

Drew, John (American actor), 324

DuBois, William E. B. (black leader), 224

## E

Einstein, Dr. Albert (scientist), 12

Eisenhower, Dwight D. (general and president, 1953-1961), 296

Ericson, Leif (Viking/Norse explorer), 59

Estevanico (black discoverer), 75

## F

Ferdinand (king of Spain), 63

Field, Cyrus W. (transoceanic telegraph cable), 268

Fisk, Pomp (black patriot), 121

Ford, Gerald (president, 1974-1977), 296, 298

Ford, Henry (automobile manufacturer), 278-279

Foster, Stephen (American songwriter), 315

Franklin, Benjamin (patriot and diplomat), 107, 137, 158-159

Frost, Robert (American poet), 318-320

## G

Garland, Charles (young philanthropist), 24

Garrison, William Lloyd (abolitionist leader), 213, 220

George III (king of England), 107, 112, 113, 116, 126-127, 159

Geronimo (Indian warrior and chief), 250, 252-253

Goddard, Robert (rocketry scientist), 267

Gompers, Samuel (union leader), 232

Goyathlay. *See* Geronimo

Grasso, Ella T. (governor of Connecticut, 1975-1980), 23

# PHOTO CREDITS

American Airlines, Republic Aviation Corporation: 306
American Federation of Labor: 233
American Telephone and Telegraph: 268
Amherst College: 318
Art by Jance Lentz-Weiner: 74, 75
Associated Booking Corporation: 315
Bel-Mar Visuals: 273
Brookhaven Laboratory: 300
Brown Brothers: 289
Bruce Coleman: 8
Carnegie Mellon University: 311
Chang Kee CACI: 7
Charles Phelps Cushing: 71, 90, 219, 247, 250, 254, 255
Chien-Shiung Wu, Columbia University: 15
Culver Pictures: 12, 14, 27
Cunard Lines: 263, 274
Cyr Color Photo Agency: 290, 294
Dan Budnik: 322
Daniel Inouye: 22
Dominick Ruggiero: 23
Eastern National Parkway and Monument Association: 70
Ed Nowak: 262
Edison Institute's Henry Ford Museum in Dearborn, Michigan: 272
Edward Brooke: 221
Ester Goddard: 266
Ford Archives: 278
Ford Motor Company: 274, 278, 279, 281, 282
General Electric Company, Schenectady, New York: 302, 303
General Foods: 277
General Motors: Chevrolet Division: 262
                Pontiac Division: 101, 109
Greyhound Bus Company: 262, 307
Historical Picture Services, Inc., Chicago: 26, 87, 88, 103, 106, 109, 113, 114, 137, 148, 159, 165, 168, 170, 174, 178, 196, 210, 229, 250, 251, 257, 259, 261, 297, 298, 314, 317
Image Group: 7, 9, 24, 204, 246, 269, 271, 272, 276, 311
International Harvester Company: 280
Jefferson Memorial Foundation: 162, 163
Job Survival Skills, Copyright ©1981. Singer Career Systems, Division of The Singer Company: 339
Karen A. Yops: 115
Karsh, Ottawa: 322
King Foundation: 225
LPGA: 17
Library of Congress: 107, 110, 112, 119, 120, 129, 140, 148, 150, 158, 162, 164, 166, 167, 171, 175, 179, 182, 185, 192, 212, 222, 227, 228, 232, 234, 235, 239, 249, 255, 262, 263, 270, 274, 287, 310, 317
Lincoln Center: 315
Malcom W. Emmons: 19, 223
Metropolitan Museum of Art: 315
Moorland-Spingard Research Center, Howard University: 18
Montana Historical Society: 248, 255
Museum of the City of New York: 156, 167, 256, 261
N.A.A.C.P.: 216
NASA: 262, 304, 305, 325
National Archives: 23, 126, 275, 282, 284, 288, 289

National Gallery of Art: 105, 184, 187
National Library of Medicine: 300
Naval Photographic Center: 291
Nemo Warr: 262
New York Department of Commerce: 261
New York Department of Health: 300
New York Historical Society: 68
New York Public Library: 183, 215, 222, 226, 286, 320, 324
North American Rockwell: 301
Photo Researchers, Inc.: 296
Radio Corporation of America: 273
Republican State, Central, and Executive Committee of Ohio: 298
Shirley Chisholm: 25
Smithsonian Institute: 86, 119, 157, 176, 252, 253
Springfield, Ohio - Chamber of Commerce: 186
Standard Oil of New Jersey: 277, 282, 309, 313
Star Spangled Banner Flag House: 170
Supreme Court of the United States: 149, 153
Swiss Foto, S.A.: 65
Taft Museum: 268, 273
The Bettmann Archive, Inc.: 65, 169, 289
Trans World Airlines: 262, 267, 274
United Nations: 277, 294, 299, 321
United Press International: 16, 27
United States Lines: 263
University of Illinois at Urbana - Champaign, Illinois: 21
U.S. Air Force: 252, 264, 265
U.S. Army: 290, 292
U.S. Department of Agriculture: 300
U.S. Department of Agriculture, Soil Conservation Service: 280
U.S. Information Agency: 289
U.S. Marine Corps: 323
U.S. Signal Corps: 194
Westinghouse Electric Company: 263, 312
Wide World Photos: 223

**COVER PHOTOS** *top left:* Courtesy of THE New-York Historical Society,
New York City; *top middle:* Sacks/Editorial Photocolor Archives; *top
right:* Cooper/Editorial Photocolor Archives; *middle left:* Dept. of
Defense; *middle:* Sacks/Editorial Photocolor Archives; *middle right:*
Tree/Editorial Photocolor Archives; *bottom left:* The Image Group;
*bottom middle:* The Image Group; *bottom right:* Michael Evans - The White House